EMERGING
VOICES
IN
GLOBAL
CHRISTIAN
THEOLOGY

EMERGING VOICES
IN
GLOBAL CHRISTIAN THEOLOGY

William A. Dyrness

ZondervanPublishingHouse
Grand Rapids, Michigan

A Division of HarperCollinsPublishers

Emerging Voices in Global Christian Theology
Copyright © 1994 by William A. Dyrness

Requests for information should be addressed to:
Zondervan Publishing House
Grand Rapids, Michigan 49530

Library of Congress Cataloging-in-Publication Data

Emerging voices in global Christian theology / William A. Dyrness, general editor.
p. cm.
Includes bibliographical references.
ISBN 0-310-60461-3
1. Theology, Doctrinal—Developing countries. 2. Theology, Doctrinal—Europe,
Eastern. 3. Evangelicalism—Developing countries. 4. Evangelicalism—Europe,
Eastern. 5. Evangelicalism—United States. 6. Christianity and culture.
7. Missions—Theory. 8. Christianity and other religions. 9. Developing countries—
Church history—20th century. 10. Europe, Eastern—Church history—20th century.
I. Dyrness, William A.
BT30.D44E44   1994
230'.09172'4–dc 20   93-46053
                                                                                          CIP

Kwame Bediako's chapter reprinted from *Jesus In African Culture (A Ghanaian Perspective)* (Ghana, Africa: Asempa Publishers, 1990).

Scripture quotations are taken from the *Holy Bible: New International Version*®. NIV®. Copyright © 1973, 1978, 1984 by International Bible Society. Used by permission of Zondervan Publishing House. All rights reserved.

Scripture quotations marked NASB are from the *New American Standard Bible* © The Lockman Foundation 1960, 1962, 1963, 1968, 1971, 1972, 1973, 1975, 1977. Used by permission. All rights reserved.

Scripture quotations marked RSV are from the *Revised Standard Version of the Bible* © 1946, 1952, 1971 by the Division of Chistian Education of the National Council of Churches of Christ in the USA. Used by permission. All rights reserved.

Scripture quotations marked NRSV are from the *New Revised Standard Version of the Bible* © 1989 by the Division of Christian Education of the National Council of Churches of Christ in the USA, and are used by permission. All rights reserved.

Note: Some Scripture quotations have been translated directly from foreign language Bibles.

Edited by Rachel Boers
Cover design by Mark Veldheer
Cover photograph by Ian O'Leary, Tony Stone Worldwide
Printed in the United States of America

94   95   96   97   98 / ❖ DH / 10   9   8   7   6   5   4   3   2   1

Contents

Asia

Latin America

Preface

This book presents a sampling of theological reflection by thinkers in non-western settings. Lest we be thought patronizing, the "emerging" character of these voices has to do with our limited western perspective rather than being a descriptive statement about these thinkers. Slowly but surely we are overcoming our provincialism and becoming aware of the importance of voices like this to our world wide theological conversation, but their value, in many cases, has long been recognized in their home areas. Indeed in some cases we are dealing with the senior figures of theology for their area. But even in 1994 the truth remains that most western theological students know very little about theological reflection outside the West. They may have heard of Gustavo Gutierrez or Nelson Mandela, but of the younger theologians in those regions they know little. It was for this reason that I wrote my brief introduction *Learning About Theology from the Third World,* which this book is meant to complement. Those who used that book as a text in class called for a sequel that would be a source book of theological reflection currently taking place in these settings.

This book then is meant to provide opportunity to "listen in" on the theological conversations going on in many different places. No attempt was made to have writers address a common set of questions, indeed we purposely avoided setting any agenda for them. We wanted them to give us an example of theological reflection that is in process and that reflects issues of concern to them. We did attempt, however, to collect a variety of perspectives from different places to give a flavor of the diversity of theology today. We will have occasion to comment on this in the introduction, but here it is important to remember that these provide the merest introduction to what is happening around the world and are meant to stimulate our appetite to further pursue the questions these essays raise.

A criticism raised about my earlier book ought to be noted here. Some readers felt that concentration on theological reflection elsewhere gives the false impression that no thinking of this kind is going on in North America (and Europe). This is clearly untrue as the vital work being done by feminist, African American, or Hispanic theologians testify. Indeed it is an important part of our theological listening in on other traditions to listen first to those nearest to us. Moreover one could well argue that a perspective on work done by minorities in our midst would provide important bridges for understanding theologians overseas. These are all valid and important points and it is a criticism to which this book is also vulnerable. This weakness is due to the fact that my primary exposure to non-western theology has been outside North America—primarily in Manila, Philippines and Nairobi, Kenya. This biographical fact is the reason for this particular approach rather than its intrinsic superiority. An important task remains for all of us to find ways to link these traditions and bring them all into our common conversation.

This being said, the authors included in this anthology are worth hearing in their own right. I want to express my gratitude to all of them for their willingness to be part of this project and their cooperation throughout. This is meant to be their book and that is why their names appear in large letters on the cover. Stanley Gundry of Zondervan Publishing House has been an encouraging supporter throughout, even though it was clear the reading public for Two Thirds World theology is still unfortunately small. Robert Cahill has held the project together since it was conceived and my gratitude is as deep and heartfelt as it is inadequate. Dave Sielaff, Anne White, and Jone Bosch of the word processing office at Fuller also deserve thanks for putting the many manuscripts into a unified and camera ready form. All of these have worked because they have shared my belief that these writers and the churches they represent deserve much more visibility among us than they have had to the present.

William Dyrness

Pasadena, California
September, 1993

Introduction

William Dyrness

That Evangelical Christians should be interested in a book of theological reflection from non-western sources may not seem strange on the surface of it. After all they have usually been quick to respond to the call to go into all the world with the Gospel. They are more likely than their mainline colleagues to have gone on short term mission trips or served on mission committees at Church. But the truth is that their missionary efforts have not always encouraged serious theological reflection. The Bible Colleges they established around the world were better at equipping students for evangelism and church planting than in stimulating them to reflect biblically on their setting.

Those churches and schools founded by mainline missionaries have by contrast encouraged theological reflection from the beginning. Pioneering work in Third World theology has come from this setting. As early as 1966 the All Africa Conference of Churches met in Ibadan, Nigeria and produced a book of reflections that set a high standard.[1] In 1976 in Dar es Salaam, Tanzania, the Ecumenical Association of Third World Theologians (EATWOT) was born, which has met regularly since then and produced an important series of books.[2]

Evangelicals continued their mission activity and met in important international conferences in Berlin (1966) and Lausanne (1974). Although this was not their primary purpose, some valuable theological reflection was beginning in this context.[3] The Lausanne movement and its sister organization The World Evangelical Fellowship, especially its Theological Commission, continued to sponsor conferences where theological themes were discussed. The most famous of these was issued in what is still a primary reference work on the Gospel and culture, by

---

1. Kwesi Dickson and Paul Ellingworth, eds., *Biblical Revelation and African Belief* (Maryknoll: Orbis, 1971).

2. See Sergio Torres and Virginia Fabella, eds., *The Emergent Gospel: Theology from the Underside of History* (Maryknoll: Orbis, 1978), and most recently K. C. Abraham, *Third World Theologies: Commonalities and Divergences* (Maryknoll: Orbis, 1990).

3. The articles were collected in Stanley Mooneyham, ed., *One Race, One Gospel, One Task* (Minneapolis, 1968) and in J. D. Douglas, ed., *Let the Earth Hear His Voice* (Minneapolis, 1975).

John Stott and Robert Coote (eds.), *Down to Earth: Essays on Gospel and Culture*.[4] Meanwhile, evangelicals were making up for lost time by founding a number of seminaries in strategic centers around the world, beginning in the late 1960s and early 1970s. Graduates of Fuller's School of World Mission (founded in 1968) and these new seminaries began to make their mark before long.

During the 1970s these younger theologians began meeting together in what were called Fraternities of Theologians.[5] Groups began meeting in Africa, Asia, and Latin America. In 1983 many of these met together for the first time for an important theological conference in Bangkok, Thailand and produced a most important collection of theological reflection edited by Vinay Samuel and Chris Sugden.[6] The work in that book, to which this collection is in many ways a sequal, demonstrated that evangelical thinkers from around the world could produce first-rate work and were ready to take their place in the world wide theological discussion.

If Third World scholars were preparing themselves for theological conversation, their colleagues in the West, it must be admitted, were not always ready to hear what they had to say. With 20,000 to 30,000 theological books pouring from western presses annually there is not much time left over to listen in on theological conversations taking place elsewhere. U. S. seminaries are usually anxious to have non-western faculty as colleagues, even to allow the latter to "listen in" on their theological conversations. But we have not reached the point where these conversations have become truly multi-lateral. This collection of pieces and the others we have noted, are all based on a fundamental and far-reaching claim: The interrelated nature of the Christian community and the demands placed on the church at the end of this millennium make genuine exchange in the theological arena not only possible, but indispensible. This point is so important, and so poorly understood, that it might be valuable here to sketch out the elements that lie behind such a claim.

First, Christians in Africa, Asia, and Latin America now outnumber those in the West by many millions. By 1992 Third World Christians numbered 974.3 million, compared to 600.8 million in the West. Those

4. Grand Rapids, Eerdmans, 1980.

5. These groups organized in the mid 1980s as the International Fellowship of Evangelical Mission Theologians (INFEMET), under the leadership of Vinay Samuel and Christ Sugden.

6. *Sharing Jesus in the "Two Thirds" World* (Grand Rapids: Eerdmans, 1983).

figures are no doubt more striking today. As Andrew Walls describes this new reality he notes that "it is nothing less than a complete change in the centre of gravity of Christianity, so that the heartlands of the church are no longer in Europe, decreasingly in North America, but in Latin America, in certain parts of Asia . . . and in Africa."[7] If theology is done by God's people wherever they might be placed, then increasingly theology will reflect its changing setting. This is not to say theological reflection will exist in isolation from that done in the West, indeed this must not be the case. But it will certainly extend that conversation to include new discussion partners.

If theology is our human reflection on God's revelation of himself in Jesus Christ and in Scripture, then it will certainly bear the mark of its humanity. We in the West have sometimes denied that this is the case believing that our reflection, or what we take as the normative expression of this truth, is a timeless product that must simply be applied in various settings. It is true that our use of Greek philosophical categories gave to theology an appearance of stability, but we are now seeing that even this universality was illusory. Indeed, our special way of abstracting theological truth from the statements of Scripture directly reflects our unique western heritage. This heritage has served us well and has facilitated renewal and allowed application in many places throughout western history. But it often does not acquit itself well when it is taken into a non-western setting.

A single example might make this point clearer. I have taught Apologetics classes in three continents for more than twenty years. In the West I have grown accustomed to introducing my students to arguments for the existence of God that have existed in our tradition for hundreds of years. These have become especially important in our century where secularism has eaten away at beliefs that were commonly held a century ago. How do we know that God exists and that he has spoken his word to us? This basic question of epistemology is at the heart of many obstacles to faith in the West.

During my first experience of teaching Apologetics to a class of African students in Nairobi, I asked as I always do what they felt to be the major objections to belief in Christianity among people they knew.

---

7. "Towards an Understanding of Africa's Place in Christian History," in *Religion in a Pluralistic Society*, J. S. Pobee, ed. (Leiden: Brill, 1976), 180. The figures are those of David Barrett which appear annually in the January issue of the *International Bulletin of Missionary Research*. See Vol. 16, No. 1, p. 27.

After some thought, one of the students (from a rural part of Zaire) raised his hand and said: "The major objection would be if the rains don't fall and the crops do not grow. That would produce a crisis of faith." After my initial shock (nowhere in my notes was I prepared to defend Christianity along those lines!), I began to realize that religion in Africa was a matter of contesting powers. Every village had its native gods or spirits and their traditional means of dealing with those powers. These powers were traditionally invoked for calling down the rains which were always a matter of life and death in that setting. How does the power of the Christian God relate to these other powers? This question was less a matter of truth than of the management of power, or as we have learned to say, of power encounters. We will see in our discussions of African theology that this is still the pertinent issue. The issues of the existence or nonexistence of God and the truth of his Word, while important forms are not the pressing questions in Africa. The question is not "does God exist" but which god is the true god? Therefore, different questions will be on the agenda of African theolgians. Similar points could be made for theology in Asia or Latin America.[8]

A second and even more important reason for us to read theologians from outside the West is their importance for our own theological maturation. We, of course, struggle over rains—we in America have had problems with too much and too little only recently—but we ordinarily do not conceive of this as a theological problem. I have said that western theology has a great deal of vitality left in it, but there are areas where it is clearly in need of renewal. Two which come to mind are the need for a theology of the earth and its processes, and a theology of ethnicity or cultural differences. Indeed because of the unique nature of our theological tradition questions like these have not usually come up. Ordinarily our reflection has taken place at such an elevated level of generality that issues related to say, the fertility of the soil, have not seemed theologically significant. Almost two hundred years ago Friedrich Schleiermacher was supposed to have called for a theology of the soil, but for various reasons his challenge went largely unheard.

Moreover, theological reflection was carried on among a largely homogenous population. Issues of cultural diversity (or gender difference) did not arise, or when they did they were immediately settled in terms of the values of those speaking. Now because of the realities of

---

8. These different agendas are sketched out in some detail in my book *Learning about Theology from the Third World* (Grand Rapids, Mich.: Zondervan, 1990).

migration, refugees and tourism people have been thrown together in unprecedented and unsettling ways. How can we reflect responsibly as biblical thinkers on these differences?

In these and many other areas of thought our brothers and sisters from non-western settings have a great deal to teach us. Indeed I would go further than merely saying these theologians will help us fill in gaps in our theological encyclopedia. I think it is safe to say that any renewal that will come to western theology will come by interaction with voices from alternative traditions. We will see in these papers that concern for relations between peoples and between First and Third World churches, relationship to the earth and its processes, are all questions pressing to these theologians. And we have much to learn from these discussions. In fact, one could argue that renewal in theological reflection in America has already been stimulated by feminist, black, and Latin American theology. We will see that much creativity is evident in the work of the thinkers featured in this book and more will be heard from them in the days ahead.

The Contemporary Character
of Non-Western Theology

These writings are not in any way intended as a scientific sample of theological reflection outside the West. Indeed they reflect the biases and contacts of the editor. But some generalizations can clearly be made from even this small body of work. First, it is clear that the agenda of theology outside the West is extremely diverse, as indeed one would expect from the great variety of settings represented. Some are probing deeply into their own non-Christian history to see what expectations for salvation were present (Okorocha); others are looking closely at their own Christian history to see how the present tensions in the church have emerged (Barrio and Balcomb). Still another dares to turn his gaze toward what he regards as the weakness of the evangelical church in America which has had such a profound impact around the world (Lim). This points up the fact that theological realities are often seen to reside in the particularities of their own historical and social situation (Miranda-Feliciano).

In the midst of the diversity of the discussions, however, there are emerging themes that can already be noted. We have pointed out the tendency to reflect theologically on their historical situation and the place of the church in that setting. Whereas we in the West have only recently begun to understand and evaluate the realities of our own "contextual-

ization," this was urgent for mission churches from the beginning. Relations with mission churches, between white and black churches, or
between warring ethnic groups, all have become occasions to reflect on
the theological reality of community and God's purposes for his creation.

Related to this we see, in the second place, the tendency to reflect
more closely on our relation to the earth, the processes of nature and
related issues of poverty. Not only African but Indian thinkers (cf. Ken
Gnanakan's article) provide examples of materials that are helpful to all
of us working toward a much needed theology of creation. A theology
of the state has been a staple ingredient of western theological reflection, but Third World reflection helps us think about the issue of political power theologically. As Samuel Escobar and Evelyn Miranda-
Feliciano show us, this is not an abstract issue but one felt in the stom-
ach when examples of raw power get out of hand. The articles by Volf
and Bediako provide examples of the shape a more systematic approach
to theology might take in alternative settings. Both are moving toward
more comprehensive perspectives in theology but do so with the tools
provided by their cultural and historical situation. In both these cases we
catch a glimpse of theology being formed close to where the people are
living and working.

All of this will be the subject of comment further on, but this brief
summary leads me to a final generalization about non-western theology
that has struck me from the beginning of my experience outside America. Theological reflection often takes place in the context of mission
and evangelism. I have hinted that this can be seen as a weakness, and
indeed, it was responsible for the relative weakness of theology early
on. But the other side of this is that theology that grows in this context
will have an immediacy and dynamic that makes it very accessible. One
of the authors, Cyril Okorocha, has described to me how he was able to
write and think in the midst of a busy life as a pastor and church leader.
He would have to steal moments while waiting for a plane or late at
night, after the last parishioner had gone home. Like most other Two
Thirds World theologians, he did not have the luxury of taking sabbaticals during which he was able to hone his thoughts in the quiet of a great
university library. This appears to us as a great disadvantage, and in a
way it is, but it reflects the realities of life in the Third World (and inci-
dentally, among racial-ethnic churches in the West as well). It is not surprising then that their work is often "engaged" and grapples with vital
and living issues.

It might be helpful for us to remind ourselves that this setting almost exactly reflects that of the New Testament, where the writers worked in the context of busy lives of ministry. Paul's theology in many respects is a theology written in mission and was intended to facilitate the advance of the Gospel. If anything reflects this situation today it is work done by Two Thirds World theologians rather than the usual academic theology produced in the West. Both are needed, of course, so that we might fulfill Paul's prayer that "all of us come to the unity of the faith and of the knowledge of the Son of God, to maturity, to the measure of the full stature of Christ" (Eph. 4:13 NRSV).

The question that arises in this context is how genuine interaction among western and non-western theologians may be facilitated. Other than reading essays like those in this book in our spare time, how might theologians from widely different settings learn from one another? My sense is that this would best be fulfilled if western and Third World theologians were able to share alternative settings—allowing our brothers and sisters from abroad to enjoy sabbaticals while we spend some time in ministry outside our usual context. They can profit from our considerable library facilities, while we "catch" some of the urgencies they live with on a daily basis.

But there are two critical, I am tempted to say insurmountable, obstacles that remain to this kind of interaction—one philosophical and one practical. The philosophical issue relates to our essentially ethnocentric attitude toward intellectual traditions. Recently I was in a meeting of influential theologians during which we were discussing the growing reality of cultural diversity and the messiness of theological discussions that resulted. I dared to say this was probably a healthy thing, since it gave us a better sense of what the world was really like (something theologians have not been famous for). Another in the circle, a denizen of an Eastern divinity school who would never call himself an evangelical, immediately responded that he knew the world was a messy place, but the role of theology is to find and promote order in the world. At that moment the gulf that separates theological reflection and training as it is ordinarily conducted in the West from that typically done in non-western traditions emerged with great clarity.

Because of our unique philosophical and social heritage we see the role of theological leadership primarily as promoting intellectual order and a grand synthesis. We want to understand and make "sense" of the diversity we see around us. Our primary concern is an intellectual one. For most people outside the West the pressing issues relate to day to day

survival and the struggle with deeply imbedded issues of social and cultural oppression. Margaret Miles has put this distinction in the following
terms. For most of western history, she argues, the normative activity by
which humanity is constituted has been subjective consciousness. But
many people in that history, and, we are arguing, most people outside of
this world today, find that "belonging to a family or a social or national
community, the struggle for physical necessities, or their position in the
life cycle of the body, . . . precede and determine their thought and activity."[9] We would not want to set thought and life in opposition to one
another, but we must frankly recognize the difference between a theology primarily carried out in an academic setting and one growing out of
the more immediate issues of everyday life. Clearly both have certain
things to learn and both have contributions to make. But the problem
remains that many theologians in the West often make an unrecognized
assumption that their heritage is privileged.

This philosophical prejudice is aided and abetted by a more readily
acknowledged historical and practical problem: up to this point the theological influence has been almost exclusively unidirectional. Because of
the ways in which patterns of communication and transportation have
emerged and the colonial history of many non-western settings, theologians outside the West are far more likely to be exposed to western theology than the other way around. One rarely meets a Two Thirds world
theologian who is not anxious to have more access to western theology
and western theologians. But finding a western theologian who is even
conscious of theology done outside the West, let alone wants to learn
something from it, is even more rare.

We have reviewed a few of the reasons why this situation needs to
change. But for readers of this book the most important consideration
remains the biblical teaching of the apostle Paul which we quoted above
from Ephesians 4. We must learn from each other for the simple fact that
maturity is a function of all of us together, that is of the whole body of
Christ, rather than of any individual or group. The gifts Christ gives to
the church are given so that we—verse thirteen is emphatic—all of us,
"come to the unity of faith and of the knowledge of the Son of God, to
maturity, to the measure of the full stature of Christ." (v.13 NRSV). The
pages which follow are important evidence of ways this is already
beginning to happen.

---

9. *Image as Insight* (Boston: Beacon Books, 1985), 17.

Eastern Europe
Introduction

The dominant religious tradition in the West has been primarily the Judeo-Christian tradition. For this reason Christian theologians have been able to shape their theologies in a religious environment that, secularism apart, has been somewhat congenial to the Gospel. Meanwhile, theologians in the Two Thirds World encounter non-Christian traditions in many different forms and thus are confronted with the challenge of speaking about a Christian God in the face of many forms of sometimes hostile religions. A place where western and non-western religious traditions come together today in unique and painful ways is the former Yugoslavia. There representatives of Catholic, Orthodox, and Moslem traditions are locked in a conflict so bitter that it has so far frustrated all efforts of mediators and peace keeping forces. Miroslav Volf who is Croatian by birth, but who has lived much of his life in what is now Serbia, represents a minority tradition in this context, that of Pentecostalism.

Having friends, even relatives on all sides of the tense and shifting borders Miroslav has felt the hatred and bitterness with a depth we can only imagine. As he put it to me a while ago, the problem for him often comes down to: "How can we understand this kind of hatred, theologically?" What do we make of this bitterness on the part of people whose history and biographies are ineluctably interconnected? In this gripping article he seeks to use the very categories that arise out of the situation—exclusion and otherness—to open the way to a theological understanding of God's presence in this situation. While his work is clearly informed and energized by the dramatic realities he has seen around him, he goes as far as anyone in this collection to suggest ways that we might move to a systematic, that is integrated, perspective on what he sees. Professor Volf is currently at work on a book that expands on these categories and elaborates this framework.

Exclusion and Embrace:
Theological Reflections in the Wake
of "Ethnic Cleansing"

Miroslav Volf

"In the Gospels, Jesus tells a puzzling story about the unclean spirit who leaves a person, only to return with seven other spirits of an even more wicked character. The new state of the person is even worse than the old (see Matt. 12:45ff.). I am sometimes tempted to apply this story to the situation in Eastern Europe after the 1989 revolution. The demon of totalitarian communism has just been or is being exorcised, but worse demons seem to be rushing in to fill the empty house."[1] This is how I introduced a paper two years ago on the tasks of the churches in Eastern Europe after the 1989 revolution. It was at a conference of Third World theologians in Osijek, Croatia. Some six months later, the Evangelical Theological Faculty, which hosted the conference, had to flee to neighboring Slovenia; Osijek was being shelled day in and day out by Serbian forces. What during the conference had only *seemed* about to happen had in fact already taken place. New demons had possessed the Balkan house and were preparing their vandalistic and bloody feast, first in Croatia and then in Bosnia. Signs of their presence in other parts of Eastern Europe are less tangible, but real nonetheless. As soon as the undivided "new Europe" appeared on the horizon, it vanished again into the thick smoke of the stubborn Balkan fire.

The task for Eastern European churches remains the same today as it was two years ago—to ward off the onrush of both the old and the new demons. What has changed is the complexity of the task. I intend, however, neither to repeat nor supplement my analysis and recommendations of two years ago. Instead of asking a primarily missiologically

---

1. Miroslav Volf, "When the Unclean Spirit Leaves: Tasks of the Eastern European Churches after the 1989 Revolution," *Cross Currents* 41 (1991), 78.

oriented question about what churches in Eastern Europe today should do,[2] I propose to discuss a more fundamental issue involving the challenge that being caught between the old and new demons presents for *theological reflection*—a reflection which, of course, must always take place under the horizon of the mission of God in the world. What are some of the key theological issues facing Christians in Eastern Europe, particularly in the Balkans? When the heat of the battle subsides and attention is focused neither on killing nor on surviving, two issues are at the forefront of peoples' minds. The first is *evil and sin*: how does one make sense of the vicious circle of hell—deep hatred and the baffling network of small and great evils that people inflict on each other? The second is *reconciliation*: how do we stop the killing and learn to live together after so much mutual hatred and bloodshed have shaped our common history? Both of these issues coalesce in the more abstract but fundamental question of *otherness*—of ethnic, religious, and cultural difference. In Eastern Europe this question is seldom posed in such abstract terms, and is often not asked consciously at all. But it frames all the other questions with which people are grappling existentially.

Those whose theological palates long for some exotic fruit from foreign soil might be disappointed with my list. Are not these same issues surfacing everywhere in the world today? Am I not offering staple foods that can be found anywhere? My answer is yes, probably. But then as a theological chef I do not think this should bother me. My responsibility is not to tickle the palates of (western) theological connoisseurs dulled by abundance and variety, but to fill the empty stomachs of people engaged in a bloody conflict. I have to prepare the food *they* need. Opinions of connoisseurs might be interesting and instructive, but nutritious value for the hungry is what matters. This is what it means to do contextualized theology. So my question will be, how do the issues of otherness, sin and reconciliation look from the perspective of the social upheaval and ethnic conflict in the Balkans?

---

2. This paper was presented at a joint conference of the Gesellschaft für Evangelische Theologie and Arbeitskreis für Evangelische Theologie in Potsdam, Germany, February 15–17, 1993. The theme of the conference was "God's Spirit and God's People in the Social and Cultural Upheavals in Europe" and the topic assigned to me "The Tasks of the Christian Community in the Social and Cultural Upheavals in Europe." Jayakumar Christian and Dr. Young-Lee Hertig have read a previous version of the paper and helped me see some issues from Indian and feminine Korean perspectives respectively. Suggestions of my colleagues and/or friends Prof. David Augsburger, Prof. Philip Clayton, and Prof. James Wm. McClendon, Jr. have helped me a great deal.

Much of my reflection on these issues took place as I was living and teaching in Osijek during the fall of 1992. By that time, the war in Croatia was over (or at least its first phase was),[3] but its traces were everywhere—broken windows, scared facades, destroyed roofs, burned and desolated houses, a ruined economy and, above all, many deep wounds in the hearts of the people. But the war was continuing with even greater brutality in the neighbors' courtyard. As Croatians were watching the unabated Serbian aggression in Bosnia and trying to cope with the never-ending stream of refugees, they were reliving their own war inferno. There was much pride over their newly won statehood, even if it had had to be paid for in blood. But there was even more trepidation about the future: When would the powerful aggressor be stopped and brought to justice? Would they ever regain the lost territories and return to their villages and cities? If they did, how would they rebuild them? The feeling of helplessness and frustration, of anger and hatred, was ubiquitous.

From the beginning of the conflict I was sharing in the destiny of my people—first from afar, from Slovenia and from my home in California; then first-hand, when I arrived in Osijek for a prolonged stay. It was then that I was forced to start making sense of what I encountered. What I present here can best be described as a "preliminary account of an exploration." This exploration would never have been undertaken and would have long since been given up had it not been for the powerful experience of the complex and conflicting social realities brought on by revolution and war. Experience goaded me on to explore. So I will not shy away from appealing to it here.

The Other

I was crossing the Croatian border for the first time since Croatia declared independence. State insignia and flags that were displayed prominently at the "gate to Croatia" were merely visible signs of what I could sense like an electrical charge in the air: I was leaving Hungary and entering Croatian space. I felt relief. In what used to be Yugoslavia one was almost expected to apologize for being a Croat. Now I was free to be who I ethnically am. Yet the longer I was in the country, the more hemmed in I felt. For instance, I sensed an unexpressed expectation to explain why as a Croat I still had friends in Serbia and did not talk with disgust about the backwardness of byzantine-orthodox culture. I am

---

3. The paper was finished in January 1993.

used to the colorful surrounding of multiethnicity. A child of a "mixed marriage," I grew up in a city which the old Habsburg Empire had made into a meeting place of many ethnic groups; and I live in the (tension-filled) multicultural city of Los Angeles. But the new Croatia, like some jealous goddess, wanted all my love and loyalty; she wanted to possess every part of my being. I must be Croat through and through to be a good Croat; I could read that between the lines of the large-lettered ethnic text that met my eyes wherever I looked. "Croatia," I thought to myself, "will not be satisfied until it permeates everything in Croatia."

It is easy to explain this tendential *omnipresentia Croatiae in Croatia*. After forced assimilation under Communist rule, it was predictable that the feeling of ethnic belonging would vigorously reassert itself. Moreover, the need to stand firm against a powerful and destructive enemy leaves little room for the luxury of divided loyalties. The explanations make sense, yet the unsettling question remains: Does one not discover in Croatia's face some despised Serbian features? Has the enemy not captured Croatia's soul along with Croatia's soil? Serbian aggression has enriched the already oversized vocabulary of evil with the term "ethnic cleansing": Ethnic otherness is filth that needs to be washed away from the ethnic body, pollution that threatens the ecology of ethnic space. But, not unlike many other countries, Croatia wants to be clean too—at least clean of its enemies, the Serbs! There is, of course, a world of difference in whether one suppresses otherness by social pressure to conform and emigrate, or even by discriminatory legislation, or whether one works to eliminate it with the destructive power of guns and fire. But is not the goal the same—a monochrome world, a world without the other?

During my stay in Croatia I read Jacques Derrida's recent reflections on today's Europe. He reflects on his own European identity:

> I am European, I am no doubt a European intellectual, and I like to recall this, I like to recall this to myself, and why would I deny it? In the name of what? But I am not, nor do I feel, European in every part, that is, European through and through. . . . Being a part, belonging as 'fully a part,' should be incompatible with belonging 'in every part.' My cultural identity, that in the name of which I speak, is not only European, it is not identical to itself, and I am not 'cultural' through and through, 'cultural' in every part.[4]

---

4. Jacques Derrida, *The Other Heading: Reflections on Today's Europe* (tr. P. A. Brault and M. B. Naas; Bloomington: Indiana P, 1992), 82f.

The identity of Europe with itself, Derrida went on to say, is totalitarian. And indeed, Europe's past is full of the worst of violences committed in the name of European identity. Europe colonialized and oppressed, destroyed cultures and imposed its religion all in the name of its identity with itself. It was not too long ago that Germany sought to conquer and exterminate in the name of its identity with itself (and Croatia participated in the project its own way). Today, Balkan is aflame in the name of Serbia's identity with itself. Identity without otherness— this is our curse!

The practice of ethnic and other kinds of "cleansing" in the Balkans forces us *to place otherness at the center of theological reflection*. The problem is, of course, not specific to the Balkans. The processes of integration in Europe place otherness high on the agenda. So do, for instance, the disintegration of the Soviet empire and the fragility of multiethnic and multi-religious nations like India. The large framework for the problem is set by developments of planetary proportions. Modern means of communication and the emerging world economy have transformed our world from a set of self-contained tribes and nations into a global city. The unity of the human race is no longer an abstract notion. And the closer humanity's unity, the more powerfully we experience its diversity. The "others"—persons of other culture, other religion, other economic status and so on—are not people we read about from distant lands; we see them daily on the screens in our living rooms, pass by them on our streets. They are our colleagues and neighbors, some of them even are spouses. The others are among us; they are part of us. Yet they remain others, often pushed to the margins. How should we relate to them? Should we celebrate their difference and support it, or should we bemoan and suppress it? The issue is urgent. The ghettos and battlefields throughout the world testify indisputably to its importance.[5] It is not too much to claim that the future of not only the Balkans but the whole world depends on how we deal with ethnic, religious, and gender otherness.

Liberation theologians taught us to place the themes of oppression and liberation at the center of theological reflection. They drew our

---

5. For a short analysis of the political and cultural, but mainly philosophical, importance of the "difference," see Mark C. Taylor, *Altarity* (Chicago: The University Press of Chicago, 1987), xxi. See also Tzvetan Todorov's classic treatment of the problem of otherness in the account of the encounter between European and American civilisations *The Conquest of America: The Question of the Other* (tr. R. Howard; New York: Harper, 1985).

attention to the God who is on the side of the poor and the oppressed, and the demands of God's people to be on the same side too.[6] Nothing should make us forget these lessons, for the "preferential option for the poor" is rooted deeply in biblical traditions. But the categories of oppression and liberation are by themselves inadequate to address the Balkan conflict—or, indeed, the problems in the world at large today. The categories are, of course, almost tailor-made for both Croats and Serbs: each side perceives itself as oppressed by the other and both are engaged in what they believe to be the struggle for liberation. Unless one is prepared to say that one side is completely right and the other wrong, this is precisely where the problem lies. Categories of oppression and liberation provide combat gear, not a pin-striped suit or a dinner dress; they are good for fighting, but not for negotiating or celebrating. Even assuming that the one side is right and the other wrong, what happens when the fight is over and (we hope) the right side wins? One still faces the question of how the liberated oppressed can live together with their conquered oppressors. "Liberation of the oppressors" is the answer that the "oppression–liberation" schema suggests. But is it persuasive? Victors are known for never taking off their soldiers' suits; liberation through violence breeds new conflicts. The categories of oppression and liberation seem ill-suited to bring about the resolution of conflicts between people and people groups. I suggest that the categories of "exclusion and embrace" as two paradigm responses to otherness can do a better job. They need to be placed at the center of a theological reflection on otherness, an endeavor I would like to term a "theology of embrace."

A "theology of embrace" would, however, amount to a betrayal both of God and oppressed people if it were pursued in such a way as to marginalize the problems of oppression and liberation. Rather, we need to see oppression and liberation as essential dimensions of exclusion and embrace respectively. Those who are oppressed and in the need of liberation are always "the others." Indeed, almost invariably the oppressed do not belong to the dominant culture of the oppressors, but are persons or people groups of other race, gender, or religion. To embrace others in their otherness must mean to free them from oppression and give them space to be themselves. Anything else is either a hypocritical tap on the shoulders or a deadly "bear hug." Thus the ques-

---

6. See the classic work by Gustavo Gutierrez, *A Theology of Liberation: History, Politics and Salvation* (tr. S. Inda and J. Eagelson; New York: Orbis Books, 1973).

tion must never be whether one should struggle against oppression, but what theological categories are most adequate to accomplish the task.

I will address the issue of otherness first by looking at the nature of Christian identity. This will provide a platform from which to talk about sin as exclusion and about salvation as embrace. At the outset I have to beg for indulgence. Within the confines of a single paper I am able neither to ground the "theology of embrace" sufficiently in the work of Christ nor to reflect extensively on its concrete implications. I am also unable to work out the differences in the way exclusion and embrace take place on individual and group levels.

Aliens

In his reminiscences entitled *From the Kingdom of Memory*, Elie Wiesel defines the stranger as "someone who suggests the unknown, the prohibited, the beyond; he seduces, he attracts, he wounds—and he leaves. . . . The stranger represents what you are not, what you cannot be, simply because you are not *he*. . . . The stranger is *the other*. He is not bound by your laws, by your memories; his language is not yours, nor his silence."[7] How should we respond to the strange world of the other? In answering this question, Christians will have to reflect on their *own identity as strangers*.

From the inception of the Christian church, otherness was integral to Christian ethnic and cultural identity.[8] Toward the end of the New Testament period, Christians came to designate themselves explicitly as "aliens and sojourners" (1Peter 2:11).[9] By the second century these metaphors became central to their self-understanding. They saw themselves as heirs to the Old Testament people of God: Abraham was called to go from his country, his kindred and his father's house (Gen. 12:1); his grandchildren and the children of his grandchildren became "aliens in the land of Egypt" (Lev. 19:34 NASB); the nation of which he and Sarah were foreparents lived as exiles in the Babylonian captivity. And even when they lived securely in their own land, Jahweh their God expected them to be different from nations that surrounded them. However, at the root of Christian self-understanding as aliens and sojourners lies not so

---

7. Elie Wiesel, *From the Kingdom of Memory: Reminiscences* (New York: Summit Books, 1990), 59f.

8. See Reinhard Feldmeier, *Die Christan als Fremde: Die Metapher der Fremde in der antiken Welt, im Urchristentum und im 1. Petrusbrief* (WUNT 64; Tübingen: J. C. B. Mohr [Paul Siebeck], 1992).

9. Gustaf Stählin, "ξένο" κτλ.," *TDNT* V, 30.

much the story of Abraham and his posterity as the destiny of Jesus Christ, his mission and his rejection which brought him to the cross. "He came to what was his own, and his own people did not accept him" (John 1:11). He was a stranger to the world because the world into which he came was estranged from God. And so it is with his followers. "When a person becomes a believer, then he moves from the far country to the vicinity of God. . . . There now arises a relation of reciprocal foreignness and estrangement between Christians and the world."[10] Christians are born of the Spirit (John 3:8) and are therefore not "from the world" but, like Jesus Christ, "from God" (John 15:19). It is not at the disposal of Christians whether to be alien in their own culture. The "difference" from one's own culture—from the concrete "world" one inhabits—is essential to the Christian's cultural identity.

But why be "different"? Simply for the sake of difference? Even that is progress in a world without the other. Belonging without distance destroys: I affirm my identity as Croatian and want either to shape everyone in my own image or eliminate them from my world. So why not dirty the walls of a monochrome culture with some spiteful, colorful graffiti? There is a value in difference even simply as difference. Yet the difference will remain sterile if it is nothing but a protest gesture. It might also turn into its very opposite. If belonging without distance destroys, distance without belonging isolates: I deny my cultural identity as Croatian and draw back from my own culture. But more often than not, I became trapped in the snares of counter-dependence. I deny my Croatian identity only to affirm even more forcefully my identity as a member of this or that anti-Croatian sect. And so, as the "positive fusion" is substituted by "negative fusion," an isolationist "distance without belonging" slips into a destructive "belonging without distance." Difference from a culture must never degenerate into a simple flight from that culture. Rather, to be alien and sojourner must be a way of living *in* a culture and *for* a culture. In biblical terminology, the kingdom of God is not *of* this world, but it is *in* this world and *for* this world. Distance must involve belonging as belonging must involve distance.

Given, then, the need for interpenetration of distance and belonging, what is the positive purpose of the distance? The category of "new creation" sets us on the trail leading to an answer. In a key passage about the nature of Christian existence, Paul writes: "So if anyone is in Christ, there is a new creation" (2 Cor. 5:17). The rebirth of a person by the

---

10. Stählin, "ξένο" κτλ.," 29.

Spirit is nothing less than an anticipation of the eschatological new creation of God, a gathering of the whole people of God and of all the cultural treasures that have been dispersed among the nations. By the Spirit, that future universal event becomes a concrete reality in each believer.

One consequence of the re-creation of a person by the Spirit is that she can no longer be thought of apart from the rich and complex reality of the new creation. The Spirit sets a person on the road toward becoming what one might call a "catholic personality," a personal microcosm of the eschatological new creation. Catholic personality is a personality enriched by otherness, a personality which is what it is only because all differentiated otherness of the new creation has been reflected in it in a particular way. The distance from my own culture that results from being born by the Spirit does not isolate me, but *creates space in me for the other.* Only in distance can I be enriched, so that I, in turn, can enrich the culture to which I belong.

Because everything belongs partly to a catholic personality, a person with catholic personality cannot belong to any one thing totally. Her only way to belong is with distance. This distance from any particular reality—from any particular person and culture—which exists for the sake of transcending the exclusion of all other reality from that person's identity, might be called "catholic foreignness." Christians are not simply aliens to their own culture; they are aliens that are at home in every culture, because they are open to every culture. Something of this catholic foreignness might have been in mind of the anonymous author of the Epistle to Diognetus when he wrote, "every foreign country is their fatherland and every fatherland is a foreign country."[11]

The notion of the catholic personality avoids exclusivism because each person has become a particular reflection of the totality of others. At the same time it transcends indifferent relativism. Each does not simply affirm the otherness as otherness, but seeks to be enriched by it. But should a catholic personality integrate all otherness? Can one feel at home with everything in every culture? With murder, rape, and destruction? With nationalistic idolatry and "ethnic cleansing"? Any notion of catholic personality which was capable of only integrating but not of discriminating would be grotesque. For there are incommensurable perspectives that stubbornly refuse to be dissolved in a peaceful synthesis, and there are evil things that we should stubbornly resist to integrate

---

11. "Epistle to Diognetus," 5:5.

into our personalities.[12] The practice of exclusion cannot be given up. The biblical category for it is "judgment." This brings us to the second positive purpose of the distance.

Distance which results from being born by the Spirit—"catholic foreignness"—entails a judgment not only against a monochrome character of one's own culture but also against evil in every culture. The new creation which an authentic catholic personality should anticipate is not an indiscriminate affirmation of the present world. Such an affirmation would be the cheapest of all graces, and hence no grace at all—not toward the perpetrators of evil, nor, of course, toward their many victims. There can be no new creation without judgment, without the expulsion of the devil and the beast and the false prophet (Rev. 20:10), without the swallowing up of the night by the light and of death by life (Rev. 21:4; 22:5).[13] The notion of "catholic foreignness" therefore necessarily involves a conflict with the world: the struggle between truth and falsehood, between justice and arbitrariness, life and death.[14] Distance from a culture that rebirth by the Spirit creates is a judgment against the evils of a culture. It creates space for the struggle against the various demons that assault it. A truly catholic personality must be an evangelical *personality*—a personality transformed by the Spirit of the new creation and engaged in the transformation of the world.

But does not talk about demons and darkness return us to the exclusion which the notion of the "catholic personality" should have overcome? Indeed, does not the notion of catholic personality presuppose exclusion because it rests not only on belonging but also on distance? The best way to tackle these questions is to look at the significance of the "centrality." It seems rather obvious that when talking about identity one cannot do without a center; otherwise, the talk of difference and its being internal to oneself makes no sense. The difference is internal to what? Jacques Derrida, who is not known to be graceful toward what he calls "hegemonic centrality," recognizes as much when he insists that self-difference "would gather this center [the human centre of an individual—M.V.], relating it to itself, only to the extent that it would open

---

12. See Richard J. Mouw, "Christian Philosophy and Cultural Diversity," *CSR* 17 (1987), 109–21, 114ff.

13. See Miroslav Volf, *Work in the Spirit: Toward a Theology of Work* (New York: Oxford UP, 1991), 120f.

14. See Jürgen Moltmann, *Der Weg Jesu Christi. Christologie in messianischen Dimensionen* (München: Kaiser, 1989), 226. Cf. also Jürgen Moltmann, "Dient die 'pluralistische Theologie' dem Dialog der Welt-religionen?" in *EvTh* 49 (1989), 528–36.

it up to" the divergence from itself.[15] Derrida cannot give up the center, for then the difference would remain everywhere and nowhere. The center seems to function, however, only as a precondition for openness for the other, as a contentless container of difference. But if the self is not a center organizing the difference, but merely a container of the difference, does one not end up—exactly contrary to Derrida's intention—with a "melting pot" (or some chaotic "salad-bowl")? The lesser trouble with the melting pot is that it never existed. The greater trouble is that it dissolves the difference. The identity with oneself—a personal centeredness—must be preserved for the sake of difference.[16] My being centered in distance from the other is not a negative act of exclusion, but a creative act of separation. The book of Genesis rightly describes creation as successive divine acts of separation (see 1:3ff.). Because I and the other can be constituted in our mutual otherness only by separation, no genuine openness to the other is possible without it. This is why the encounter with a stranger is creative only if, as Elie Wiesel puts it, you "know when to step back."[17]

In the case of Christians, superimposed on the center which creates their human identity is another center which creates their *Christian* identity. Emergence of this new center is also an act of creation—the new creation—and it takes place through separation. But why this new center? Why the additional separation? Because a human center is not an impersonal axis, but a personal self—a heart—that cannot exist without a "god," without a framework of meaning and value. The god of the self is the doorkeeper who decides about the fate of the otherness at the doorsteps of the heart. To embrace a Christian God does not mean to place a doorkeeper at the entrance of one's heart which was without one

---

15. Derrida, *The Other Heading*, 10. He says as much when he speaks of the contradictory demand that the European cultural identity not be dispersed but that at the same time it not accept "the capital of a centralizing authority" (38f.).

16. In his Gifford lectures entitled *Oneself as Another*, Paul Ricoeur distinguishes categorically between *idem*-identity and *ipse*-identity. In the circle of *idem*-identity the other is "distinct" or "diverse" and it functions as the antonym of "same." In the circle of *ipse*-identity, the otherness is constitutive of sameness; here the selfhood of oneself "implies otherness to such an intimate degree that one cannot be thought of without the other" (Paul Ricoeur, *Oneself as Another*, tr. K. Blmey [Chicago: The University of Chicago Press, 1992], 3). So when we speak of the loss of identity—of *Ichlosigkeit*—then the "I" of which the subject says that it is nothing is "a self deprived of the help of sameness" (166).

17. Wiesel, *From the Kingdom*, 73. A stranger, he writes, "can be of help only as a stranger—lest you are ready to become his caricature. And your own" (65).

before, but to *re*place the one doorkeeper with another. One cannot get rid of one's gods; one can only change them. And when one thinks one has gotten rid of them, a restless demon who wanders through waterless regions looking for a resting place but finds none has already taken their place (see Matt. 12:43). So the question is not whether one has a doorkeeper, but who the doorkeeper is and how the doorkeeper relates to otherness. Does the Christian doorkeeper prohibit anything non-Christian from entering in?

There are two injunctions which persistently surface in the Bible. One is to have no strange gods; the other is to love strangers. The two injunctions are interrelated: one should love strangers in the name of the one triune God, who loves strangers. This triune God is the center that regulates a Christian's relationship to otherness, a doorkeeper who opens and closes the door of the self.[18] To be a Christian does not mean to close oneself off in one's own identity and advance oneself in an exemplary way toward what one is not. It means rather to be centered on this God—the God of the other—and participate in *God's* advance toward where God and God's reign is not yet. Without such centeredness, it would be impossible either to denounce the practice of exclusion or demand the practice of embrace.

Exclusion

What strikes one immediately in the Balkan war is the naked hate, a hate without enough decency—or shall we say hypocrisy?—to cover itself up. Not that hate is unique to this conflict. Most wars feed on hate, and the masters of war know how to manufacture it well. It is the proportions of the Balkan hate, and its rawness right there on the fringes of

---

18. The metaphor of the door is helpful insofar as it implies a necessary demarcation, but it is also misleading insofar as it suggests a sharp and static boundary. In analyzing the category "Christian," missiologist Paul Hiebert suggests that we make use of the mathematical categories of "bounded sets," "fuzzy sets," and "centered sets." Bounded sets function on the principle "either/or": an apple is either an apple or it is not; it cannot be partly apple and partly a pear. Fuzzy sets, on the other hand, have no sharp boundaries; things are fluid with no stable point of reference and with various degrees of inclusion—as when a mountain merges into the plains. A centered set is defined by a center and the relationship of things to that center, by a *movement* toward it or away from it. The category of "Christian," Hiebert suggests, should be understood as a centered set. A demarcation line exists, but the focus is not on "maintaining the boundary" but "on reaffirming the center" (Paul G. Hiebert, "The Category 'Christian' in the Mission Task," *International Review of Mission* 72 [1983]: 421–27, 424). The center of a person who is a new creation in Christ is constituted by separation, but around the center there is space for otherness.

what some thought to be civilized Europe, that causes us to stagger. Think of the stories of soldiers making necklaces out of the fingers of little children! Never mind whether they are true or not—that they are being told and believed suffices. The hate that gives rise to such stories and wants to believe them is the driving force behind the ruthless and relentless pursuit of exclusion known as "ethnic cleansing." This is precisely what hate is: an unflinching will to exclude, a revulsion for the other.

It might be that the most basic sin is pride, though this way of defining sin does not seem to capture with precision the experiences of most women.[19] But I doubt that it is helpful to go about reducing all sins to their common root;[20] the Bible at any rate does not seem to be interested in such a business. I will not pursue here the search for the one basic sin, but indicate a fundamental way of conceiving sin: *sin as exclusion*.[21] For those who are interested in exploring the connection between exclusion and pride, one could point out that exclusion, which is a form of the contempt toward the other, might be considered "the reverse side of pride and its necessary concomitant in a world in which self-esteem is constantly challenged by the achievements of others."[22]

One of the advantages of conceiving sin as exclusion is that it names as sin what often passes as virtue, especially in religious circles. In the Palestine of Jesus' day, "sinners" were primarily social outcasts, people who practiced despised trades, failed to keep the Law as interpreted by the religious establishment, and Gentiles and Samaritans. A pious person had to separate herself from them; their presence defiled because they were defiled. Jesus' table fellowship with social outcasts, a fellowship that belonged to the central features of his ministry, turned

---

19. See Judith Plaskow, *Sex, Sin and Grace: Women's Experience and the Theologies of Reinhold Niebuhr and Paul Tillich* (University Press of America, 1980); Daphine Hampson, "Reinhold Niebuhr on Sin: A Critique," *Reinhold Niebuhr and the Issues of Our Time* (ed. R. Harries; Michigan: Eerdmans, 1986), 46–60.

20. So also Jürgen Moltmann, *The Spirit of Life: A Universal Affirmation* (tr. M. Kohl; Minneapolis: Fortress Press, 1992), 127.

21. "Exclusion" as I am using the term here should not be confused with "separation." Separation, as I noted earlier, is a creative act through which otherness is constituted. If one speaks of sin as separation (see, for instance, Barry Ulanov's reflections on sin as separation in "The Rages of Sin," *USQR* 44 [1990]: 137–50) one should think of it as a second-order separation—a rendering asunder of things that in their otherness belong together.

22. Reinhold Niebuhr, *The Nature and Destiny of Man: A Christian Interpretation I: Human Nature* (New York: Charles Scribner's Sons, 1961), 211.

this conception of sin on its head: *The real sinner is not the outcast but the one who casts the other out.* As Walter Wink writes, "Jesus distinguishes between those falsely called sinners—who are in fact victims of an oppressive system of exclusion—and true sinners, whose evil is not ascribed to them by others, but who have sinned from the heart (Mark 7:21)."[23] Sin is not so much a defilement but a certain form of *purity*: the exclusion of the other from one's heart and one's world. In the story of the prodigal son, the sinner was the elder brother—the one who withheld an embrace and expected exclusion. Sin is a refusal to embrace the other in her otherness and a desire to purge her from one's world, by ostracism or oppression, deportation or liquidation.

The exclusion of the other is an exclusion of *God*. This is what one can read between the lines of the story of the prodigal son. The departure of the younger brother from the father's home was an act of exclusion. He wanted his father—and maybe his brother too—out of his world. Yet in his life of exclusion, in the far country, he was closer to the father than was his older brother who remained at home. For like the father, he longed for an embrace. His older brother kept the father in his world, but excluded him from his heart. For the older brother an act of exclusion demanded retaliatory exclusion. But for the father, an act of exclusion called for an embrace. By excluding his younger brother, the older brother excluded the father who longs for an embrace.

But did not *both* brothers exclude the father? Are they not *both* sinners? Are they not both *equally* sinners? This brings us to the problem of the universality of sin.

From a distance things look fairly simple in the Balkan war: Croatians (and Muslims) are the victims and Serbians are the aggressors. Has any city in Serbia been destroyed, any of its territories occupied? The macro-picture of the conflict is clear, and it does not seem likely that anything will ever change it. I approached the clear contours of this picture with a pre-reflective expectation that the victim is innocent and the oppressor guilty. This natural presumption was aided by my belonging to the victimized group. I had, of course, never doubted that Croatians share some blame for the outbreak of the war (just as I never doubted that only Croatia's renunciation of sovereignty would have prevented the conflict from breaking out in the first place). But I expected Croatians to be more humane victims. At night in Osijek, I would hear explo-

---

23. Walter Wink, *Engaging the Powers: Discernment and Resistance in a World of Domination* (Minneapolis: Fortress Press, 1992), 115–6.

sions go off and know that another house or a shop of a Serb who did not emigrate had been destroyed; and rarely was anyone brought to justice. Refugees, those who were victimized the most, looted trucks that brought them help; they were at war with *each other.* Are these simply necessary accompaniments of a war? If so, they prove my point: the more closely one looks at the picture, the more the line between the guilty and the innocent blurs and all one sees is an intractable maze of small and large brutalities. I was tempted to exclaim: "All are evil, equally evil!" But then I heard those same words broadcasted by the Serbian propaganda machine. The logic was simple: If evildoers are everywhere, then the violence of the aggressor is no worse than the violence of the victim. All are aggressors and all are victims. Placing the micro-picture of the maze of evil so close to our eyes was calculated to remove the macro-picture of aggression and suffering from our field of vision.

Christian theology has traditionally underlined the universality of sin. "All have sinned and fall short of the glory of God," writes the apostle Paul, echoing some central Old Testament passages (Rom 3:9ff.). In the bright light of the divine glory, stains of injustice appear on all human righteousness and blemishes of narcissism, indifference and sometimes hate on all human love. In addition to freeing us "from delusions about the perfectibility of ourselves and our institutions,"[24] the doctrine of the universality of sin pricks the thin balloons of self-righteousness of aggressor and victim alike and binds them in the solidarity of sin, thus preparing the way for reconciliation. This is why the doctrine of the universality of sin should not be given up.

However, if all are sinners, are all sins equal? Reinhold Niebuhr, who in our century most powerfully restated the doctrine of the universality of sin, thought so. But he sought to balance the equality of sin with the inequality of guilt.[25] If one affirms the equality of sin, then such a balancing-act becomes unavoidable. But why assert the equality of sin in the first place? From "all are sinners" *does not* follow "all sins are equal."[26] Aggressors' destruction of a village and refugees' looting of a truck are equally sin, but they are not equal sins. The equality of

---

24. Wink, *Engaging the Powers*, 71.

25. Niebuhr, *The Nature*, 222ff.

26. So already William John Wolf, "Reinhold Niebuhr's Doctrine of Man," *Reinhold Niebuhr: His Religious, Social, and Political Thought* (ed. C. W. Kegley and R. W. Bretall; Library of Living Theology 11; New York: Macmillan, 1956), 240.

sins dissolves all concrete sins in an ocean of undifferentiated sinfulness. This is precisely what the prophets and Jesus did not do. Their judgments are not general but specific; they do not condemn everyone and anyone, but the rich and mighty who oppress the poor and crush the needy. The sin of driving out the other from her possession, from her work, from her means of livelihood, the sin of pushing her to the margins of society and beyond, weighs high on their scales. How could there be universal solidarity in *this* sin? The mighty are the sinners and the weak are the sinned against. Even if all people sin, not all sin equally. To deny this would be to insult all those nameless heroes who refused to participate in power-acts of exclusion and had the courage to embrace the other, even at the risk of being ostracized or imprisoned. The uprightness of these people demands that we talk about sin concretely.[27]

But if we always speak of sin concretely—if we speak of it only in the plural—do we not reduce sin to sinful acts and intentions? Is this not too shallow a view of sin? And does it not lead to unhealthy and oppressive moralizing? The answer would be yes, if it were not for the *transpersonal dimension of sin and evil.*

"Eruption" might be a good word to describe the conflict in the Balkans. I am thinking here less of the suddenness by which it broke out than of its insuppressible power. It does not seem that anybody is in control. Of course, the big and strategic moves that started the conflict and that keep it going are made in the centers of intellectual, political, and military power. But there is too much will for brutality even among the common people. Once the conflict started it seemed to trigger an uncontrollable chain reaction.[28] These were decent people, helpful neighbors. They did not, strictly speaking, *choose* to plunder and burn, rape and torture—or secretly enjoy these things. A dormant beast in them was awakened from its uneasy slumber. And not only in them: the motives of those who set to fight against the brutal aggressors were self-defense and justice, but the beast in others enraged the beast in them. And so the moral barriers holding it in check were broken and the beast went after revenge. In resisting evil, people were trapped by it. After World War II,

---

27. See Moltmann, *The Spirit*, 126.

28. On the eve of World War II, Carl Gustav Jung wrote: "The impressive thing about the German phenomenon is that one man, who is obviously 'possessed,' has infected a whole nation to such an extent that everything is set in motion and has started rolling on its course towards perdition" ("Wotan," *Collected Works of C. F. Jung*, ed. H. Read et al; tr. R. F. C. Hull; Bollingen Series XX [New York: Pantheon Books, 1964], 179–93, 185).

Carl Gustav Jung wrote, "It is a fact that cannot be denied: the wickedness of others becomes our own wickedness because it kindles something evil in our own hearts."[29] Evil engenders evil, and like pyroclastic debris from the mouth of a volcano, it erupts out of the aggressor and the victim alike.

In a fascinating book, *Engaging the Powers*, Walter Wink accesses the problem of the power of evil by looking at what he calls the "Powers" and their perversion into the "Domination System." The Powers, he claims, are neither simply human institutions and structures nor an order of angelic (or demonic) beings. They are both institutional and spiritual; they "possess an outer, physical manifestation . . . and an inner spirituality or corporate culture."[30] The Powers are essentially good, but when they became "hell-bent on control," Wink claims, they degenerate into the Domination System. This System itself is neither only institutional nor spiritual; rather the "forces of this present darkness" (see Ephesians 6:2) are the interiority of warped institutions, structures and systems that oppress people. I will modify Wink's terminology and substitute the "Exclusion System" for his "Domination System," for as a rule the purpose of domination is to exclude others from scarce goods, whether they are economic, social or psychological. But Wink is right that it is through the operation of the System that the power of evil imposes itself so irresistibly on people. Caught in the *System* of exclusion as if in some invisible snare, people begin to behave according to its perverted logic. Should we call this anything but "possession"?

Yet persons cannot be reduced to the System. The System needs persons to make it "breathe" with the spirit of evil, and persons can escape the logic of the System, as the noble history of resistance demonstrates. So if people do acquiesce, it is not because the System forces them to acquiesce, but because there is something in their souls that resonates with the logic of exclusion. Could the culprit be the desire for identity—the instinctive will to be oneself—that is written into the very structure of our selves, as Wolfhart Pannenberg has recently suggested?[31] The will to be oneself is essentially healthy, of course. Yet it

29. Carl Gustav Jung, "After the Catastrophe," *Collected Works of C. F. Jung* (ed. H. Read et al; tr. R. F. C. Hull; Bollingen Series XX; New York: Pantheon Books, 1964), 194–217, 198.

30. Wink, "All Will be Redeemed," *The Other Side* (Nov.–Dec. 1992): 17–23. See Wink, *Engaging the Powers*, 33–104.

31. So Wolfhart Pannenberg, *Systematische Theologie II* (Göttingen: Vandenhoeck & Ruprecht, 1991), 298f.

always carries within it the germs of its own illness. To remain healthy, the will to be oneself needs to make the will to be the other part of itself. And so, because the other must become part of who we are as we will to be ourselves, a tension is built into the desire for identity. It is the antipodal nature of the will to be oneself that makes the slippage into exclusion so easy. The power of sin from without—the Exclusion System— thrives on both the power and the powerlessness from within, the irresistible power of the will to be oneself and the powerlessness to resist the slippage into exclusion of the other.

The desire for identity could also explain why so many people let themselves be sinned against so passively—why they let themselves be excluded. It is not because they do not have the will to be themselves, but because one can satisfy that will *by surrendering to the other*. Their problem is not so much exclusion of the other from their will to be oneself, but a paradoxical exclusion of their *own* self from the will to be oneself (what in feminist theology is called "diffusion of the self"). I call this exclusion a "problem," not a "sin," for it often comes about as a result of introjected acts of exclusion that we suffer.[32] Sin "is lurking at the door" when the introjected exclusion of ourselves by others results in our exclusion of the others—when we start looking for everything dark, inferior, and culpable in them. Like Cain, we then became ready to kill the otherness of the other.

Embrace

What do we do about the terrible sin of exclusion that lurks at our door or has already entered our soul? How do we master it? Is there a way out of the circle of exclusion to an embrace? The tragedy of the Balkan situation is that very few people seem to be asking these questions. Vengeance is on everybody's mind. Serbs want to avenge the slaughter of their compatriots in World War II and to repay others for their injured sense of national pride during the post-War years. Croatians and Muslims want revenge for Serbian atrocities, some from the present war and some from the previous one, and for their economic exploitation. And the greater their success at revenging themselves, the more Serbs feel justified in their aggression. An evil deed will not be owed for long; it demands an instant repayment in kind. Vengeance, as Hanah Arendt wrote in *The Human Condition*,

---

32. Such introjection is possible, of course, because our will to be one with ourselves can be satisfied in part by giving ourselves to others.

acts in the form of reacting against an original trespassing, whereby far from putting an end to the consequences of the first misdeed, everybody remains bound to the process, permitting the chain reaction contained in every action to take its unhindered course; . . . [vengeance] encloses both doer and sufferer in the relentless automatism of the action process, which by itself need never come to an end.[33]

The endless spinning of the spiral of vengeance has its own good reasons that are built into the very structure of our world. If our deeds and their consequences could be undone, revenge would not be necessary. The undoing, if there were will for it, would suffice. But our actions are irreversible. Even God cannot change them. And so the urge for vengeance or for punishment seems irrepressible. Arendt called this "the predicament of irreversibility" (237). The only way out of it, she insisted, was through an act of *forgiveness.*

Yet forgiveness is precisely what seems impossible. Deep within the heart of every victim, hate swells up against the perpetrator. The Imprecatory Psalms seem to come upon their lips much more easily than the prayer of Jesus on the cross. If anything, they would rather pray, "Forgive them not, Father, for they knew what they did" (Abe Rosenthal). If the perpetrators were repentant, forgiveness would come more easily. But repentance seems as difficult as forgiveness. It is not just that we do not like being wrong, but that almost invariably the other side has not been completely right either. Most confessions, then, come as a mixture of repentance and aggressive defense or even lust for revenge.[34] Both the victim and the perpetrator are imprisoned in the automatism of exclusion, unable to forgive or repent and united in a perverse communion of mutual hate.

In the Imprecatory Psalms, the torrents of rage have been allowed to flow freely, channeled only by the robust structure of a ritual prayer.[35] Strangely enough, it is they that point to a way out of the slavery of hate to the freedom of forgiveness. For the followers of the crucified Messiah, their main message is: hate belongs before God, not in a reflec-

---

33. Hanah Arendt, *The Human Condition* (Chicago: The University of Chicago Press, 1958), 240f.

34. See Carl Gustav Jung, "Epilogue to 'Essay on Contemporary Events,'" *Collected Works of C. G. Jung* (ed. H. Read et al; tr. R. F. C. Hull; Bollingen Series XX; New York: Pantheon Books, 1964), 227–43, 240f.

35. See Christoph Barth, *Introduction to the Psalms* (New York: Scribners, 1966), 43ff.; Erhard S. Gerstenberger, "Enemies and Evildoers in the Psalms: A Challenge to Christian Preaching," *Horizons in Biblical Theology* 4/2 (1983): 61–77.

tively managed and manicured form of a confession, but as a pre-reflective outburst from the depths of our being. Hidden in the dark chambers of our hearts and nourished by the system of darkness, hate grows and seeks to infect everything with its hellish will to exclusion. In the light of the justice and love of God, however, hate recedes and the seed is planted for the miracle of forgiveness. Forgiveness flounders because I exclude the enemy from the community of humans and exclude myself from the community of sinners. But no one can be in the presence of God for long without overcoming this double exclusion, without transposing the enemy from a sphere of monstrous inhumanity into the sphere of common humanity and herself from the sphere of proud innocence into the sphere of common sinfulness. When one knows that the torturer will not eternally triumph over the victim, one is freed to rediscover his humanity and imitate God's love for him. And when one knows that the love of God is greater than all sin, one is free to see oneself in the light of the justice of God and so rediscover one's own sinfulness.

Yet even when the obstacles are removed, forgiveness cannot simply be presumed.[36] It always comes as a surprise—at least to those who are not ignorant of the ways of men and women. Forgiveness *is* an outrage, not only against the logic of the Exclusion System but also "against straight-line dues-paying morality," as Lewis Smedes puts it.[37] The perpetrator *deserves* unforgiveness. When forgiveness happens, there is always a strange, almost irrational, otherness at its very heart, even when we are aware that, given the nature of our world, it is wiser to forgive than to withhold forgiveness. Could it be that the word of forgiveness that must be uttered in the depths of our being if it is uttered at all, is an echo of Another's voice?

Forgiveness is the boundary between exclusion and embrace. It heals the wounds that the power-acts of exclusion have inflicted and breaks down the dividing wall of hostility. But it leaves a distance, an empty space between people that allows them either to go their separate ways in what is called "peace" or fall into each other's arms.

"Going one's own way"—a civilized form of exclusion—is what the majority of the people in the Balkans contemplate in their most

---

36. See James Wm. McClendon, *Systematic Theology I. Ethics* (Nashville: Abingdon Press, 1986), 224ff.

37. Lewis B. Smedes, *Forgive and Forget. Healing the Hurts We Don't Deserve* (San Francisco: Harper & Row, 1984), 124.

benevolent and optimistic moments. "Too much blood was shed for us to live together," I heard almost every time I participated in conversations about what might happen after the clamor of battles dies down. Never mind geographic proximity, never mind the communication lines that connect us, our similar languages, our common history, our interdependent economies, the complex network of friendships and relations created by the years of living with each other and making love to each other! A clear line will separate "them" from "us." They will remain "they" and we will remain "we," and we will never include "them" when we speak of "us." Each of us will be clean of the other and identical with herself. And so there will be peace among us. What muddies this clean calculation is the fact that the war broke out in the name of Serbian identity with itself. By what magic does one hope to transform exclusion from a cause of war into an instrument of peace?

The only way to peace is through embrace—that is, after the parties have forgiven and repented, for without forgiveness and repentance embrace is a masquerade. An embrace involves always a double movement of *aperture* and *closure*. I open my arms to create space in myself for the other. The open arms are a sign of discontent at being myself only and of desire to include the other. They are an invitation to the other to come in and feel at home with me, to belong to me. In an embrace I also close my arms around the other—not tightly, so as to crush her and assimilate her forcefully into myself, for that would not be an embrace but a concealed power-act of exclusion; but gently, so as to tell her that I do not want to be without her in her otherness. I want her to remain independent and true to her genuine self, to maintain her identity and as such become part of me so that she can enrich me with what she has and I do not.[38] An embrace is a "sacrament" of a catholic personality. It mediates and affirms the interiority of the other in me, my complex identity that includes the other, a unity with the other that is both maternal (substantial) and paternal (symbolic)[39]—and still something other than either.[40]

---

38. See Wiesel, *From the Kingdom*, 61.

39. For the categories see Julia Kristeva, *Au commencement était l'amour. Psychoanalyse et foi* (Textes du xxe siècle; Hachette, 1988), 35ff.

40. This rather schematic analysis of embrace needs to be fleshed out concretely, of course. The identity of a person or social group cannot be abstracted from its history. An embrace must include both individual histories and a common history, which is often a history of pain. The mutual inclusion of histories and of common memory is therefore essential to a genuine embrace.

Why should I embrace the other? The answer is simple: because the others *are* part of my own true identity. I cannot live authentically without welcoming the others—the other gender, other persons, or other cultures—into the very structure of my being. For I am created to reflect the personality of the triune God. The Johannine Jesus says: "The Father is in me and I am in the Father" (John 10:38). The one divine person is not that person only, but includes the other divine persons in itself; it is what it is only through the indwelling of the other. The Son is the Son because the Father and the Spirit indwell him; without this interiority of the Father and the Spirit, there would be no Son. Every divine person *is* the other persons, but he is the other persons in his own particular way. Analogously, the same is true of human persons created in the image of God. Their identity as persons is conditioned by the characteristics of other persons in their social relations. The others—other persons or cultures—are not filth that we collect as we travel these earthly roads. Filth is rather our own monochrome identity, which is nothing else but the sin of exclusion at cognitive and voluntative levels—a refusal to recognize that the others have *already* broken in through the enclosure of our selves and unwillingness to make a "movement of effacement by which the self makes itself available to others."[41] In the presence of the divine Trinity, we need to strip down the drab gray of our own self-enclosed selves and cultures and embrace others so that their bright colors, painted on our very selves, will begin to shine.

But how do the bright colors shine when the Exclusion System is dirtying us incessantly with its drab gray paint? How do we overcome our powerlessness to resist the slippage into exclusion? We need the energies of the *Spirit of embrace*—the Spirit who "issues from the essential inward community of the triune God, in all the richness of its relationships," who lures people into fellowship with the triune God and opens them up for one another and for the whole creation of God.[42] The Spirit of embrace creates communities of embrace—places where the power of the Exclusion System has been broken and from where the divine energies of embrace can flow, forging rich identities that include the other.

---

41. Riceour, *Oneself*, 168.
42. Moltmann, *The Spirit*, 219.

Africa

Introduction

The bewildering cultural diversity of the continent of Africa makes any generalization impossible. But ironically its common history with western powers has given it a unity that is impossible to ignore and one that must figure in any theological reflection that takes place. Ever since the Berlin conference in 1885 when the continent was divided up among the European powers according to maps that were wildly inaccurate, Africa has been struggling to discover (or rediscover) its spiritual soul. While no Third World country has escaped the influence of non-western colonizers and settlers, no part of the world has felt more keenly the colonists presence as a scar on their cultural soul.

On the one hand the Christianity that the colonizers brought early became an important factor in the development of Africa. From small beginnings in the last century, associated with names like David Livingstone and Robert Moffat, the church in Africa has grown until today in many countries sixty to eighty percent of the population are counted as Christian.[1] According to David Barrett, during the last decade the number of Christians in Africa has grown at an astounding rate of 16,000 converts per day.[2] On the other hand there has been the continuing presence and influence of the deep seated traditions of African Traditional Religions—the management of the many friendly and unfriendly powers by the offering of gifts and sacrifices. While these traditions have been roundly and uniformly condemned by the missionaries as demonic, they continue to attract millions of adherents—some of whom also nominally follow the teachings of Christianity. But the persistent influence of these faiths suggest that religious needs in Africa will inev-

---

1. Still the best source for basic information on the introduction of Christianity into all the non-western areas represented in this book is Stephen Neill, A *History of Christian Missions* (Middlesex: Penguin, 1964).

2. His statistics have appeared regularly in the January issue of the *International Bulletin of Missionary Research* (New Haven, Conn).

itably focus on the management of the powers that threaten to disrupt life, rather than, say, the quest for personal fulfillment as in America.

All of this raises an inescapable question: what do we make of this new thing in Africa which the missionaries brought? Is there such a thing as African Christianity, and if there is what form should it take? Most importantly, what relation does it have to the indigenous traditions of the continent? Since no single answer is possible to this question, we are fortunate that the three articles published here represent three very different kinds of response that reflect very different settings.

Tony Balcomb began his life as a minister of an all white Assembly of God church. Little by little he began to see not only the obvious evil of apartheid, but the insidious and systematic ways that the white and "Christian" society denied the Gospel by their behavior. This for him began to pose the fundamental challenge the Gospel faces in a post-apartheid world: How can people who have been systematically excluded from the goods of society hear the Gospel, when it has been associated in their minds with their oppressors? How can Christianity be freed from these associations?

As our newspapers remind us day after day, the answers to these questions will not come easily and they will not come apart from great misunderstanding and violence. It is precisely this anguish that Dr. Balcomb's article captures so well. The stories of Christians in South Africa today are not simplistic testimonies of deliverance from sin and evil. They are anguished accounts of self doubt and suspicion. They represent the first stammering attempts to open a conversation in which each side will, at least initially, surely misunderstand the other. But the follower of Christ cannot wish this situation away. These questions are not optional. And if the traditional readings of Scripture in that setting appear escapist, this fact itself is not without significance for the world church. We have to ask why this is so and what can be done about it. We who do not live in this setting may wish that the testimonies of these people were more positive, but testimonies like this would not ring true in South Africa today. And we who belong to the body of Christ must listen and somehow seek to stand with them through this time of national trauma.

A very different perspective on the role of Christianity is given by Cyril Okorocha from his context among the Igbo in Nigeria. Impetus for this study, which builds on his doctoral dissertation written for Andrew Walls at Aberdeen, grew out of the amazing conversion of the Igbo people in the first decade of this century. This turning, which we would call a people movement today, raises interesting questions about religious and social motivation. Typically these questions have been troubling to researchers in the West. The social and economic factors figuring in a peoples' conversion have sometimes, or better yet, have usually been ignored by mission students because they appear to contradict claims made for the power of God's spirit. People come to God because God draws them; if they come for any other lessor motivation we fear they will become "rice" Christians. On the other hand these external factors are sometimes seized upon by secular researchers as sufficient motivation for social change. People are drawn to follow any social (or religious) movement if it promises sufficient benefits; any further religious explanation is unnecessary.

Dr. Okorocha grasps this nettle in a refreshing and straightforward way. What researchers in the West often ignore, he implies, is their own sacred/secular dichotomized worldview. Our western view of things is straightforward: If God is involved no social or economic cause is relevant; if economic factors are causal God need not be invoked. What this simplified schema ignores is that for the African, and for the Igbo in particular, social needs inevitably raise religious questions. As Dr. Okorocha notes in another place, this is because

> The world around [the African] is peopled by a whole universe of beings and therefore his whole religious effort is to find the way or means whereby he can manipulate to his own advantage through prayer and ritual, the powers inherent in the "spirit forces."[3]

The social and religious are interrelated in such a way that not only does one cause not exclude another, but it actually implies the other. So one must not exclude any element of a peoples' expectation when examining their notion of salvation. For the African, Okorocha notes, salvation will always be seen as an encounter between two systems of expectation resulting in a movement by the people in the direction of power.

The implications of this argument are extremely important and it is not possible to elaborate on all of them here. But a single example might underline one potential direction of study. Because we in the West have assumed that physical and spiritual causes are mutually exclusive we have been perennially troubled with the question of how to "integrate" these dimensions. As a result, we have argued endlessly about the relationship between evangelism and social action. But what if we assumed,

---

3. Cyril Okorocha, *The Meaning of Religious Conversion in Africa: The Case of the Igbo of Nigeria* (Aldershot, Hampshire: Avebury-Gower, 1987), 52.

with the African, that the world was an interrelated causal nexus? The problem of relationship simply does not arise if social and spiritual realities are not separated in the first place. Instead a whole series of potentially fruitful questions emerges: what if this separation comes not from our biblical worldview but from our unique history?[4] What is lost when the African worldview is assumed? What might be gained? At the very least Dr. Okorocha's study provides an angle of vision that puts the nature of salvation in a whole new light.

Kwame Bediako is a Presbyterian pastor and theologian from Ghana who directs an important study and research center, the Akroki-Christaller Memorial Center for Mission Research and Applied Theology in Ghana. Though he has doctorates from universities in France and in Scotland his work is nourished by the traditions of his Akan people. Unlike Cyril Okorocho, his article takes its starting point not from the history of the conversion of his people but from the theological meaning of his Akan cultural practices. In the light of this setting he turns his attention to the theological tradition of Christianity, especially the meaning of Christ's incarnation. He begins with an innocuous question: What does it mean to call Jesus the universal savior? But then he goes on to put an important twist on this confession: what now does it mean to call this universal savior, the savior of the African world? The question becomes more pressing in the light of the fact that the teaching of this Jesus in Africa has all too often not touched the African reality.

Here the uniqueness of his question raises issues not only for Africans, but also for those of us who follow Christ in the West. What if we added a similar addendum to our confession of faith: What does it mean to call this universal savior the savior of our western world? What have we made of the universality of Christ's lordship? How does it reflect unique ways we have tended to think about ourselves and our world— i.e. since, from our western technological perspective, there is one interrelated world there must be one kind of savior for all. But what if this one savior seems to hold out salvation primarily for our kind of people? Has this universality served to keep others from seeing and understanding how Jesus is specially the savior for them?

Interestingly, Dr. Bediako has not asked these questions. They occurred to me when I read his article. He is wrestling with his own situation, but his honesty and his willingness to say that the presentation of

---

4. I have argued along these lines in *Let the Earth Rejoice: A Biblical Theology of Holistic Mission* (Pasadena: Fuller Seminary Press, 1983, reprinted 1991).

Christ has not always touched the African soul, immediately makes me think about why this is so and whether I have not done things that confuse rather than clarify who this Jesus is for people in my setting.

Two aspects of Dr. Bediako's essay are worthy of note. First the sacral nature of the rule of Akan chiefs and their relation to the power of the ancestors immediately raise the question of how power is mediated and managed for the benefit of the community. Now, typically missionaries have encouraged converts to replace the local version of "power management" with that of Christ and the Holy Spirit. But this has two dangers. One is that what Christ does might be seen as irrelevant to the longings of the people. If, for example, Christ's major work is seen as forgiveness of sins and the culture seeks power for living well, Christianity might appear irrelevant. But there is an additional danger. If the African opts for the Christian story the danger is that he or she will lose their identity as Africans. How does this new story of Christ connect with my own special history?

Here Dr. Bediako's work is especially important for he is able to show by a wise and illuminating use of Hebrews that Christ both meets and surpasses the longings of the culture for power. It meets these needs so that the social structure and its processes are validated. But it surpasses them so that the character of Christ as Lord and Savior of all is underlined.

This latter move becomes more important as Dr. Bediako's argument proceeds. For as he uncovers what Christ is said to do in Hebrews, against the backdrop of the Ghanaian concept of kingship and its relation to the ancestors, one begins to see elements of the work of Christ that have previously been overlooked. One sees, for example, how his desacralizing of political power can actually raise the whole political process to a place of service to God and one's neighbor. Or one can understand how this larger adoptive past which Christ brings gives the Akan Christian a new point of identity that makes real fellowship across cultures possible. And notice how the illumination of the West African notion of the mediation of the ancestors gives Christ's continuing priestly mediation a new importance.

In our setting, when biblical teaching about sacrifice and priesthood has become an historical curiosity it may well be that scholars like Bediako and Okorocha will be the instructors who will help us recover these central themes of biblical truth. For the best contextual readings of Scripture not only open culture to biblical truth, but unwrap dimensions of Scripture that decontextualized readings have overlooked.

South Africa:
Terrifying Stories of Faith from the Political Boiling Pot of the World

Tony Balcomb

You said one could be deformed by this country, and yet it seems to me one can only be deformed by the things one does to oneself. It's not the outside things that deform you, it's the choices you make. To live anywhere in the world, you must know how to live in Africa. The only thing you can do is love, because it is the only thing that leaves light inside you, instead of the total, obliterating darkness.[1]

South Africa is struggling, with the rest of Africa, to come to terms with the meaning of democracy. This is a struggle that cannot exclude God. Our history is a history that is steeped in the Christian Gospel, and our society continues to be unable to escape this reality. This makes theological reflection an exercise that is to do with the whole of life. Not a single issue of life can escape the fact of our faith. Our faith demands of us that we ask the questions to do with our lives. Our lives demand of us that we ask the questions to do with our faith. Our conversation is therefore to do with politics, economics, the environment, religion, culture, and community and our conversation is with each other and with God. It is this conversation, this living dialogue with God, with each other, and with our context, that shapes theological reflection within the South African situation at this time. It is the kind of conversation that we find in the scriptures—the conversation that takes place among God and the patriarchs, prophets, apostles, and ordinary men and women of God as they wrestled with life, with each other and with God, around the issues of life, of each other and of God. It is the conversation of those who cannot escape each other, even though at times they long to. For

---

1. Words of Creina Alcock, quoted by Rian Malan, in *My Traitor's Heart: A South African Returns to Face His Country, His Tribe, and His Conscience* (New York: Atlantic Monthly Press, 1990).

almost four centuries in South Africa we fought and killed each other. When we tired of this we shouted abuse at each other across great divides of race, culture, and ethnicity. When we tired of this we slammed the door on each other, each pretending the other was not there, each hoping the other would go away. But when we squatted at the keyhole and squinted through to the other side, we saw each other there, as large as life, waiting. And we knew that one day we would have to do it. One day we would have to talk.

And now that day has come.

But what is the nature of our conversation? Certainly it is not the conversation of those who have long been apart and wish to catch up on news. Neither is it the conversation of a repentant married couple who wish to make up after an argument. Most significantly it is not the conversation of the victor over the vanquished, though there was a time in our history when this was so, and each side no doubt wishes that it could continue to be so. Rather it is the conversation of those who have begrudgingly come to realize that conversation is the only way out, because those who do not talk, fight. It is therefore conversation steeped in suspicion, resentment, fear, and hate. But it is, nevertheless, conversation.

Few realize the enormity of this task of conversation in South Africa. Conversation between socioeconomic equals of one race, class, and culture is one thing, conversation between those whose only reason to speak to each other (or fight each other) in the past has been influenced, in one way or another, by interests of power or money, is another thing altogether. Historically we have spoken to each other only as victor and vanquished, master and servant, oppressor and oppressed. The terms, therefore, of our conversation have been entirely dictated by those who have had the power to control the outcome of the conversation. This situation has gone forever in South Africa. The oppressed will no longer communicate with the oppressor on his terms alone. The basis of communication must be equality. But equality does not come about until it is agreed upon, and it cannot be agreed upon until it is discussed. We are thus in a "catch 22" situation. We cannot speak except as equals and we cannot become equals unless we speak. The only way out of such an impasse is to rely not on the outcome of conversations but on the way in which they are conducted. The controllable factor in our conversation, in other words, is no longer result, but process. We speak about a process of negotiation, a process of dialogue, and a process of change. And the centrality of process means the suspension of most other concerns. For those concerned with "getting on" with outcome so we can "get on" with the economy, or "get on" with life, the business of waiting while the politicians talk is a desperately frustrating affair. But our history of getting on with the economy and treating people as though they were simply cogs in the economic machine has finally caught up with us. What we are working for now is survival on a far more basic level even than economic survival, it is survival as a nation. I want to illustrate the nature of the communicative task lying before us in South Africa by telling three stories and then reflecting on the theological significance of these stories. The first is the story of a young black woman called Nonqawuse, the second is the story of a young black man called Sipho, and the third of a middle-aged white man called Peter. All of them are true stories. Because Nonqawuse's story is famous and set in the last century I have used her real name. Because the story of Sipho and Peter are contemporary I have used pseudonyms for them.

Nonqawuse was a young Xhosa woman living in the 1850s in a region in South Africa today called the Ciskei but in the 1850s called British Kaffraria. It was a rich and fertile region during that period, and much coveted by the European settlers as farm land. Because of this it was the scene of what has been known as the Eighth Frontier War. This was a war, as were the seven others, waged by the colonizers against the indigenous people in order to get their land. The Xhosa spears and shields were no match for the European canons and guns. Besides which the Xhosas were not, as were their Zulu neighbors to the North, a war-like nation. They were easily defeated. But defeating a people is one thing, destroying them is another. A process of subjugation began in which the Xhosa's were gradually stripped of their land and made to be vassals. Sir Harry Smith, the governor of the Cape at the time, entered into this region as victor, ordering the people to kiss his feet while red-coat soldiers with bayonets stood by. He told the people that their land would be broken up into countless towns and villages bearing English names. "You shall all learn to speak English at the schools which I shall establish for you" he said, "You may no longer be naked and wicked barbarians, which you will ever be unless you labour and become industrious . . . You must learn that it is money that makes people rich by work."[2] The only way in which the Xhosa's could now survive was to work on the white-owned farms. A "Masters and Servants" Act was sub-

---

2. *Reader's Digest Illustrated History of South Africa*, 136.

sequently passed, greatly favoring white employers and painstakingly covering virtually every conceivable circumstance, imposing harsh penalties on offending servants. Their political structures fragmented and their beliefs eroded by a mixture of missionary teachings and European technology, the Xhosas were truly a desperate and subjugated people. Inevitably, they looked elsewhere, anywhere, for help.

And this is where the young adolescent girl called Nonqawuse came in. One day, the story goes, she was addressed by her ancestors, the *amadlozi*, who, while they had passed on, were believed to be living in the spirit world and still intimately linked with the affairs of the people. "Tell that all the community," they said, "is to rise again from the dead! Tell that all cattle must be slaughtered, for they are herded by hands defiled with witchcraft! Tell that there should be no cultivation, but that the people should dig new granaries, build new houses, erect great and strong cattle-folds . . ."

The paramount chief of the Xhosa, Sarhili, believed the story and ordered all the subordinate chiefs to carry out the wishes of the ancestors as they had been communicated to the prophetess Nonqawuse. The belief was that the ancestors would rise and chase away all the whites who had taken their land if the injunction was obeyed. The date of the first resurrection was set for 11 August, 1856.

To understand the implications of such a command one has to understand that cattle constituted the economic backbone of the Xhosa people. To destroy the cattle was to effectively decimate the people.

A massive slaughter of cattle ensued. When 11 August came and went and there was no resurrection, those who had refused to kill their cattle were blamed and further carnage ensued. Disappointment followed disappointment, bringing the Xhosa people to the brink of civil war. When Sarhili finally denounced the prophecy in July 1857, some 15 months after it all began and thousands of people having died of starvation, the Xhosa people were effectively decimated.

The story of the Xhosa cattle killing of 1857 is a tragedy of mega-Shakespearean proportion. Popular belief has it that the colonial authorities themselves spread the story about the appearance of the ancestors to Nonqawuse in order to destroy the Xhosa. But the point is not so much who it was that spread the story that the cattle should be killed, but that the story was believed, and that it was believed because the people were in a state of such terrible oppression that they would desperately cling to anything that indicated a way out for them. What is clear, in any case, is that one does not have to believe the story that the colonialists spread the rumor about the necessity to kill the cattle to accept their culpability in the whole affair. Quite clearly they were fundamentally culpable. This story is profoundly significant for so many reasons. It reflects the tragic consequences of western greed and imperialism in Africa, it demonstrates the helpless pathos of a subjugated people looking to their own resources and traditions to explain and overcome their subjugation, it raises the question of the impossible possibility of accepting western ideas and western technology to overcome the dominance of western oppressors, it emphasizes the profoundly important role, that "magic" played, and continues to play, in Africa, it points to the possibility of an entirely legitimate yet tragically misplaced understanding and analysis of a situation and illustrates the power of rumor to reinforce such an analysis in the corporate mind of an African people, it reminds us that the more crushed a nation's spirit is the more desperate the measures become that that nation takes to overcome the dehumanizing effects of its subjugation, it shows us that the innocent victims of oppression experience and interpret that oppression on a level that is far deeper than the merely political, and it illustrates the damage that a nation can inflict on itself in the process of its struggle against its oppressors.

The importance of the Nonqawuse story is that the dynamics that it contains have been repeated again and again throughout the history of the struggle for justice and liberation in South Africa. Nonqawuse lives on in the minds and actions of thousands of conquered people in South Africa wherever and whenever these people interface with the conqueror. She lives on in the toyi-toying[3] masses of young people on the township streets, she lives on in the sit down strikes of the factory floors, she lives on in the consumer boycotts, the protest marches, the riots, the demonstrations and the funerals of those slain in battle. There are still young people who visit the *sangoma* (witchdoctor) to obtain special *muti* (medicine) that will protect them from the bullets of the security forces. There are still wildfire stories that spread throughout communities and end up with necklace killings of potential "sellouts" to the white oppressor. There are still perplexed and disturbed whites, looking on from the comfort of their middle class homes, failing to recognize their own culpability in all this madness. And there are still angry, anguished, frustrated, dehumanized, and demoralized blacks who, having inflicted

---

3. The toyi-toyi is a kind of war dance accompanied by singing done in perfect unison by crowds of people and is unique to the struggling masses of black South Africans.

on themselves and their communities a kind of mindless self-destruction, simply do not understand how or why it is that what they do seems to have no effect in displacing the oppressor.

The story of Nonqawuse is the story of the clash of two cultures, two worldviews, and two political systems and the shattering impact that one of these systems has on the psyche of the other. The mental construction of reality of the one forces itself on the mental construction of the reality of the other and ultimately destroys it. The destroyer is left with the spoils of destruction and the destroyed is left with all the anomie that accompanies those whose material and symbolic world has been shattered.

This is the context in which our conversation with God and with each other is to take place.

My second story is the story of Sipho, the angry young black who is fighting a bitter war of survival against a system which in every facet he perceives to be implacably set against him. Sipho lives in a two-roomed tin house with his mother and two sisters in a township situated in one of the strongholds of white political reactionism in South Africa. As a young person he was extremely mild mannered, shy and retiring. He did not get involved in any way in the political struggle, even though many of his peers did. His concern was with survival for himself and his family, and to get on the wrong side of the system when you were already on the edge of survival potentially spelt disaster. All he wanted to do was keep his nose clean with the white bosses. He worked as a "garden boy" for the whites while not at school to try to earn some money for his family. One day Sipho heard the Gospel being preached. He was immediately seized by the good news that Jesus loved him, cared for him and died for him. It was the first time that he had heard of anyone who really cared. He embraced this Christ as one who, he was sure, would help him to get on in life. So strong did his love for Christ become that his whole life was absorbed with serving Him. He was determined, indeed, to know nothing but Christ and Him crucified. When asked to introduce himself he would say "I am Sipho Mazibuko, born again, Spirit filled, and bound for heaven!"

Sipho felt called to the ministry and joined a Bible school. To learn about the Bible every day was heaven for him. He believed it with all his heart. But going to Bible school cost money. He worked hard as a garden boy to pay his way but his wages were a miserable pittance. Anyhow, he believed that God would help him in all things.

There came a time in Sipho's life at Bible school where his greatest need was a pair of shoes. He began to pray for these shoes, certain that God would provide them. One day the white principal of the Bible school gave him a box with some shoes in them. Full of excitement he opened the box. To his astonishment he found that it contained a pair of woman's shoes. Sipho was shattered. God must surely have understood that he was a male and not a female. Why, therefore, did He give him women's shoes? If he had received no shoes at all he would have understood—but women's shoes! God was surely playing games with him. But how could God do this when his need was so desperate? Gradually the idea came to Sipho that this God was in some sort of pact with the white principal who had given him the shoes. What did this man think he was playing at? There was no other answer but that they both, the principal and God, were mocking him.

Thus began the making of Sipho into a revolutionary. He was not "conscientized" by his radical friends, neither by the brutality of the system. He was conscientized by a white Bible school teacher who gave him a pair of women's shoes. This, of course, was not the only ingredient that made him what he is today. But this experience, preceded as it was by the sincerity of his faith and mixed with the failed expectations that followed, began to change his perceptions towards the world in which he found himself. From a person adopting a posture of supplication towards his world, pleading with it to help him survive, believing that he could win it around to be basically benevolent towards him, he began to adopt a posture of fundamental antagonism towards it. From here on the same logic that drove him towards trusting in Christ, the Bible, and the church, began to drive him towards mistrusting Christ, the Bible, and the church. Note that I say mistrusting, I do not say, disbelieving. In other words it was not as though he no longer believed that these things existed. If that were the case it would have been far easier for him, for he would have been able simply to turn his back on them. But it became far more serious than the straightforward adoption of atheism. For him the devastation was not in that there was no God or no Christ, but that this God and His Christ had failed him. He had believed them to be with him and they had shown themselves to be against him. He found himself in a kind of marriage to things from which he was unable to get a divorce. He could not leave Christ, he could not disbelieve in Christ, all he could do was live with Him in a relationship of antagonism, bitterness, resentment, and mistrust.

And this is how Sipho is today. He still lives in a tin shack with his family, he is still subject to grinding poverty, and he is still a student of theology. He is marginalized from the church and from society, fighting all those things that hurt and destroyed him in the past, fighting those who fight against him, and using all his will and determination to press gang others into joining his side in this fight.

Now it may be difficult for us to take Sipho's story seriously. We could easily dismiss it as a naive and misinformed response to the Gospel. But in adopting this attitude we would rather be showing ourselves to be naive and misinformed. Sipho's experience is paradigmatic for young black Christians in this country. There are thousands like him who have had very similar experiences. Confused, uncertain, insecure, and resentful young people who have an ax to grind with society, with the Gospel, and with the Bible.

And we have to reflect on the role of the church in this phenomenon. The Gospel by definition is good news. We cannot expect to preach good news to the poor and oppressed without them thinking that by accepting this good news they will soon be liberated from their poverty and oppression. Sipho made the mistake of believing, simply and emphatically, what he had heard the Christian missionaries say. He interpreted it according to his own life situation, and, through a process of events, he has turned, quite simply, into a fairly dangerous member of human society. Hannah Arendt's words become chillingly reminiscent.

> The masses of the poor, this overwhelming majority of all men, whom the French Revolution called *les malheureux*, whom it transformed into *les enrages*, only to desert them and let them fall back into the state of *les miserables*, as the nineteenth century called them, carried with them necessity, to which they had been subject as long as memory reaches, together with the violence that had always been used to overcome necessity. Both necessity and violence, made them appear irresistible—*la puissance de la terre*.[4]

The missiological challenges arising out of such a story are, of course, profound. We need to ask ourselves the question—What is the meaning of Christian mission in South Africa in the light of Sipho's experience?

---

4. Cf. *On Revolution*, Faber and Faber, London, 1963.

My last story is the story of Peter, the middle-class white who thought he could take sides with the poor and oppressed. Peter came to Christ in his second year of university and immediately felt strongly called to the Christian ministry. He started prayer meetings and Bible studies in his residence at university and many others came to Christ. He joined a Pentecostal church situated in a white working-class part of town. His whole life was absorbed in the ministry. The church in which his spiritual formation took place scorned formal theological education. God gave ministries in terms of Ephesians 4:11 and those ministries were to be developed and nurtured in the local church—around the Lord's table, in the open air, in the fellowship meetings, at the Bible studies and in the gospel meeting. With a science degree, no formal theological education, three years of ministry in the local church, and a heart bursting with love for God and His word, Peter was sent out into the ministry. His first pastorate was a small fundamentalist church amongst the white working class. God brought a mini-revival to that church. Many new people joined the church, many were baptized, many "cottage" meetings and Bible studies were started in the outlying areas, some of which later became churches. These were the days before the mega-charismatic churches which were a middle- rather than working-class phenomenon. They were the days of Pentecostalism in the Azusa street tradition—the apartheid version. Apartheid meant that Peter could live in South Africa and be largely unaware of what was happening among four-fifths of its population. His theology, in any case, was dismissive of worldly affairs. The Soweto riots of 1976, one of the major turning points in the history of South Africa in which hundreds of people were killed, passed as simply another event that signified God's judgment on the world and Christ's imminent return to fetch his church out of the mess.

By the early eighties, however, Peter's theological horizon had begun to broaden. He had studied theology through correspondence and gained a degree in theology. He became especially fascinated with the theology of Jurgen Moltmann whose theology of the cross both deeply disturbed and fascinated him. It resonated with something, perhaps, that he was experiencing week after week around the Lord's table. Working-class people, he discovered, relate with the cross of Christ in a way that the middle class do not. The prayers and supplications of these people focused in lurid detail around the sufferings of Christ. There was obviously something in the cross of Christ which resonated deeply with the experience of their lives.

It was this dimension of suffering that began slowly to seep into Peter's spirit. Luther was right—a theology of the cross contradicted a theology of glory. A theology of glory blinded one to the living realities of life. Its crass insensitivity further bruised an already bruising humanity. Peter began to learn lessons there that were to be reinforced again and again in the future. The poor, oppressed, and suffering of this life were alienated by a middle-class religion that refused to come to terms with the pain of their existential reality. Once embraced, the Gospel could become a powerful means of articulating this pain, but it could also prevent this articulation and therefore alienate oneself from one's own reality. The choice became simple—faith could either be an opiate that caused escape from reality or a challenge that caused engagement with reality. These theological developments in Peter's thinking inevitably began to orient him towards his context. A new conversion was in the making—a conversion to context—and it was to be a conversion as powerful, meaningful, and transformatory as his conversion to Christ.

Peter's first meaningful encounter with those living on the receiving end of the apartheid system happened when he developed a friendship with a black trade union leader who also happened to be an active lay minister in his local church. Thus came an introduction not only to the struggle for liberation but an introduction to this struggle within the context of the church. The trauma of the realization of what apartheid had done to his country was matched only by the trauma of the realization that he had for so long been blind to it.

From now on worship and the practice of the faith could not but take place within the framework of this new found realization. As a pastor of an all white and, by now, middle-class congregation, the natural thing was to share his convictions with his congregation. But the sheer intensity of the outrage with which he was faced when drawing attention to these things taught him another great lesson—that when you preached about the evils of a political system to those who benefited from that system you were touching the gods of the inner sanctuaries of their lives. Here awaited another traumatic discovery—that in all the departments that constituted our service of God there was one department that had a huge KEEP OUT sign—the department of the political. The strenuousness of the reaction against "political" sermons far exceeded anything else that had ever been preached of a controversial nature from the pulpit. Quite clearly there were interests at stake here that were the strongest of all the interests amongst God's people. The essential idol had been discovered, the essential ideology exposed. Thus was Peter led into direct confrontation with his church and his tradition, and thus did he find his way into the circles of the downtrodden.

New and bitter lessons had to be learned here too. The deficit chalked up against white males through the history of South Africa is so big that the odds against them being accepted into the circles of the oppressed are great indeed. Yet Peter's commitment to the struggle was not based merely upon a political conviction or the desire for acceptance among those whose cause he had embraced, it was a commitment based upon the conviction that for him to deny the struggle against apartheid was to deny the faith. This did not mean, of course, endorsing everything in that struggle, but rather to endorse its essential goals of justice. The fact that this commitment was to do with faith means the presence of a transcendent factor within such commitment. God was on the side of the oppressed, God was with them in their struggle—and Peter's faith was in God. It is not easy, of course, to make such a statement as "God is on the side of the oppressed" without having to ask some fundamental questions about the nature of God. Indeed many times Peter heard the oppressed themselves asking such questions.

Despite his commitment and despite the gracious recognition of this commitment by the downtrodden, Peter realized that the possibility of complete identification with the oppressed was remote. Indeed it was more than remote—it was outrageous. Outrageous because the black people's struggle against oppression is essentially and uniquely their own. And when the oppressor, who has taken away all from the oppressed, now claims to be able to own the struggle as well, it is indeed the final insult. Thus it was made quite clear to Peter from the beginning that this was the black people's struggle, not the white's, and that whites were there by invitation, appreciated for the price they had paid, appreciated for their usefulness, but nevertheless essentially marginal in the struggle. So it was that Peter joined that beleaguered group of whites in this country who find themselves in the middle. They constitute a subculture of their own, marginalized by mainstream whites who consider them, at worst, dangerous communists, and, at best, "loony lefties," and marginalized by mainstream blacks who, at best, tolerate them in the ranks of struggle, and, at worst, suspect them of having ulterior motives directed against the struggle.

The story of Peter, as that of Nonqawuse, is deeply significant. I have told it because it surfaces some fundamental questions of meaning in our present context. What is the possibility of meaningful conversation amongst the peoples of South Africa? What is the meaning of the Gospel and of Christian discipleship in the context of just revolution? What is the meaning of reconciliation in a situation of severe economic and political discrepancy? And what is the meaning of participation by whites in the struggle against a system that they have participated in establishing? Moreover it underlines an extraordinary irony, the irony of the necessity of working *against* the sharp boundaries dictated by the apartheid system from a position that situates you clearly *within* those boundaries. It is a grave irony indeed that amongst those most respected from the point of view of the community of the oppressed are those who are the most hated. This is because the oppressed know best those who locate themselves most clearly in the camp of the oppressor. These are the best understood, for they fit most clearly into the ideological frame of reference of the revolutionary. When you know your enemy you can fight him. When your enemy says he is not your enemy but your friend it is much more difficult. The boundaries must not be confused, they must be clear, then everyone knows where he or she stands. So, for the Peters of this life, South Africa is a no-man's land. But this story is important also because it indicates that the process of negotiation must quite clearly be a *political* process. Trust and goodwill may be important factors, but where they are all but nonexistent the situation is made worse when you pretend that they are there. At the end of the day we will have to rely on a political process and political instruments to help bring us to a place of political equality. When that has happened relationships may be normalized. Christians will have to take this into account when they do their theological reflection in the context of political transition.

There are many far more terrifying stories that can be told from this the political cauldron of the world. South Africa, today, is simply a terrifying place in which to live. Terrifying not because it is a dangerous place to live. Indeed there are probably many other far more dangerous places to live in the world. But it is terrifying in that so much seems to be at stake. And of all the things that are at stake the most significant is the Gospel of Jesus Christ itself. Not that events in South Africa will prove or disprove the validity of this Gospel. Rather they will test once again, possibly in a way unprecedented in human history, whether believers in that Gospel will be able to respond to these events in such a way that brings it credit, and not discredit.

Kyrie Eleison, Lord have mercy on us.

The Meaning of Salvation: An African Perspective

Cyril Okorocha

The nature of salvation in African religious experience is the focal point of this brief study. There are three reasons why I consider this study crucial for the study of religion and theology, especially in relation to the proclamation of the Christian Gospel in cross-cultural contexts, and to pastoral care in the non-western world where vibrant Christianity has its highest numerical growth at present and where the future of Christianity now appears to lie.[1]

The first is that my studies among the Igbo of Nigeria show that it is a people's inherited ideas about salvation as the goal of humanity's religiousness that determines their response to a new religious system.[2] In other words, religious conversion in Africa is seen as a power encounter: an encounter between two, or several, systems of salvation resulting in a movement on the part of the people in the direction of power.[3] This power, or what R. H. Codrington observes among the Melanesians as *mana*, is not occult, economic, political, or humanistic power. It is a mysterious "something" which the Igbo of Nigeria describe as *ihe* (an inexplicable "something") which is at once attractive and mystifying. In Rudolf Otto's classic study, it is a mysterious *tremendum et fasinosum*. But in African religiology, this *ihe* must lead to the enhancement of life

---

1. David Barret, *World Christian Encyclopedia* (Oxford: OUP, 1982); Andrew F. Walls, "Towards Understanding Africa's People's Place in Christian History," ed. J. S. Pobee, *Religion in a Pluralistic Society* (Leiden: E. J. Brill, 1976, 108–9; and John V. Taylor, "The Future of Christianity," ed. John McManners, *The Oxford Illustrated History of Christianity* (Oxford: OUP, 1990), 628–85.

2. Cyril C. Okorocha, "Religious Conversion in Africa: Its Missiological Implications," *Mission Studies*, IX–2, 18, 168–81; "What Is Religious Conversion in Africa?" (Dept. of Theology University of Upsalla, Sweden: Consultation on Religion in Africa, Oct. 1992).

3. See Cyril C. Okorocha, "Salvation in Igbo Religious Experience: Its Influence on Igbo Christianity" (Ph.D. thesis, University of Aberdeen, Scotland), ch. 7.

or salvation. The Igbo describe this enhanced, superior or viable life as *Ezi Ndu*. It is desirable life, the joy of human desiring. A life worth living; the *summun bonum* of Igbo religiousness. The point here is that inherent religious ideas are the determinative factors in a people's response and conversion to a new religious system. In that encounter, socioeconomic and even political factors are important as catalysts affecting the *rate* of conversion but not the determinants of their decision. When a movement that leads to conversion appears to be a pursuit of "material things" it is so only from the point of view of a westernized observer. For African peoples such a pursuit, properly understood, is viewed as a religious journey.

Furthermore, for African peoples, every religious quest is a quest for salvation and the central theme of African religiosity is salvation: the enhancement of life or *Ezi Ndu* in Igbo. Vatican II suggests that this axiom is not unique to the Igbo or African peoples, for "men look to their different religions for an answer to the unresolved riddles of human existence." In other words, salvation is the goal of humanity's religiousness, even though conceived and defined differently. G. van der Leeuw[4] holds a similar view on the ultimate concern of every *homo religiosus*.

This, then, is why it is missiologically important that we understand a people's idea of salvation if we wish to communicate the Gospel meaningfully to them. Their response to a new religious system is usually an extension of the search for salvation. That is, African peoples, subject existing as well as innovative religious forms to continuous scrutiny, in an attempt to reconcile alternative innovations with prior principles so as to enhance the capacity of their core institutions for meeting contemporary contingencies. (We shall return to this point later.) The implication of this observation is that the proclaimer of a new religious system would be utterly naive to expect either passive acceptance of what is proclaimed on the part of the hearers, or complete apathy. There is a need to listen attentively to the inarticulate concerns of the people and the yearnings expressed through their core institutions so that one learns in the course of teaching to present the Gospel relevantly and meaningfully. The point here is that

> The Gospel . . . is presented, whether the missionaries wish it or not, whether they know it or not, in accordance with what the hearer

---

4. Geradus H. van der Leeuw, *Religion in Essence and Manifestation*, E. T., E. J, Turner (London: George Allen and Unwin, 1938), 281.

thinks, desires, believes. He may be wrong; but the Gospel is in fact
presented to him, at least, at first, as *he* sees it.[5]

This means that a people listen to the proclamation of a new religious system with judicious inquisitiveness and will respond to the new
system to the degree to which they perceive within it, as proclaimed or
presented, the possibility of realizing in and through it, aspirations and
hopes desired but not experienced in the old. Thus, according to van der
Leeuw,

> Conversion would then be the assumption of what has for long been
> accumulating beneath the threshold of consciousness, which finally
> and forcibly makes its way into the open . . . the consciousness of
> something . . . which overwhelms the convert . . .[6]

That "something" is salvation. The "eruptive force" that makes it
tangible or makes it "attractive" or "irresistibly overpowering" for the
potential convert is the *mana* or *ihe* inherent in the vehicle of salvation,
the new religious system as proclaimed by the evangelist or missionary.
This is important for the missionary as well as the pastor. Our studies
among the Igbo and other African peoples show that African peoples
will remain faithful to a new religious system for as long as, and only in
so far as, the new system is able to prove itself a viable vehicle of salvation in contemporary terms. After all, the New Testament teaches that
the "Gospel is the power of God that brings salvation to everyone who
believes."[7] For African people, religion is about salvation. The salvific
capacity or religiousness of any religious system is measured in terms of
its "*mana* content" and its viability in terms of the contemporaneity and
tangibility of its "*mana* effect." Thus, it is the inherent ideas about salvation that determine the conversion to, faithfulness within, and possible
evolutions of new religious systems in Africa.

The second missiological significance of the theme of salvation, as
already stated, is that it is the central theme of the religiousness of all
homo sapiens. In short, wherever there is a religion, there is a notion of
salvation. This is because

---

5. R. H. Codrington, "The Gospel as Presented to Savage Peoples," *The Wittering
Lectures* (Rhodes House Library, Oxford: Rhodes House Library, 1902), 3–4; Codrington
papers, pkt. S.30, *The Wittering Lectures* (Rhodes House Library, Oxford: Rhodes House
Library, 1895–1907), S.30.

6. Op. cit., 533.

7. Romans 1:16.

The search for salvation is recorded in the very dynamism of the human mind, indeed it appears as the fundamental and universal aspect of it . . . Whatever else religion may or may not be, it is essentially a reaching forward to the ideal of salvation.[8]

In short, any religion that is worthy of that name is about salvation,[9] even though expressed differently by different belief systems. Therefore, to understand what a people mean by salvation is to enter into the heart of their worldview and thus into the source of their socioreligious behavior. This study has a multidisciplinary usefulness. To understand a people's idea of salvation is to understand the way they express and desire to experience religious values. It also gives us an insight into the spring of their social behavior. In short, what a people believe about salvation is the window into their soul and thus into their core socioreligious institutions. For example, the western idea of religion as primarily a means to forgiveness and atonement compared with the African concern for power and provision is explained in this light by H. W. Turner: Whereas the West is concerned with a God who forgives and the average westerner finds *guilt* a constant threat to full happiness, the African is preoccupied by "an overriding concern for spiritual power from a mighty God to overcome all enemies and evils that threaten *human life and vitality.*"[10]

The third missiological import of the study of the meaning of salvation follows naturally from this last point. If all true religions are about salvation, then the theme of salvation becomes at once a ready and universal water table which may be touched from whatever local context one stands on the religious landscape. In the study of religions and religious behavior, rather than look for cultural and cultic institutions to dismantle in order to understand the people, the theme of salvation gives us an immediate point of contact and a total revelation of a people's whole life and ethos. Thus, in evangelism and mission, as in incarnational theologizing, the theme of salvation becomes a most versatile common denominator. For, as Robertson Smith asserts:

---

8. The Vatican, *Religions: Fundamental Themes for a Dialogistic Understanding*, (The Vatican, 1970), 87, 175.

9. Edward Geoffrey Parrinder, *A Dictionary of Non-Christian Religions* (Philadelphia: Westminster Press, 1973), 189.

10. H. W. Turner, "Contribution of Studies on Religion in Africa to Western Religious Studies," eds. Fasholé-Luke and Glasswell, *NT Christianity for Africa and the World* (London: SPCK, 1974), 174.

no positive religion worthy of the name, can expect a hearing in a new context if it presumes to start on a *tabula rasa*: a new scheme of faith can find a hearing only by appealing to religious instincts and susceptibilities that already exist.[11]

Salvation, however, is at once a common water table and a divide. African people's definition of salvation is highly sensitive to contemporary realities. Therefore a religious system is considered outmoded if its definition of, or *mana* for, salvation, does not keep pace with the observable contemporary form that *Ezi Ndu* (or "the good life") has acquired in a given context and epoch in human life and history.

What, Then, Is Salvation in African Piety?

This question may be phrased empirically thus: what do African peoples mean when they say they are saved? This question became gripping for me as a result of two encounters I had with two different people in Nigeria. The first, a very wealthy business woman, was asked if she was saved. "O yes," she replied and then proceeded to narrate how in fifteen years in the long distance haulage business none of her vehicles had ever been involved in a road accident. Furthermore, she was very wealthy, had several houses in town and above all had two grandsons and a third was on the way. I then asked how her husband and sons-in-law felt about her progress in life and her grandsons. She was furious. She had never been married, neither were her daughters. How then did she acquire so much wealth? That was a private area of her life I must not intrude into. For her, salvation meant wealth, health, and posterity with no reference to moral scruples. Yet the experience of these material benefits was viewed as a religious affair. Such a utilitarian attitude to religion may be the greatest obstacle in the way of social transformation and total Christianization in Africa.

Is salvation, simply and squarely, material prosperity and no more? Does *Ezi Ndu*, viable life, include more than material prosperity?

Another woman in Northern Nigeria came forward in an evangelistic meeting in response to an "altar call" during which the preacher had stressed that the "Gospel is the source of the power of God that brings salvation." She looked very moved by the message and visibly agitated emotionally. When I called her aside and enquired why she came forward, she replied, tears rolling down her cheeks:

---

11. Robertson Smith, *Religion of the Semites* (London: A & C Black, 1957), 2.

> My husband who comes from a different tribe, has been nasty and unfaithful to me. He beats me. My friends told me about this Church and that your preaching and prayer have power. I am not a Christian, but I need this power that the preacher referred to today.

"And what will you do with the power when you get it?" I enquired.

> I just want a little strength for revenge. That man is really wicked I want to show him that my God can answer my prayers and can also save me. He will see what a woman can do if God answers my prayer.

"But why don't you pray for him and ask God to help you to forgive him?" I appealed gently. She burst out in furious rage:

> God forbid! How can you ask me to forgive such a wicked man? May God reject evil. What will God tell me when I die if I should just let him go on like that? Please pray for me, let God help, yes I need his power, I need his salvation. If God can save me from this man, I will be happy.

To African peoples, religion has to do with power. The missionary, preacher, or pastor is expected to be a bearer and medium of the power that brings salvation in context. But what did this woman mean by salvation? Both the missionary/evangelist and the pastor need to wrestle with this question so that religious conversion may be real and pastoral care relevant.

A different incident from Islamic Northern Nigeria further buttresses this point. In 1987, I sent a student of mine to spend a fortnight living with, observing, and interviewing the Maguzawa people of the Ikara Local government area of the Zau Zau Emirate of Northern Nigeria, as part of his university degree project.[12] The Maguzawa were the original Hausa people of the now Sokoto Caliphate, who fled their homes to take refuge in bushes at the advance of the Arab (Fulani) Muslim jihadists in the 18th/19th century. They were thus nicknamed Maguzawa (those who ran away). But beginning in 1982–1983 these people began to turn to Christianity *en masse*. The last Christian preacher in their area had been expelled by the colonial government in 1913 at the behest of the Islamic leaders, because conversion to Christianity appeared to signal rejection of Islam and especially, oppression or domination of one race or cultural group by another, whether Hausa-

---

12. K. Daniel, "The pagan religion among the Ibos of Owerri," *Nigerian Teacher* (Sept. 1987): 16–17.

Fulani Feudalism or British imperialism. Questioned as to why they now chose to surrender to a new religion and reject Islam, opting for Christianity even though it was not to their political advantage, their Sarikin or chief, spoke for the people: "We reject coercion. We choose Christianity. In so doing, we choose freedom and progress." See and compare my study of the Igbo rejection of Islam,[13] and note also G. T. Basden:

> Why has Mohammedanism not won converts from among the Ibos [Igbo] yet? Because the Ibo is sturdy of character. He is also acute and an observer of things as they are. *He judges by results.* [In trading], the principles adopted generally by the Mohammedans make clear to him that their religion exercises no better influence in methods of business than his own, in fact the Ibo is inclined to believe that of the two his religion is to be preferred, as far as the ethics of trade are concerned.[14]

Basden concluded that his enquiries showed that the Igbo would normally not "forsake paganism for Mohammedanism."[15]

The preacher as well as the pastor needs to know that in Africa, the definition of salvation must keep pace with progress in terms of contemporary realities. But that is not all. There is also an ethical as well as a ritual dimension. To understand these and much more about salvation in African piety, we need to examine a selection from the prayers of African peoples.

What Is Salvation in African Piety?
A Study of African Prayers

Prayer gives us the best key for understanding the complexities of any particular belief system. "Not in dogmas and institutions, not in rites and ethical ideals, but in *prayer* do we grasp the peculiar quality of the religions of any people."[16] Prayer is a theological exercise whose primary concern is with the realization of salvation as idealized in the religious system in which one prays. These concerns are articulated practically through the petitions.[17]

---

13. Cyril C. Okorocha, op. cit. 1987: 212–21

14. G. T. Basden, *Among the Ibos* (London: Frank Cass, 1966), 127ff. (Italics mine.)

15. Ibid., 306.

16. Friedrich Heiler, *Prayer: A Study in the History and Psychology of Religion*, ET: S McCombe (London: OUP, 1932), xv. (Italics mine.)

17. See also Christian R. Gaba, "Man's Salvation: Its Nature and Meaning in African Traditional Religion," *Christianity in Independent Africa*, eds. Fasholé-Luke, et al., (London: Rex Collings, 1978), 389ff.

1. Morning Prayers

This is the most comprehensive of all African prayers. Every traditional African *pater familias* regards it as a *sine qua non* for beginning a new day; the Igbo are an outstanding example.

The Igbo Morning Prayer:

The Igbo traditional morning prayer or *Ikwo aka ututu*—literally "washing one's hands in the morning," but meaning *revitalizing life for a new day*, is a fascinating ritual.

The *pater familias* rises at the crack of dawn, squats in front of his *obi* (the patriarch's private residence, or in some areas, the communal open hall at the centre of the compound) facing the main entrance to the family homestead and beside his *chi* tree (symbolic *totem* tree), which is normally planted by the main door into his *obi*. After ritually washing his hands, face, and feet and rinsing his mouth with water (or preferably with gin or palm-wine) for cleansing or sanctification, he chews a piece from his *kolanut* and forcefully spits it on his *ofor* stick to feed and thus vitalize it. He also spits some gin on it for extra "power" and effectiveness. He now feels ready to address the Ancestors and spirits in prayer. He marks off the circular boundary of sanctification by means of *nzu* (*kaolin* or white chalk); squats within this circle, and places his *ofor*, now vitalized, on the ground in front of him, but within the circle. (There are no books, special vestments, or other distracting or cumbersome abstract items).

Within the circle and with his *ofor* stick in front of him, he is conscious of a sacred assembly: the living, represented by himself, and the "mighty dead" or Ancestors, symbolized by the *ofor* stick which is the embodiment of the whole *ethos* of the Ancestors.[18] The circle enclosed by the white chalk includes the good spirits but excludes the *agwu, akalogoli*, and other such capricious spirits or *ajo mmuo*. The dome of this circular temple is the blue sky above, the abode of *Chineke*, Creator God, *Obasi-bi-n'elu*, King of Heaven, or *Osebiluwa*, the Creator and Owner of the Universe. The sky is also the highway of the chief messenger of *Chineke, Amadioha* of the thunderbolt.

He maintains a hallowed moment of measured silence, staring lividly at the gate in deep concentration. He clears his throat loudly, takes a pinch of snuff and sneezes with deliberate noisiness (perhaps to awaken his household!), and says loudly *Ndu! Ndu! Ndu! Ndu!,* Let there be *life*.

---

18. See Okorocha 1987: 96–100.

He strikes his *ofor* stick symbolically four times on the ground while repeating the traditional names of the Igbo week: *Eke, Orie, Afor, Nkwor.* Thus nature and the natural order are invited to witness his prayers. There is no mediator. His own personal integrity and birthright as a freeborn, or *Diala*, mediate for him. He is free to approach *Chineke*, the Ancestors, simply because he is *Nwadiala*, a freeborn of freeborn descent, and an upright person, or *Ezimmadu*.[19]

Self introduction: [Emphasis—birthright, rite of inheritance]

> A stranger does not chase a kite [i.e. has no right to interfere
> in family matters].
> I am a *Nwadiala* the son of Okorocha, the son of Nnadi, the son of
> Aluruoha, son of Egolu, son of Okwu, son of Oma, son of Ede
> [the Apical Ancestor].[20]

Greeting and adoration: [adoration, praise, and adulation of the spirits]

> Our fathers, have you seen a new day?
> Amadioha of the thunderbolt, Canon of the Sky,
> I salute you.

> My personal *Chi*, who owns and controls
> My destiny, I salute you.
> The Land of Nekede [i.e., Earth goddess, *Ala*]
> I salute you.
> Ala of Okwu, I salute you.
> Otamiri [the river] of Nekede, greetings
> I am a freeborn, [*Nwadiala*].

> The soul of this day, greetings
> I am holding on to *ogu* [moral rectitude]
> *Eke, Orie, Afor, Nkwor* [He hits his *ofor* stick rhythmically on the
> ground as he recites the days of the week].

Adoration of Chineke, or Creator God, the Almighty:

> *Obasi* who dwells above
> Glorious and powerful King
> The incomprehensible and ineffable One.

---

19. A *Diala*, or freeborn, is one whose genealogy can freely and readily be traced to the Apical Ancestor in a patrilineal descent Group. The chronological span is between 300 and 500 years.

20. See Cyril Okorocha, "God the Father and Hunger in Africa," in Gitari et al. (eds.), *The Living God* (Nairobi: Uzima), 57.

Unfathomable waters
King of the Heavens
The King who dwells above and is above all [i.e., *the Transcendent
    One, the wholly "other"*],
And yet whose garments reach the earth
The Immanent One [i.e., *Chineke* is at once Transcendent and
    Immanent].
I submit entirely to you in homage
We are still here
The land and place you allotted to us
And in the condition in which you last met with us [i.e., in utter
    dependence on your providence].

(Silence, then the ofor stick is hit on the ground rhythmically as he
recites the days of the week. This may be followed by a second chant,
and a further period of silence before the next part of the prayer
session).

Invocation of justice: [note the use of proverbs and local idioms]

He who pursues the day old chick
Keeps falling to the ground,
But the day old chick jogs on [silence].

Chineke, may you arbitrate:
I am innocent; I am a child [i.e., innocent],
May the one who comes to destroy me—
The innocent one, destroy himself instead.
Eha, Eha, Eha, Eha [or Ise. . . five i.e., five fingers on one complete or
    just hand]. . . So be it!
(He hits the *ofor* on the ground. Silence, and then the petitions).

Petitions: [These are couched in proverbs, idioms and logic]

- *Life and Posterity*: (At this point his voice is deep and the plea
  is impassioned. He is moved almost to tears and sobbing. This
  is the heart of his petitions.)

Our beloved fathers,
Please hear my voice.
Give us life, worthwhile life [*Ezi Ndu*]
Life is superior to wealth
Give us life
Life is supreme
Give us "childbearing"

Give us children one at a time
[i.e., *no twins*, as this is thought to be against nature due to the
    complications it brings!]
Until our homestead is full of children
May I never lack a successor [Ahamefula]
Earth goddess, please hear [He pleads passionately]
Do give us "child bearing" [Omumu]
Children are superior to wealth
But do not deny us wealth
Children and wealth are closely related
For if children are given
It is only reasonable that the means for their upbringing is given

- *Ezi Ndu,* or viable life: emphasized and described

Chase sickness away from us
Give us health
Give us well being [total well being]
Sickness is evil and terrible Life is supreme
Therefore give us life
Viable life
Long life
Life with a living hope
Life that knows posterity
Worthy life
 (Eha, Eha . . .),

- *Intercession*: (for those away from home)

The traveller is bound to come home
[i.e., East or West, home is best]
He is not condemned to the road
My beloved father [i.e., Ancestor]
Please guard your children
You travelled to other lands in your time
And returned safely home
Those in "government jobs," in big cities
Do bring them safely home
Give them favor before their employers
Give them wisdom and understanding
Travellers' guardian Spirit [*Ukwu na ije*]
Please guard them
To travel implies that coming home is guaranteed [by you]
May they acquire wealth—honest wealth

May they marry
Good and worthy wives [here husbands are implied if daughters are
     in mind]
Free born wives [as opposed to osa or outcast]
Those who are our type—who understand us [culturally]
And we understand them
Worthy and obedient wives
Whose wombs are full of children
It is a terrible curse to marry and still
Lack children and successors
Give them, one baby at a time
Until the house is full of children

Long life, viable life [*Ezi Ndu*]
Please give them life

Ikenga, you spirit of personal achievement
Guard and protect them
May no one harm them
May they harm no one
May their hands be clean
May they never be guilty of any crime—Whether in thought
     or action—
May *ofor* and *ogu* be their guardians and friends
May there be no cause for us to
Avenge their blood [i.e., give them peace with and protection from
     their neighbors and others]
Prosper them and may they go and return safely
That we may be like others
So as not to lag behind in progress . . .
[Eha, Eha, . . . and silence, clears throat and then concludes]

Summary and conclusion:

My fathers, I am only a child
An innocent child who knows nothing
You have heard me
May your judgement be just and fair
You always judge justly
Since you know everything
Justice and innocence [ofor na ogu]
Hear and judge
Let the kite perch [on the tree]
Let the eaglet also be free to perch on the same tree
[This is fairness—justice, equity, and liberty for all]

But the one who denies the other
The right or freedom to perch on or access
To this common tree, may his wings break off
The one who denies others the right to live
May you, O death, be his guardian and guide!

Eha-a-m,
Eke, Orie, Afor, Nkwor [and *ofor* stick rhythm]

Four days that make one week
[i.e., the truths and petitions expressed in these prayers are valid
    irrespective of the days of the week—the invocation of the "spirit
    of the days" guarantees this]
Ndu, Ndu, Ndu, Ndu. Life, Life, Life, Life
Ezi Ndu, Ezi Ndu. Ezi Ndu, Ezi Ndu: viable life
[and ofor rhythm]

The prayer session is now over. He throws the water of purification
forcefully in the direction of the exit gate of his homestead, packs up,
and feels ready to face the new day.

Morning Prayer for Mali:

The prayer is addressed at once to Amma (God Almighty) and the
Ancestors as those who give life.

Amma, accept the morning greeting
Things which come after Amma [i.e., good but lesser spirits]
Accept morning greetings
Yeben, Andumbulu, Guinu [Ancestor/forbears]
Kumogu [seeing] trees [i.e., the ethos or spirit of certain sacred trees]
Kumogu [seeing] stones
Everything
Accept my morning greetings
You who placed the stone [Creator]
Accept my morning greetings . . .
Take and drink [i.e., the libation he pours out]

If you have drunk
Give me a long old age
Give me eight grains [prosperity]
And the fruit of the calabash [wine i.e., reasons for celebration
    and merriment]
For a ninth
Make me a gift of children
And let me reach tomorrow [refers to life and health]

Prayer for Life:

These and other prayers show that the central theme of African religiousness is life. Even if there is a vagueness about eschatological future life in the Occidental sense, the preoccupation with life, abundant life, *Ezi Ndu*, is intense. Prayers are engaged in with such seriousness in order to enlist the help and power of the gods to affirm and enhance life. Mbiti[21] corroborates this observation in his study of the prayers of several African peoples. In prayer, they engage the divinities in a paradoxical and intricate mixture of logic and plea, addressing the spirits as if they saw them face to face, arguing and pleading their preference for life, qualitative life which includes health and prosperity, that is total well being:

> We have come to thee, Odo [God]
> To ask for life
> Help us to cling to it. Hasten to help us cling to life . . .

And from an Ashanti [Ghana] *pater familias*/Priest-King:

> [Our fathers],
> The edges of the years have met
> I take sheep and new yams
> And give you that you may eat:
> Life to me
> Life to these my Ashanti people . . .
> Grant that food comes forth in abundance
> Do not allow illness to come.

Here again we note the emphasis on *life*, worthwhile life: a life blessed with health and material prosperity in terms of good crops and general well being.

2. What Kind of Life is Ezi Ndu?

Salvation Is Ezi Ndu

From the prayers cited, from a study of Mbiti,[22] and from my field studies among the Igbo of Nigeria in particular, life appears to be the central theme of African religiousness. But is this true of every kind of life? From our study of African prayers, the answer is NO! It has to be

---

21. John S. Mbiti, *Prayers of African Religions* (London: SPCK, 1975), 36–44.
22. Mbiti, op. cit.

worthwhile life. The Igbo speak of *odi ndu onye nwuru anwu ka mma* "the curse of living a life of which death is to be preferred." Therefore, the Igbo qualify their quest for life in terms of *Ezi Ndu*: viable life, full life, a life which is worth living. Life is important, life is supreme for African peoples. Ilogu[23] asserts that to the Igbo this good life, or *Ezi Ndu*, is the *summum bonum*. In their prayers, the yearning is for viable life, *Ezi Ndu*. All efforts in day to day existence are made, ritually and in other ways, to exclude death

> To live here and now is the most important action of African religious activities and beliefs. This is an important element of traditional religion and one which will help us understand the concentration on earthly matters with man at the centre of religiosity.[24]

With this affirmation of life goes a stress on anthropocentrism. Humankind is the centre and the existential present is the focus, of African religious life. This preoccupation with the present is only a projection of the African peoples' fear of death. Wherever one turns, African peoples are heard to cry out against death. Thus among the Ganda of Uganda, salvific terms, such as *kuwonya* and *kulokola* signify deliverance from trouble and misfortunes, including childlessness and especially death. Troubles such as poverty and ill health are precursors to death and must be excluded in order to exclude death. The religious life of African peoples reveals a deep and incapacitating fear of death.[25] The Igbo show this fear of death in the names they give their children.[26] Here are a few examples:

Onwuamaenyi:	Death knows and respects no friends
Onwubuya:	Death is a nuisance [i.e., makes nonsense of all humankind's achievements]
Onwukamike:	Death is stronger than I [humanity]
Onwukanjo:	Death is the greatest evil
Onwuegbuchulam:	May I not die before my work on earth is completed

---

23. Edmund Ilogu, *Christianity and Ibo Culture* (Leiden: E. J. Brill, 1974), 123–24, 129.

24. John S. Mbiti, *African Religions and Philosophy* (London: Heinemann, 1969), 5.

25. Cf. Heb. 2:14–16.

26. On the religious import of Igbo names, see P. I. Anozia, *The Religious Import of Igbo Names* (Rome: PUU, Ph.D. Thesis, 1968) and S. N. Ezeanya, "The Use of Igbo Names," *WAR* 3: 2–8.

Wherever one goes in Africa, no matter how lofty an idea they may hold of their religious values, their Ancestors, and the Creator, there lurks behind every mind this consciousness of the capricious nature of the spirits, the uncertainty of life in the present and the imminence of the monster of death. Nowhere in the religious schemes of African peoples do we encounter any expressions of clear hope, certainty, and triumph in relation to the future life as in Paul's eulogy:

> Death is swallowed up in victory
> O death, where is your victory?
> O death, where is your sting?[27]

Or David's affirmation of faith:

> Even though I walk through the valley of the shadow of death,
> I fear no evil;
> For Thou art with me.[28]

The Igbo and other African peoples do not taunt death. They dread it. Therefore, life must be affirmed as the only way to *exclude* death and to create an air of hope in a situation in which hopelessness is writ large everywhere.

To the Igbo therefore, salvation, the ultimate concern of *homo religiosus* is desired and expressed in the form of viable life or *Ezi Ndu*. This life must be constantly enhanced and affirmed in the existential immediacy. Such is the Igbo passion for life. Igbo names that corroborate this emphasis on life include:

Ndubuisi:	Life is supreme
Ndubueze:	Life is *summum bonum*
Ndukauba:	Life is superior to wealth
Ndukwe:	May we live
Chinyendu:	May God give us life as a priority

Among the Yoruba of Western Nigeria, this fear of death and the preference for life are equally strong. In prayer, as Awolalu[29] shows, the emphasis is on life and prosperity. For example, the Elekole of Ikole, in Ikole-Ekiti, during the Oro Eku festival is greeted by the chief as follows:

---

27. 1 Cor. 15:54–55 (NASB).

28. Ps. 23:4 (NASB).

29. J. Omosade Awolalu, "Sin and its removal in African traditional religion," *Orita* X/1 (June 1976): 58–59, 103–4.

Hail your majesty!
May [your] sacrifice be auspicious
May you live till old age, Oboja
May your time be prosperous
May there be good leaders in your time
May the barren have issue in your time

May the town be peaceful
May the town have elders [i.e., old people]
May you live to see and celebrate another festival

The emphasis here, as in the prayer of other African peoples already cited, is on life—life in the existential here and now. But it must be a life worth *celebrating*. Even though Awolalu[30] argues rather romantically that the Yoruba believe in a heaven with God, he nevertheless admits that they are not able to assert with St. Paul that "to die is gain" or "to be with Christ is far better" nor do they pray for and look forward to the coming of that kingdom or heaven as a tangible renewal in the form of an eschatological anastasis, the final resurrection culminating in the renewal of all creation. Rather, what we see among them, as with most other African peoples, is a hazy and complex concept of reincarnation and life in an Ancestral *sheol* or abode. Hence Bediako[31] rightly argues that the Christian doctrine of resurrection and the hope of renewal of all things at the *eschaton* is an important differentia in the meaning of salvation which African religions are unable to match. Mbiti puts it even more strongly by stating that in spite of shadowy and fleeting glimpses, primal African peoples have the original state of humankind in their religion and myths when it comes to the issue of death and resurrection. "African religions must admit defeat: they have supplied no solution."[32] They offer no rescue from the monster of death and no hope for regaining immortality and attaining the gift of the resurrection. As their stress on life in prayer suggests, they find these goals deeply tantalizing, yet finally elusive.

Salvation Is Well-Being

In spite of their lack of a clear concept of immortality in the Christian eschatological sense, African peoples still think of salvation as *total*

---

30. Ibid.

31. Kwame Bediako, *The Gospel and Contemporary Ideologies* (Lagos: NIFES, 1977).

32. John S. Mbiti, *African Religions and Philosophy* (London: Heinemann, 1969), 99.

well-being. A life lived in the sacred presence where no destructive forces dwell is their ultimate goal. According to Gaba, the Anlo of Ghana view

> salvation as total well being of life in its individual as well as corporate dimensions, and this is reflected in all spheres of human existence. Human existence, in the language of Mircea Eliade, may comprise sacred and profane dimensions. But in the Anlo *milieu*, there must be a total dissolution of the sacred and profane, of spirit and matter, before human existence can be realised. In short, this concept of salvation which links salvation with material prosperity is the way that the Anlo people objectify a universal human concept . . .[33]

Salvation Is a Holistic Experience

The African understanding of salvation in the form of *Ezi Ndu* among the Igbo or Dagbe (Anlo) represents a fusion of the "sacred and secular" into a unified but sacrosanct whole. This is perhaps the greatest contribution of the study of salvation in African piety to wider missiological studies. Just as the African view of life, as seen in their prayers and other forms of religious experience,[34] is holistic, so the Christian mission must be a holistic venture with no dichotomy between the Gospel presented in the form of proclamation, and as practicalized in the form of creative and altruistic social action. The Gospel must be presented "by word and deed."[35] Viewed in this way, the mission of the Church as encapsulated in the Great Commission[36] becomes a *holistic venture* in which the Church as Christ's bride and representative on earth unites all resources at her disposal—material and spiritual—in a relentless effort to bring God's Good News to everyone in context. This Good News is the *summum bonum* of the religious efforts of *humanis generis*, which means to experience Yahweh's *Shalom* in context.[37]

---

33. Christian R. Gaba, "Man's Salvation: Its Nature and Meaning in African Traditional Religion," *Christianity in Independent Africa*, eds. Fasholé-Luke, et al (London: Rex Collings, 1978), 339.

34. See Cyril C. Okorocha, "Title Taking in Igbo Society," Preamble to "Ahiajioku Lecture 1990," Imo State Council for Arts and Culture colloquium on Igbo Social Values, (Owerri, Nigeria: Library/Archives).

35. See Colin Craston, ed. *By Word and Deed* (London: Church House, 1992).

36. Matt. 28:18–20; Mark 16:16ff.

37. See Cyril C. Okorocha," The Church Exists for Mission," *EFAC Bulletin* 44(i), 1992.

In other words, the African insight into the meaning of salvation insists that both in proclamation and catechesis and therefore in practice, our presentation of *soteria* as the ultimate goal of humankind's religiousness must be holistic. It must involve a unification of the material and spiritual an equal emphasis on both the divine (gift and initiative) in the salvific movement and the human response to that altruistic display of the *hesed*, *agape*, of the sovereign LORD. The logic here is that, in African cosmology, as our studies among the Igbo show,[38] the spiritual *soteria* or *Shalom*, given by God is experienced by, and indeed, becomes meaningful to humankind in tangible material form as *yesa*, *Ezi Ndu*, or Dagbe. This is because the spirit does not operate *ex nihilo*. Matter, redeemed matter, is the vehicle of the spirit's saving movements.

But both aspects must be held together in dynamic equilibrium in our missionizing efforts. An overemphasis of one aspect could lead to counterproductive distortions of the meaning of the Gospel. An excessive stress on the "spiritual" or even the "purely divine" side of the meaning of salvation and how it is experienced could lead to apathetic otherworldliness or even a near-Islamic determinism. On the other hand, an exclusive or undue preoccupation with the material aspect could mean that the initiative, sovereignty, love, and justice of the Almighty are lost sight of. This could lead to the impression that salvation, even though vaguely thought of as coming from God, is largely achieved through the work of humankind. Perhaps this is the greatest weakness of the African or primal understanding of salvation. Even in more modern terms, and sometimes in the name of Christianity, certain schools of thought present the whole question of the coming of the kingdom of God as though it was a matter of human achievement. Even though it is said to belong to God, in this view the Kingdom refers only to the rule of God, not necessarily to its coming from God, *ek Theou*. Therefore, it has to be achieved by some humanistic tour de force, even if that would mean further injustice, war, and the destruction of lives. Such a view constitutes a complete negation of, or at least an absence of, an experience of the grace of God received in Jesus Christ. The central theme of New Testament soteriology is the perfect revelation of the grace of God in Jesus Christ[39] and epitomized in the dying Saviour's impassioned plea from the cross: "Father, forgive them, for they do not know what

---

38. See Cyril C. Okorocha, op. cit., 1982, ch. 2.
39. John 1:14–16.

they are doing."[40] No wonder one of the executioners exclaimed, "this man must be a Son of a God!" or possibly "this man must be God."[41]

The African primal concept of salvation does not seem to have a clear concept of a forgiving God. The religious in Africa

> are very sincere in observing their religious ceremonies, for they believe that once a member has provoked the wrath of the gods, he may not be forgotten without being punished in one way or other.[42]

My previous studies[43] show that Igbo pray for salvation or *Ezi Ndu* to come from *Chineke,* the Creator God. Yet they live as though this *Ezi Ndu* was essentially a matter of the survival of the determined and the upright—those who by sheer force of will conduct their lives according to *ofor no-ogu,* justice and fair play as enshrined in the intricate interdictions of their *omenala,* the traditional decorum. They hold that "*onye kwe chi ya ekwe,*" "a person's *chi* consents to whatever the person by sheer personal determination affirms." Similarly, Evans-Pritchard,[44] in his studies among the Nuer, shows that the Nuer believe that *life* comes from God in answer to *prayer*; but they also stress that those who must expect deliverance from evil, that is salvation, must be careful always to ensure that they are in the right. The central point here is that the gods act only on behalf of the *just.* The Igbo, in their insistence that *Chineke* must always reject evil, have no room for the justification of the unjust and the salvation of the weak. This excludes grace. Hence Harry Sawyer's conclusion that "the Christian teaching of salvation does not easily fit into the tribal African concept of salvation."[45]

But do the two ideas have to fit one into the other? Our studies show that the Igbo, for instance, do not expect a simplistic and total fusion of the old and the new religious values on becoming Christians. They know that there is a difference. Their pastoral need is for a dexterous integration of the old and the new. Their need is to eliminate the harrowing contradiction of "two faiths in the one mind," which unfortunately is the

---

40. Luke 23:34.

41. Matt. 27:54; Mark 15:39.

42. K. Daniel, "The Pagan Religion among the Ibos of Owerri," *Nigerian Teacher* (Sept. 1936), 17.

43. See for example *The Meaning of Religious Conversion in Africa* (Aldershot, UK: Avebury [Gower Publishing Co.], 1987), 80, 81.

44. E. E. Evans-Pritchard, *Nuer Religion* (Oxford: OUP, 1965), 27.

45. Harry Sawyer, "Sin and Salvation: Soteriology Viewed from the African Situation," *Relevant Theology for Africa,* ed. Hans Jurgen Becken (Durban, South Africa: Lutheran Publishing House, 1973), 136.

lot of a people rooted out of an old and familiar system of values and not adequately fitted into a new one. These find themselves in the air, hanging precariously as it were between two worlds.[46] The pastoral implications of this problem for the Church in Africa are immense. But it was this same primal view of salvation as *Ezi Ndu* that led to Igbo conversion to Christianity in the first place. To the Igbo, conversion to Christianity was an encounter between two systems of salvation, resulting in a movement on the part of the people in the direction of *power.*[47]

3. The African View of Salvation Is Anthropocentric: Now Is the Symbol of Tomorrow

If the African view of salvation seems too preoccupied with mundane things, it is because the African perception of reality is holistic. "Matter is the vehicle of the spirit and the two are so much joined that what affects one, affects the other."[48] Therefore, African peoples think, not in terms of salvation today as opposed to tomorrow, or vise versa, but in terms of salvation today and tomorrow, or better still—salvation tomorrow, because, and as, received today.

For African peoples, now is the symbol of the future. Nevertheless, a "this-worldly" concept of salvation is not less spiritual because of its stress on present needs. It is only a Gnostic understanding of spirituality that fails to accept that when religion assumed a tangible focus and God a human face in Jesus Christ, he did so not as *Logos pneumatikos*[49] but as *Logos ensarkos.*[50] The Word became flesh, thus sanctifying all things. This, perhaps, is a central aspect of the African contribution to our understanding of the religious experience of mankind: to remind us that the secular is also spiritual because it is sanctified in and through the Word of God; that because God assumed human (but sinless) flesh in Christ, the physical and spiritual are fully united into one indivisible and sacrosanct whole. Africans pray for life as well as the means to make life worth living—this includes the exclusion of life-vitiating factors. The greatest evil therefore in this worldview is the vitiation of life, because what is desired is life-enhancement, which brings with it con-

---

46. See Cyril C. Okorocha, op. cit., 1977, ch. 8; see also Dilim Okafor-Omali, *A Nigerian Villager in Two Worlds* (London: Faber, 1965).

47. See Cyril C. Okorocha," The Church Exists for Mission," *EFAC Bulletin* 44(i), 1992.

48. Christian R. Gaba, "Prayer in Anlo Religion," *Orita* 1–3 (1967–69): 75–76.

49. Even though that might have impressed the Pharisees and Sadducees: John 7:27.

50. John 1:14, 18.

tentment and happiness.[51] The Igbo, like other African peoples, are not ashamed of this "humanistic" view of religion and life. From their point of view, if life is the *summum bonum* then *people*, not abstract ideas, constitute the focal point of the religiousness of *homo Africanus*. To be religious and at the same time fail to be humane, to be oppressive and exploitative of others, or to fail to respond humanely to pressing practical needs of others, is "double think." I have argued this point at length elsewhere in my critique of Jeremias and Lohmeyer's overtly otherworldly interpretation of the meaning of *artos epiousios* in the Lord's Prayer.[52] African piety is more of a lived religion than a fideistic set of dogma and philosophical romanticism. Africans through their view of life and religion, remind us not only of the sacredness of humankind as "living souls," but in their totality as living beings. And this sacredness extends to their environment and all the means of sustaining life, that is, the sacredness of all creation. Kaunda puts it more strongly thus:

> Let the West have its technology and Asia it mysticism, Africa's gift to the world . . . must be in the realm of human relationships. The way things are going, Africa may be the (only) place where man can still be man.[53]

This is because *homo sapiens* as *living* beings constitute the focal point of all aspects of African life. Africans insist by word and deed that people are more important than programs and that human life is sacred and priceless.[54] This, according to Kaunda, is what technology has displaced from western society. In the West, one no longer sees a solidarity of persons living in relation and united in a joint struggle for survival, but a motley mob of individuals in a world whose foundation in God has been largely eroded. To the African, salvation has to do with humankind in their immediacy and in their totality as beings living in a cosmos that is regarded as sacred because it is thought to be filled with life. For this purpose *homo religiosus Africanus* expects power, in the form of mana, to emanate from religious forms for the enhancement of life.

---

51. Desmond Tutu, "African Ideas of Salvation," *Ministry Theological Review*, 10 (4) (1970): 120.

52. Cyril C. Okorocha, "God the Father and Hunger in Africa," *The Living God*, eds. Gitari et al. (Nairobi: Uzima, 1987), 196–211.

53. Kenneth Kaunda and Colin Morris, *The Humanist in Africa* (Nashville: Abingdon, 1966), 22.

54. See also Matt. 12:12.

4. Central Themes in the African Concept of Salvation as Ezi Ndu

Ezi Ndu Depends on Moral Rectitude and Fair Play:

The Igbo passion for justice is an important controlling factor in their otherwise materialistic conception of salvation as *Ezi Ndu*. For the Igbo, to live according to *Ofor-na-ogu*, or justice and moral rectitude, is the *sine qua non* for enjoying *Ezi Ndu*. This implies that salvation is for the righteous and to be virtuous is the precondition for prosperity. In Igbo terms, *Ogaranya bu ezi mmadu*—the prosperous is assumed and expected to be a virtuous person. To them, might is not right. Rather right or justice is might. Igbo names corroborate this point. For example:

Ofor bu ndu (Ofondu): Justice is life [i.e., to enjoy life—*Ezi Ndu*—one must live justly]

Ogu bu ndu (Ogundu): Moral rectitude is the source of life. *Ogu bu ike (Oguike)*: Moral rectitude is true strength [i.e., *not* vise versa]

Ofolee (Ofoleta): Let *justice* see to it that justice is ultimately done. [i.e., Ofor, justice, the spirit and ethos of the Ancestors will ultimately vindicate the righteous. Cf., the Nemesis motif in Greek mythology]

Oguzie: May virtue, innocence, moral rectitude ultimately triumph [i.e., may the truth triumph. Let Ogu or innocence not be perverted in judgement and therefore may the innocent be ultimately vindicated]

Oguzoma: May my *innocence* or moral rectitude see to my deliverance

Ofozota: May *Ofor* [justice] deliver me or see to my vindication

Ofonagoro: Justice [i.e., my innocence or the justness of my cause] pleads for me and will see to my vindication and acquittal

This is not a socioreligious philosophy unique to the Igbo. According to Evans-Pritchard[55] the interdependence of the dual concepts of personal virtue or *justness*, and deliverance from evil are basic to Nuer

---

55. Evans-Pritchard, op. cit., 27.

religion. If the Igbo insist that *Chineke* must always reject evil, then whoever will enjoy the favor of *Chineke* and the spirits, the Igbo argue, must "depart from evil" in all its manifestations. This is because, the Igbo say, *Ogu bu ndu* (or as a name *Ogundu*), "moral probity is the fount of true life or *Ezi Ndu*." To the Igbo, viable life or *Ezi Ndu* hinges upon the dual concept of justice and moral probity, *Ofor na ogu*. Thus a full understanding of the idea of salvation among African peoples, especially among the Igbo, must take into account this dualistic socioreligious phenomenon. Life is not viable or abundant life unless it includes *ofor na ogu*. This is because the Igbo do not expect the gods to bless or favor an evil person. The success or prosperity of the wicked is expected to be short lived.

Ezi Ndu Includes Vitality or Total Well-Being

On the personal level, Africans expect salvation or life to be full only when it is experienced in terms of *abuntu obulamu* (among the Baganda), the "living essence" of human life.[56] This living essence embodies the *magara*, vital forces,[57] among the *Bantu* which has to be constantly revitalized through ritual means and kept in place by holding to *Ofor na ogu Igbo*. Elsewhere, I have tried to show that power, *mana* or *ihe*, is the hermeneutic for interpreting African religiousness. The religiousness of any religious system depends on its *mana* or *power* content and its viability on its *mana* effect.[58]

The Igbo, for example, believe their cosmos to be populated by life-vitiating spirit forces locked in an internecine battle at the centre of which is humankind. The power to free humankind from this deadly entanglement is believed to come from the good spirits and through religion. Therefore, in order to enjoy a life free from life-vitiating factors, one has to espouse a religious form which is known to be "powerful" enough to provide, as well as sustain, this *Ezi Ndu*.

A Kikuyu bishop from East Africa corroborated this point as he told me the story of his father's conversion to Christianity.

---

56. John V. Taylor, *Primal Vision* (London: SCM, 1963), 173.

57. Placide Tempels, *La Philosophie Bantone* (Elizabethville: Editions Lovania, 1945), 89ff.

58. Cyril C. Okorocha, op. cit., 1987: 15 et passim; see also "Christianity and African Primal Religions: A Study in Change and Continuity," Edinburgh Lecture Series (Edinburgh: Centre for the Study of Christianity in the Non-Western World, University of Edinburgh, June 1988); and "The Church Exists for Mission," *EFAC Bulletin* 44(i), 1992.

My father told me that the God of the missionaries appeared to have more power than the native divinities. When they wanted to settle, we gave them land in the evil forest where the most wicked spirits lived. We expected them to die within days. But they lived on. They cleared the forest and built houses, including a house for their God and schools for those children who were foolish enough to associate with such strange people. Besides, we saw by their robust health, that they were in possession of a better quality of life. We decided to discover the secret of this power that gave them such superior quality of life. That was how my father got converted to Christianity. Before then he was a "native doctor" and "juju" worshipper. He passed his attractive and vibrant new faith on to me as you can see today.

Wherever African peoples see a better or viable quality of life, they conclude that *Ezi Ndu* is present. They look for the source of that life in the religion professed by its possessor and go for it.

Among the Igbo, the converse is also true. A religious form that fails to provide *Ezi Ndu* for its adherents is soon discarded. Basden observes that:

> the natives often neglect their gods and, on occasions, go further to exhibit symptoms of actual contempt towards them. Shrines are allowed to fall into decay and gods left to fend for themselves. Either the deity was incapable of intervening [in the face of trouble or could not provide the vitality to maintain, *Ezi Ndu* or ward off the life vitiating forces], or failed to exercise his protective *power*. In consequence, he was denounced as an imposter; a useless encumbrance demanding sacrifices for which he gave no return.[59]

African primal peoples have no disinterested love for their gods. Worship is given only in return for protection and life-enhancing benefits. This pragmatic and almost utilitarian attitude to religion is the key to Igbo conversion to Christianity. But it is also the explanation for the rise of new religious movements, including the African Independent Churches.[60] When the native gods retreated and failed to act in protection of their adherents at the forceful advance of British imperialism, the people panicked. They thought that the world had suddenly come to an end. But most auspiciously, Christianity appeared on the scene just at this precise moment of panic and confusion. For the first time in their history, the natives were presented with a divinity whose claim to

---

59. Basden (1938/1966): 36.
60. See John S. Pobee, *AD 2000 and After* (Accra, Ghana: Asempa Press, 1991), passim.

almightiness was at once universal and authenticated by tangible results. They turned to this new religion with characteristic zeal and almost revolutionary enthusiasm.

Ezi Ndu Includes Desire for Posterity or Children

In our examination of a selection of African prayers we saw the emphasis on both life as the *summum bonum* and the gift of children as the crown of human achievements.

The morning prayer from Mali is emphatic on this request: "make me a gift of children."

The reason is so "that *your name* may not be obliterated." The perpetuity the Africans pray for is not an endless life in a blissful heaven but an extension of their being into the Ancestral *sheol*. They desire a situation which ensures a continuous relationship with the living through the Ancestral cult, but especially a returning in the form of a hope of reincarnation. In this way the lineage name is perpetuated. The Igbo emphasize this desire in the names they give their children. For example:

Ahamefula:	May my name never be obliterated
Azuatalam:	May I never lack a successor or posterity [usually male offspring]
Nwabueze:	A child is supreme or the best of gifts
Nwabuko (*male*):	A child is precious
Nwadiuto (*female*):	A child is precious [a delight]
Maduagwu:	May the human race never become extinct
Nnamdi:	"My father is still alive" [i.e., The lineage name lives on in *this* male offspring; because this male child has been born, we now affirm that our lineage will never become extinct.]
Nnanna (*male*) *Nnenna* (*female*):	My grandfather [or grandmother (f)] lives on in this child [i.e., my forebears will never be forgotten, because this child has now become an extension of their being. Also an indication of belief in reincarnation.]

Marriage is primarily for, and in order, to have children. When a marriage fails to provide children, traditional steps are taken to rectify the situation.[61]

---

61. See Okorocha, op. cit., 1987: 168–172.

As already observed, African peoples have no anticipation of a final day when the present cosmic order will be "judged, or dissolved" and replaced by a "new heaven and a new earth." There is no clear hope of a hereafter free from suffering, a hope which could give courage to the saint and reason to forgive one's enemy. On the contrary, to suffer in the present life is suggestive of the absence of *Ezi Ndu* and indicative of a comfortless future. In short, today is the oracle of tomorrow. One may hope for future salvation only if there has been a tangible evidence and experience of salvation *today*.

The Igbo *pater familias* includes his morning prayer and the Mali with a petition for a secure future:

Let the children have good health
Let the women have childbirth
So that your name may not be obliterated.[62]

The name *Ahamefula* summarizes the African concept of the eschatological dimension of salvation as *Ezi Ndu*. A person lives righteously or virtuously, being an *ezi mmadu*, by holding on to *ofor na ogu*, so that their good deeds outlive them as they are thus remembered. Male offspring are desired to perpetuate the name of the line both in reality and in character. At death the good person expects to be received into the abode of the Ancestors and especially reincarnated. Thus, the eschatological dimension of *Ezi Ndu* is a quest for continuity, which is admissive of a dualism of personality whereby the dead are at once "the departed" and essentially those who are actively present.

Contemporaneity of Salvation

Ezi Ndu is expected to manifest itself in tangible contemporary terms. This will normally include keeping pace with others in progress. If a divinity fails to provide *Ezi Ndu* in this way, it is discarded. In their prayers, the Igbo ask for wealth and riches in modern terms "so that we may not lag behind in progress,"—*ka anyi wee di ka ibe*.[63]

Religion is expected to bring social progress. *Ezi Ndu* is always desired in terms of contemporary status symbols. When this does not happen the people turn to more "reasonable" religious forms. A recent interview with the son of a founding bishop of the Anglican Church in

62. Ibid., chapter 5.
63. Ibid., 198ff.

Namibia (who would prefer to remain incognito) corroborates this point. He reports:

> The new Churches from America are growing but ours is losing members to these new churches because they not only preach powerfully and fervently, they pray for the sick and especially take care of the practical needs of their members. They have built several schools and hospitals. They symbolize progress. And who, in these modern times, would hang on to an outmoded and insensitive religious system no matter how colorful or prestigious, when the good life is abundantly evident elsewhere and within easy reach. So I don't blame them. What we need as Anglicans to grow as well, is not new or better liturgy and dogma, but a religion with power and the resources to meet human needs [in tangible contemporary terms: a religion that makes real the almightiness and the nearness of God].

Ezi Ndu Includes Peace with the Gods

To be saved includes a state of being at peace with the spirit world by living one's life in line with the traditional decorum or *Omenala*. When a breach of these elaborate commands occurs, recourse is made to the intricate ritual provisions to restore the situation. Sacrifices, which may range from such trivial items as a piece of *kola* nut, a whole roast yam, or an egg, to major items such as a goat or cow, depending on the gravity of the breach committed, feature prominently in the African cultus.

Salvation from sin in Igbo piety is seen in two forms. The *lustrative* aspect which is effected by the blood of the sacrifice[64] and the *apotropaic* aspect which is as a result of the dedication of a scape goat or an *osu*. This *osu* may vary from a chick to a cow or even a human being in the case of a terrible sin or abomination such as homicide. But at other times an *osu* is dedicated as a perpetual priest/sin-bearer on behalf or instead of his master. This is the case where on *osu* is regarded as a cult slave.[65]

Primarily, the *osu* object is that which contains the returning nature of the consequences of sin in the African worldview. Awololu[66] gives us an example from the Yoruba of Western Nigeria: The *télé* is the Yoruba

---

64. Francis Arinze, *Sacrifice in Igbo Religion* (Ibadan, Nigeria: Ibadan University Press, 1970).

65. See Okorocha 1987: 146ff.

66. J. Omosade Awololu, "Sin and Its Removal in African Traditional Religion," *Orita*, X/1 (June 1976): 19.

osu, or "human (usually male) scapegoat": The people symbolically bind their sins on him on the day of the ritual cleansing and warding off (after the cleansing sacrifice of the animal had been offered). The sins are tied to the back of the *télé* in the form of a heavy load (made up of all kinds of rubbish, often including human waste) which he bears to the sacred grove, the evil forest. The people throw the *télé* into the forest and chant:

Take sins away!
Take misfortunes away!
Take disease away!
Take death away!

Sin is regarded as any conduct or occurrence which may incur the wrath of the gods and therefore lead to the vitiation of life. It is not the vitiation of life that constitutes sin, but the breach that brought about the wrath which is evidenced in the removal of the *force vitale*. The sequence is thus: *sin—wrath—vitiation of life*. Where such a vitiation exists, life cannot be described as *Ezi Ndu*. Therefore, every effort is made to avoid whatever will contradict it or mean loss of favor or peace with the gods.

Ezi Ndu Is Communal Order or Tranquility of Order

African society is not individualist or isolationist. The Igbo insist that *Igwe bu ike* "Our unity is the source and guarantor of our collective strength and victory."[67] The African concept of societal salvation or *Ezi Ndu* is summed up in one word—*communalism*. Communalism as an aspect of *Ezi Ndu* has four characteristics: *solidarity, mutuality, reciprocity,* and *altruism* (living for others).

These four virtues characterize what the Igbo world describe as an *Ezi-mmadu*, a virtuous person. Solidarity is the group consciousness which does not exclude individual rights. The Igbo concept of *chi*[68] shows that they are astute believers in the right of the individual. They argue that there would be no "we," if there was no "I." Yet they expect the "I" to draw strength from, and merge into the "we," for greater effectiveness without losing its personal identity. In East Africa the same reality is seen in the *Harambee motif* often exploited by political libera-

---

67. MISAG II, *Towards Dynamic Mission*, eds. C. Okorocha and J. Clark (London: ACC, 1992), 27.

68. See B. I. Chukwukere, "Individualism in an Aspect of Igbo Religion," *The Conch* 3 (2): 109–17.

tion movements. It is an inexplicable and compelling consciousness that
"we belong together." We live or die together. What affects one affects
the other. The Igbo put it rather negatively thus: "When one finger is
dipped into red palm oil, it soon touches the other fingers on the hand."
No one lives or dies alone. We need each other, and whatever one does,
whether good or bad, is enjoyed or suffered by all. Thus, the care of the
environment and the concept of community and mutual responsibility
come naturally to the primal African. Igbo names that indicate the solidarity motif include:

Nwanneka:	My brother/sister/kinsfolk is/are the great-est possession/gift
Onyeaghalanwanneya:	Never forget your brother; we need each other
Maduakolam:	May I never stand alone [i.e., in time of trouble]
Umunnakwe:	My success in life depends on the good will of the kin group
Umunnabuike:	My kinsfolk are my [pride], source of strength or encouragement
Nwannediuto:	My brother/sister/kinsfolk is/are precious or my delight
Ibezimako:	May I learn to be wise through and because of the group interdependence

Mutuality means taking each other seriously. A consciousness that
we are all equal means that no one has a God-given right to rule over or
dominate the other. Hence the prayer to be like others, *idi ka ibe* [i.e.,
not to lag behind in progress], so as not to be ignored or taken for
granted. Mutuality also means learning to treat others as one would like
to be treated. The Igbo value generosity, but so that generosity does not
degenerate into paternalism which can be a source of pride for some and
humiliating for others, they expect those who give to learn the blessing
of receiving from others. So the Igbo name their children:

Omenichekwa:	Bear other people's needs and rights in mind in all your activities in life; think of others; don't be selfish
Ucheakolam:	May I never lack a sharp and lively conscience
Akobundu:	Wisdom [pure conscience] is the source of true life [*Ezi Ndu*]

Nkemakolam: May I never lack what is personal to me [i.e., may I never live depending on others for everything]

But also:

Maduakolam: May I never lack people [i.e., I need others]

Reciprocity has to do with *interdependence*. No one lives or dies alone. The Igbo say to a selfish rich person, "No one buries himself, if he does, one of his hands will have to be outside the grave"! Gifts are given and received with unrestrained generosity as a means of redistributing wealth and excluding poverty, and also as a way of indicating that one is an *ezi mmadu*, a good or saved person. African generosity, which has become almost proverbial as western missionaries, tourists, and visitors always testify, has its roots in this concept. To enjoy *Ezi Ndu* is to be generous. A stingy person is considered wicked. Olauda Equiano, back in the 18th century, argued that Igbo individualism and an achievement-oriented culture did not negate their belief in group solidarity, just as their commitment to the virtue of generosity did not encourage indolence and sponging:

> Everyone contributes something [through their own hard work] to the common stock, and as we are unacquainted with idleness, we have no beggars . . . The benefits of such a mode of living are obvious. [The Igbo are known for] their hardiness, intelligence, integrity and zeal; . . . general healthiness . . . vigor and activity.[69]

Again the Igbo say, *Aka nri kwoo aka ekpe, aka ikpe, kwoo aka nri, ha abua adi ocha*, "both hands become clean as each hand washes the other in turn."

Igbo names that indicate mutuality also indicate reciprocity, e.g., *Igwebuike*; but also, *Obileke*, my family [kinsfolk] together with my destiny [*eke*] determine what I become in life. Through their philosophies of solidarity, mutuality, and reciprocity, the Igbo assert "we need each other."

Altruism or living for others in the African concept of *Ezi Ndu* is the *onye aghala-nwanneya* motif in Igbo social philosophy. It is the motivating *ought* behind the solidarity motif or group survival. The Igbo believe that living for others is the highest expression of true *Ezi Ndu*.

---

69. Olaudah Equiano, *Equiano's Travels* (first published 1789, 2 vols.), abridged ed. Paul Edwards (London: Heinimann, 1967), 7–8.

They believe that whatever they are or have is best used when it becomes a property for the good of others. In short, the Igbo believe that living for others is the highest expression of true spirituality. An *oga-ranya* is essentially a person for others.

Names that indicate this altruistic motif include:

Adaora:	The people's daughter; Daughter beloved of the people
Obiora:	Son beloved of the people
Ahamba:	
(*Ahaejuejemba*)	My name and resources belong to my people wherever they go
Nwaora:	A child given to the people [i.e., an only son or first/only son born after a protracted and anxious period without one; during that waiting period the people share the anxiety, now that a child has been born the parents believe that the child belongs to all]

Achievements are visualized and celebrated publicly through public displays of generosity in the form of festivity and, sometimes, *"title taking."*

Conclusion

We have tried to show in this brief study what African peoples think of salvation in terms of *Ezi Ndu*, viable life. It is a life that incorporates *total wholeness*. Such life, according to the Igbo, is not just materially abundant: it must include justice and moral probity as its precondition and undergirding. *Ezi Ndu* is enhanced through the power that is found in religious forms. The eschatological dimension of *Ezi Ndu* is desired in terms of *Ahamefula*: may my name never be obliterated. This desire for continuity is pursued with equal energy in three main areas of life: a "good name," earned through one's generosity and other good deeds; offspring which makes the desire for children sometimes seem excessive and frenzied; and reincarnation and attainment of Ancestorhood so that even if physically dead, one is *essentially present* with the living.

But salvation must include the good life expressed in terms of contemporary realities. When a religious form is unable to provide for, or protect, its adherents, it is discarded and a more effective one is sought. This we found to be the key to understanding the nature and meaning of religious conversion in Africa and the rise of African Independent

Churches and new religious movements. African conversion is a search for *salvation*.

The question of the adequacy of this view of salvation as a manifestation of the religious experience of *humanis generis* will need another study to explore. Meanwhile, it is important to restate that the main watershed between the primal African and New Testament revelations of the meaning of salvation or *Ezi Ndu* is the issue of *grace*. How can *Chineke* maintain his own justice while justifying the unjust and rejecting injustice and evil? If personal justness always leads to fullness of life, how do we explain the suffering of the righteous—the Job motif? And if *Ezi Ndu* is indicative of the justness of the one who has it, how do we explain the prosperity of the wicked?[70] If *Ezi Ndu* depends on *Ofor na ogu*, how can we find a permanent solution to the problem of evil in the world and sin as a personal experience? If life is the *summum bonum*, how can humankind overcome the monster of death? These and other questions need further comparative and theological exploration in the study of this most fascinating subject.

Pastorally and missiologically speaking however, if the search for *Ezi Ndu* is the putative force behind African conversion to Christianity, it then means that that same factor will determine both their allegiance to, and continuity in, Christianity, as well as the shape and meaning of Christianity in Africa.

This places a threefold onus on the leadership of the Church in Africa: the first is that theological scholarship in Africa is no longer optional. Leaders need to engage in serious theological reflection to learn how to translate the essential truths of the historic Christian faith into the idiom of the African peoples without losing its moorings biblically and in the historic Christian continuum. That is, they need to help African Christians to be *Christians* of Africa who through a dexterous integration of the "old" and the "new" discover and continually enjoy fullness of life *en Christo* universally and in context. Furthermore, through a continuous renewal of the power that set the process of conversion in motion, the leadership are to help African Christians to match fideistic vitality with practical ethical conduct so that the Holy Spirit may use redeemed Africans in Christ to redeem and transform African society. Third, that African Christians should engage in serious theologizing so as to fill a serious hiatus present in the life of the Church—that of making a unique African contribution to the theology, life, and *mis-*

---

70. In Ps. 73, for example.

sion of the one Church, Catholic and Apostolic, to the glory of God the Father. This calls for a serious and mature African initiative in the missionary and theological agenda of the Church.

Meanwhile, we are aware of the current demographic shift in Christendom, away from the West and towards Africa and the so-called Third World.[71] This seems to point to the emergence of a "Second Great Reversal,"[72] in the direction of Christian missionary movement, but certainly suggests that the theology of the Church and the shape of Christianity in Africa could be determinative for the future of World Christianity.

---

71. Andrew F. Walls, "Towards Understanding Africa's People's Place in Christian History," *Religion in a Pluralistic Society*, ed. J. S. Pobee (Leiden: E. J. Brill, 1976), 108–9.

72. Cyril C. Okorocha, "What is the Spirit Saying?" *Compasrose/Anglican World* (London: ACC, June 1993), and John Paul II, "Encyclical on Missionary Activity," *Redemptoris Missio Origins* (Rome: The Vatican, CNS Documentary Service, Jan 1991) 20 (34), 31, pp.541–68.

Jesus in African Culture:
A Ghanaian Perspective

Kwame Bediako

Introduction
Christian Faith and African Traditional Religion in Retrospect

One of the most telling commentaries on the presentation of the Gospel of Jesus Christ in Africa is the following statement:

> Christ has been presented as the answer to questions a white man would ask, the solution to the needs that western man would feel, the Saviour of the world of the European worldview, the object of the adoration and prayer of historic Christendom. But if Christ were to appear as the answer to the questions that Africans are asking, what would he look like?[1]

It was made by one of the more perceptive and sensitive missionaries to Africa of our time and describes neatly the general character of western missionary preaching and teaching in Africa since the arrival of missionaries on our continent during the 19th century. It also raises a question which must be faced by African churches and African Christians of today who are convinced that Jesus Christ is the *Universal* Saviour and thus the Saviour of the African world, and who feel that the teaching they have so far received is inadequate.

And yet the negative side of missionary history in Africa must not be exaggerated, for several reasons. First, the vitality of our Christian communities bears witness to the fact that the Gospel really was communicated, however inadequate we may now consider that communication to have been. There is always more to the "hearing" of the Word of God than can be contained in the actual preaching of it by the human agents;[2] the Holy Spirit is also present to interpret the Word of God

---

1. John V. Taylor, *The Primal Vision: Christian Presence amid African Religion* (London: SCM Press, 1963), 16.

2. John V. Taylor, *The Growth of the Church in Buganda: An Attempt at Understanding* (London: SCM Press, 1958).

directly to the hearers. Therefore we must allow the mercy and providence of God to override the shortcomings of human achievements.

Second, African theological thinkers now share in the inheritance of the Gospel as the apostle Paul proclaimed it, the Gospel that set the early Gentile Christians free from Jewish Christian attempts to impose upon them the regulations of the Jewish Law.[3] Paul grasped firmly the universality of the Gospel of Jesus the Messiah, and by insisting that the Gospel includes all peoples without reserve, gave Gentile Christians the essential tools for assessing their own cultural heritage, for making their own contribution to Christian life and thought, and for testing the genuineness and Christian character of that contribution. For many years now African theologians have refused to accept the negative view of African religion held by western missionaries and have shown consistently the continuity of God from the pre-Christian African past into the Christian present.[4] They have therefore, like the apostle Paul, handed to us the assurance that with our Christian conversion, we are not introduced to a new God unrelated to the traditions of our past, but to One who brings to fulfillment all the highest religious and cultural aspirations of our heritage. In this way the limitations in our missionary past need no longer hinder the growth of Christian understanding and confidence in our churches.

A further reason touches on the nature of African Traditional Religion itself, and its encounter with the Christian faith. The common western missionary view of Traditional Religion was that it formed "the religious beliefs of more or less backward and degraded peoples all over the world,"[5] and that it held no "preparation for Christianity." Yet in more recent years, it has been shown that Christianity has spread most rapidly in "societies with primal religious systems,"[6] that is, religious systems akin to African Traditional Religion. These societies are the Mediterranean world of the early Christian centuries, the ancient peoples of northern Europe and modern "primalists" of Black Africa, Asia, South America and Oceania. This fact of history has led to the question

---

3. See Acts 15 and also Paul's Letter to the Galatians.

4. See, among others, E. Bolaji Idowu, *Olodumare: God in Yoruba Belief* (London: Longmans, 1962); J. S. Mbiti, *Concepts of God in Africa* (London: SPCK, 1970); G. M. Setiloane, *The Image of God among the Sotho-Tswana* (Rotterdam: A. A. Balkema, 1976).

5. W. H. T. Gairdner, *Edinburgh 1910. An Account and Interpretation of the World Missionary Conference* (London: Oliphant, Anderson and Ferrier, 1910), 139.

6. A. F. Walls, "Africa and Christian Identity," *Mission Focus*, vol. IV, no. 7 (Nov. 1978): 11–13.

whether there might be "affinities between the Christian and primal traditions?" It shows clearly that the form of religion once held to be the furthest removed from the Christian faith has had a closer relationship with it than any other.[7] Indeed, since primal religions have been "the most fertile soil for the Gospel," it has been argued that they "underlie therefore the Christian faith of the vast majority of Christians of all ages and all nations."[8] John Mbiti, probably the best-known African theologian outside of Africa has repeatedly argued that Africa's "old" religions have been a crucial factor in the rapid spread of Christianity among African peoples.[9] They were a vital preparation for the Gospel.

This argument stands the western missionary view of African religions on its head and so opens the way for a fresh approach to how we may understand the relation of Jesus as Lord and Saviour to the spiritual realities of our context.

Christ and Spirit Power
Jesus as Divine Conqueror in the African World

On the wider African scene, John Mbiti has written two articles which deal with African understandings of Christ, drawn largely from evidence from the Independent Churches. His view was that it is within these churches that African Christians have been able to express more freely their experience of the Christian faith than in the mission-dominated or historical churches (that is, the mainline denominations).[10] Though the distinctions between "independent" and "historical" churches are now less meaningful than they once were,[11] Mbiti's articles did indicate that there was something to write about, that there are characteristically African understandings of Christ. In this area, as in much else, he has been a pioneer.

---

7. H. W. Turner, "The Primal Religions of the World and their Study" in Victor C. Hayes (ed.), *Australian Essays in World Religions*, Australian Society for the Study of Religions (Bedford Park: South Australia, 1977), 37.

8. A. T. Walls, "Africa and Christian Identity," 11.

9. See John S. Mbiti, "The Encounter between Christianity and African Religion" in *Temenos*, 12 Helsinki (1976), 125–35.

10. See John S. Mbiti, "'Our Saviour' as an African Experience" in B. Lindars and S. Smalley (eds.), *Christ and the Spirit in the New Testament (Essays in Honour of C. F. D. Moule)* (Cambridge University Press, 1973), 397–414.

11. Cf. A. F. Walls, "The Anabaptists of Africa? The Challenge of the African Independent Churches" in *Occasional Bulletin of Missionary Research* 3, no. 2 (April, 1979): 48–51.

By way of illustration I shall highlight two major points he makes in those studies. The first is that Jesus is seen above all else as the *Christus Victor* (Christ supreme over every spiritual rule and authority). This understanding of Christ arises from Africans' keen awareness of forces and powers at work in the world which threaten the interests of life and harmony. Jesus is victorious over the spiritual realm and particularly over evil forces and so answers to the need for a powerful protector against these forces and powers.

The second important point is that for African Christians the term "our Saviour" can refer to God and sometimes to the Holy Spirit, as well as to Jesus. Jesus, as our Saviour, brings near and makes universal the almightiness of God. This means that he "is able to do all things, to save in all situations, to protect against all enemies, and is available whenever those who believe may call upon him." It also means that the humanity of Jesus and his atoning work on the Cross are in the background, and Jesus is taken to belong essentially to the more powerful realm of divinity, in the realm of spirit-power. Though Mbiti considers this view of Christ as inadequate, he does stress that the methods and context of present-day evangelism need to be reexamined and that there needs to be also a "deeper appreciation of the traditional African world, whose grip is so strong that it exercises a powerful influence on the manner of understanding and experiencing the Christian message, however that message may be presented."

These considerations bring us near the heart of the problem that confronts us now: how to understand Christ authentically in the African world. To make my reflections more concrete, I propose to relate them as far as possible to the religious belief and worldview of the Akan peoples. Being an Akan myself, I shall be dealing with realities with which I can easily sympathize, for I believe such reflection can be authentic only in context. I shall be setting forth some of my own concerns with regard to my own Akan world of ideas and beliefs.

Jesus and the Ancestors in Akan Worldview

Accepting Jesus as "our Saviour" always involves making him at home in our spiritual universe and in terms of our religious needs and longings. So an understanding of Christ in relation to spirit-power in the African context is not necessarily less accurate than any other perception of Jesus. The question is whether such an understanding faithfully reflects biblical revelation and is rooted in true Christian experience. Biblical teaching clearly shows that Jesus is who he is (i.e., Saviour) because of what he has done and can do (i.e., save), and also that he was able to do what he did on the Cross because of who he is (God the Son), cf. Colossians 2:15ff. Since "salvation" in the traditional African world involves a certain view of the realm of spirit-power and its effects upon the physical and spiritual dimensions of human existence, our reflection about Christ must speak to the questions posed by such a worldview. The needs of the African world require a view of Christ that meets those needs. And so who Jesus is in the African spiritual universe must not be separated from what he does and can do in that world. The way in which he relates to the importance and function of the "spirit fathers" or ancestors is crucial.

The Akan spirit world on which human existence is believed to depend, consists primarily of God, the Supreme Spirit Being (*Onyame*), Creator and Sustainer of the universe. Subordinate to God, with delegated authority from God, are the "gods," (*abosom*), sometimes referred to as children of God (*Nyame mma*), and the ancestors or "spirit fathers" (*Nsamanfo*). The relative positions of the "gods" and the ancestors are summed up by Dr. Peter Sarpong, the Catholic Bishop of Kumasi and an authority on Akan culture:

> While God's power surpasses all others, the ancestors would appear to tilt the scale in their favor if their power could be weighed against that of the lesser gods. After all are the deities not often referred to as "the innumerable gods of our ancestors," the spokesmen of the human spirits?[12]

John Pobee formerly of the University of Ghana, has also underlined the importance of the ancestors in the religious worldview of the Akan. He has devoted a whole book to developing some aspects of an Akan Christian theology. He concludes that

> Whereas the gods may be treated with contempt if they fail to deliver the goods expected of them, the ancestors, like the Supreme Being, are always held in reverence or even worshipped.[13]

We shall not discuss here whether ancestors are worshipped or simply venerated. We need only to recognize that the ancestors form the most prominent element in the Akan religious outlook and provide the

---

12. Peter Sarpong, *Ghana in Retrospect: Some Aspects of Ghanaian Culture* (Accra-Tema: Ghana Publishing Corporation, 1974), 43.

13. John S. Pobee, *Toward an African Theology* (Nashville: Abingdon, 1979), 48.

essential focus of piety. Pobee's comment on the ancestors is therefore well-founded:

> Perhaps the most potent aspect of Akan religion is the cult of the ancestors. They, like the Supreme Being, are always held in deep reverence or even worshipped. The ancestors are that part of the clan who have completed their course here on earth and are gone ahead to the other world to be elder brothers of the living at the house of God. Not all the dead are ancestors. To qualify to be an ancestor one must have lived to a ripe old age and in an exemplary manner and done much to enhance the standing and prestige of the family, clan or tribe. By virtue of being the part of the clan gone ahead to the house of God, they are believed to be powerful in the sense that they maintain the course of life here and now and influence it for good or ill. They give children to the living; they give good harvest, they provide the sanctions for the moral life of the nation and accordingly punish, exonerate or reward the living as the case may be.[14]

Ancestors are essentially clan or lineage ancestors. So they have to do with the community or society in which their progeny relate to one another, and not with a system of religion as such, which might be categorized as "the Akan religion." In this way, the "religious" functions and duties which relate to ancestors become binding on all members of the particular group who share common ancestors. Since the ancestors have such an important part to play in the well-being (or otherwise) of individuals and communities, the crucial question about our relationship to Jesus is, as John Pobee rightly puts it: "Why should an Akan relate to Jesus of Nazareth who does not belong to his clan, family, tribe, and tradition?"

Up to now, our churches have tended to avoid this question and have presented the Gospel as though it was concerned with an entirely different compartment of life, unrelated to traditional religious piety. As a result, many of our people are uncertain about how the Jesus of the church's preaching saves them from the terrors and fears which they experience in their traditional worldview. This shows how important it is to relate Christian understanding and experience to the realm of the ancestors. If this is not done, many of our fellow African Christians will continue to be men and women "living at two levels"—half African and half European—but never belonging properly to either. We need to meet God in the Lord Jesus Christ speaking immediately to us in our particu-

---

14. John S. Pobee, *Toward an African Theology*, 46.

lar circumstances, in a way that assures our people that we can be authentic Africans and true Christians.

John Pobee suggests that we "look on Jesus as the Great and Greatest Ancestor" since, "in Akan society the Supreme Being and the ancestors provide the sanctions for the good life, and the ancestors hold that authority as minister of the Supreme Being."[15] He considers some of the problems involved, but because he approaches the problem largely through Akan wisdom sayings and proverbs, he does not deal sufficiently with the religious nature of the question. In addition, he does not let the biblical revelation speak sufficiently in its own terms into the Akan situation. He too easily assumes similarities between Akan and biblical (for him "Jewish") worldviews, underestimating the potential for conflict, and so does not achieve real encounter. For if we claim as the Greatest Ancestor one who, at the superficial level, "does not belong to his clan, family, tribe and nation," the Akan non-Christian might well feel that the very grounds of his identity and personality are taken away from him. It is with such fears and dangers, as well as the meanings and intentions behind the old allegiances, that a fresh understanding of Christ has to deal.

The Universality of Jesus Christ and Our Adoptive Past

I suggest that we should read the Scriptures with Akan traditional piety well in view. In this way we can arrive at an understanding of Christ that deals with the perceived reality of the ancestors. I also recommend that we make the biblical assumption that Jesus Christ is not a stranger to our heritage. I therefore start from the universality of Jesus Christ rather than from his particularity as a Jew. By doing this I do not disregard the Incarnation; rather I affirm that the Incarnation was the incarnation of the Saviour of all people, of all nations, and of all times. Also, by insisting on the primacy of Jesus' universality, we do not seek to reduce his incarnation and its particularity to a mere accident of history. We hold on to his incarnation as a Jew because by faith in him, we too share in the divine promises given to the patriarchs and through the history of ancient Israel (cf. Eph. 2:11–22). So those promises belong to us also, because of Jesus. Salvation, though "from the Jews" (John 4:22), is not thereby Jewish. To make Jesus little more than a "typical" Jew is to distort the truth. There is clearly more to him than Jewishness. His statement in John 8:43–44 that a Jew could have for a father not

---

15. John S. Pobee, *Toward an African Theology*, 94.

Abraham at all, but the devil, was outrageous from the Jewish point of view. What counts is one's response to Jesus Christ. Here we find one of the clearest statements in Scripture, that our true human identity as men and women made in the image of God, is not to be understood primarily in terms of racial, cultural, national, or lineage categories, but in terms of Jesus Christ himself. The true children of Abraham are those who put their faith in Jesus Christ in the same way that Abraham trusted God (Rom. 4:11–12).

Consequently, we have not merely our natural past, for through our faith in Jesus, we have also an "adoptive" past, the past of God, reaching into biblical history itself. This also—aptly described as the "Abrahamic link"—is our past.[16]

In the same way, Jesus Christ, himself the image of the Father, by becoming one like us, has shared our *human* heritage. It is within this *human* heritage that he finds us, and speaks to us in terms of its questions and puzzles. He challenges us to turn to him and participate in the new humanity for which he has come, died, been raised, and glorified.

The Good News As Our Story

Once this basic, universal relevance of Jesus Christ is granted, it is no longer a question of trying to accommodate the Gospel in our culture; we learn to read and accept the Good News as *our* story. Our Lord has been, from the beginning, the Word of God for us as for all people everywhere. He has been the source of our life, and illuminator of our path in life, though, like all people everywhere, we also failed to understand him aright. But now he has made himself known, becoming one of us, one like us. By acknowledging him for who he is, and by giving him our allegiance, we become what we are truly intended to be, by his gift, that is, the children of God. For he himself is the Son of God, originating from the divine realm. If we refuse him that allegiance, we lose that right of becoming children of God. Our response to him is crucial because becoming children of God does not stem from, nor is it limited by, the accidents of birth, race, culture, lineage, or even "religious" tradition. It comes to us by grace through faith.

This way of reading the early verses of John's gospel, from the standpoint of faith in Jesus Christ as *our* story, is valid and necessary. The beginning of the Gospel echoes the early verses of Genesis 1. We

---

16. A. F. Walls, "Africa and Christian Identity," 13.

are meant to appreciate the close association of our creation and our redemption, both achieved in and through Jesus Christ (Col. 1:15ff.). We are to understand our creation as the original revelation of God to us. It was in the creation of the universe and especially of the man and woman that God first revealed his Kingship to our ancestors and called them and us to freely obey him. Working from this insight, that our creation is the original revelation to, and covenant with, us, we, from the African primal tradition, are given a biblical basis for discovering more about God within the framework of the high doctrine of God as Creator and Sustainer, which is deeply rooted in our heritage. More significantly, we are enabled to discover ourselves in Adam (cf. Acts 17:26) and come out of the isolation which the closed system of clan, lineage, and family imposes, so that we can recover universal horizons.

However, "as in Adam all die. . ." (1 Cor. 15:22). Adam sinned and lost his place in the garden. Where the biblical account speaks of the expulsion of the man and woman (Gen. 3), African myths of origins talk of the withdrawal of God, so that he is continually in people's thoughts, yet is absent from daily living in any practical sense. The experience of ambiguity which comes from regarding the lesser deities and ancestral spirits as both beneficent and malevolent, can only be resolved in a genuine incarnation of the Saviour from the realm beyond. But trinitarian doctrine is preserved, for the God who has become so deeply and actively involved in our condition is the Son (John 1:18), whom to see is to "see" the Father (cf. John 14:15ff.; Acts 2:38ff.), and this is made possible through the Holy Spirit (John 14:23).

Jesus As "Ancestor" and Sole Mediator

Thus the gulf between the intense awareness of the existence of God and yet also of this "remoteness" in African Traditional Religion and experience is bridged in Christ alone because "there has been a death which sets people free from the wrongs they did while the first covenant was in force" (Heb. 9:15). How does this death relate to our story and particularly to our natural "spirit-fathers"? Some suggest that ours is a "shame-culture" and not a "guilt-culture," on the grounds that public acceptance is what determines morality, and consequently a "sense of sin" is said to be absent.[17] This view is oversimplified and is

---

17. See F. B. Welbourn, "Some Problems of African Christianity: Guilt and Shame" in C. G. Baeta (ed.), *Christianity in Tropical Africa* (London: Oxford University Press), 182–99; cf. John V. Taylor, *The Primal Vision*, 166–69.

challenged by African theologians and sociologists.[18] However, in our tradition the essence of sin lies in its being an antisocial act. This makes sin basically injury to the interests of another person and damage to the collective life of the group. Busia's comment on the Ashanti is significant:

> The Ashanti conception of a good society is one in which harmony is achieved among the living, and between the living and the gods and the ancestors . . .[19]

Such a view of morality does not resolve the real problem of the assurance of moral transformation within the human conscience. For the real problem of our sinfulness is the soiled conscience, and against this, purificatory rites and sacrificial offerings to achieve social harmony are ineffectual. And yet the view of sin as antisocial seems to be also biblically valid: sin is indeed sin against another person and the community's interest. But human beings are the creation of God, created in God's image, so social sin is also sin against God. The blood of Abel cried to God against Cain (Gen. 4). The Good News underscores the valid insight about the social nature of sin, but brings the need for expiation into a wider context. Sin is more than the antisocial act; the sinner sins ultimately against a personal God who has a will and purpose in human history.

Seen from this angle, our needs in our tradition make the insights about Jesus Christ in the epistle to the Hebrews perhaps the most crucial of all. Our Saviour has not just become one like us; he has died for us and his death has eternal sacrificial significance for us. It deals with our moral failures and the infringements of our social relationships. It heals our wounded and soiled consciences and overcomes, once and for all and at their roots, all that in our heritage and our somewhat melancholy history brings us grief, guilt, shame, and bitterness. Our Saviour is our Elder Brother who has shared in our *African* experience in every respect, except in our sin and alienation from God, an alienation with which our myths of origins make us only too familiar. Being our true Elder Brother now in the presence of God, his Father and our Father, he displaced the mediatorial function of our natural "spirit-fathers." For these themselves need saving, since they originated from among us. It is

---

18. John S. Pobee, *Toward an African Theology*, 102ff.; cf. K. A. Busia, "The Ashanti" in Daryll Ford (ed.), *African Worlds: Studies in the Cosmological Ideas and Social Values of African Peoples* (London: Oxford University Press, 1954), 207.

19. K. A. Busia, "The Ashanti" in Daryll Forde (ed.), *African Worlds*, 207.

known from African missionary history that sometimes one of the first actions of new converts was to pray for their ancestors who had passed on before the Gospel who proclaimed. Such an action is an important testimony to the depth of these people's understanding that Jesus is sole Lord and Saviour. Jesus Christ, "the Second Adam" from heaven (1 Cor. 15:47) becomes for us then the only mediator between God and ourselves (cf. 1 Tim. 2:5). He is the "mediator of a better covenant" (Heb. 8:6), relating our human destiny directly to God. He is truly our high priest who meets our needs to the full. (We shall have more to discuss on this all-important epistle of the New Testament later.)

From the kind of understanding held about the spirit-world, the resurrection and ascension of our Lord also come to assume great importance. He has now returned to the realm of Spirit and therefore of power. From the standpoint of Akan traditional beliefs, Jesus has gone to the realm of the ancestor spirits and the "gods." We already know that power and the resources for living are believed to come from there, but the terrors and misfortunes which could threaten and destroy life come from there also. But if Jesus has gone to the realm of the "spirits and the gods," so to speak, he has gone there as Lord over them in much the same way that he is Lord over us. He is therefore Lord over the living and the dead, and over the "living-dead," as the ancestors are also described. He is supreme over all "gods" and authorities in the realm of the spirits. So he sums up in himself all their powers and cancels any terrorizing influence they might be assumed to have upon us.

The guarantee that our Lord is Lord also in the realm of the spirits is that he has sent us his own Spirit, the Holy Spirit, to dwell with us and be our protector, as much as to be Revealer of Truth and our Sanctifier. In John 16:7ff., our Lord's insistence on going away to the Father includes this idea of his Lordship in the realm of spirits, as he himself enters the region of spirit. It also includes the idea of the protection and guidance which the coming Holy Spirit will provide for his followers in the world. The Holy Spirit is sent to convict the world of its sin in rejecting Jesus, and to demonstrate, to the shame of unbelievers, the true righteousness which is in Jesus and available only in him. But he is also sent to reveal the spiritual significance of God's judgment, this time not upon the world, but upon the devil, who deceives the world about its sin and blinds people to the perfect righteousness in Christ. Our Lord therefore, entering the region of spirit, sends the Holy Spirit to his followers to give them understanding of the realities in the realm of spirits. The close association of the defeat and overthrow of the devil ("ruler of this world") with the death, resurrection, and exaltation of Jesus (cf. John 12:31) is significant here. In addition, the thought of the "keeping" and the protection of his followers from "the evil one" forms an important part of Jesus' prayer recorded in John 17 (cf. John 17:9), which is aptly described as his "high priestly" prayer.

These are some of the areas for us to investigate when we begin to reflect on the Good News from the standpoint of the worldview of our heritage. Some important insights are in store for us, not from isolated passages of Scripture, but from entire and significant bodies of teaching in the Word of God.

The Lordship of Christ Amid Sacred Power
The Position of the Chief: The Problem of Ambiguity

So as to make concrete the Lordship of Christ in relation to the natural "spirit-fathers" or ancestors, let us focus on the way in which Christ's Lordship may be related to the significance of Kingship in our society. This close connection between the place and role of the ancestors and the meaning of kingship on the one hand, and the place and role of Christ on the other, is due to the fact that the reigning Chief occupies the stool of the ancestors, particularly his royal ancestors. There is more to the Chief's position than simply succession to the office of his deceased predecessors. In the Akan worldview these do not die but simply go "elsewhere," that is, into the realm of the "spirit-fathers" from whence they continue to show interest and to intervene in the affairs of the state. The installation of the Chief renders his very person sacred. This is done by bringing him into a peculiarly close contact with the ancestors. The ceremony at which this is effected is known to be quite simple. Upon the ritually preserved stool of his most renowned ancestor, the Chief is briefly lowered and raised three times. Once enstooled in this way, the Chief, as Dr. Sarpong explains, is "now more than just a head of state. He is, in a sense, an ancestor himself. From that moment everybody must call him Nana (grandfather)"[20] The Akan royal title, Nana, is itself an ancestral title. The ancestors are Nana-non Nsamanfo, that is, ancestor spirits or "spirit-fathers."

Since the cult of the ancestors is the most powerful aspect of religious life in traditional Akan society, the Chief's sacred office has great religious significance. Because the traditional belief is that the well-

---

20. Peter Sarpong, *The Sacred Stools of the Akan* (Accra-Tema: Ghana Publishing Corporation, 1971), 54; cf. 26.

being of the society depends upon the maintenance of good relations with the ancestors on whom the living depend for help and protection, the Chief acquires a crucial role as the intermediary between the state and the ancestors. He is the central figure at the organized religious ceremonies which ensure the maintenance of harmony between the living and the spirit-fathers. So closely is religion bound up with Akan kingship that in his authoritative study of Ashanti kingship Dr. Busia concluded:

> No one could be an adequate chief who did not perform the ritual functions of his office. There have recently been elected as chiefs in different parts of Ashanti men who are both literate and Christian. But they have all felt an obligation to perform the ritual acts of their office. They were enstooled in the stool house, where they poured libations to the ancestors whom they had succeeded . . . It is as successors of the ancestors that they are venerated and their authority respected, and they could not keep the office without maintaining contact with the ancestors through the traditional rituals.[21]

While Busia rightly insists that "the Chief's position is bound up with strong religious sentiments," his conclusions also indicate that there is some ambiguity about the position of the Chief who wishes to embrace the Christian faith. Busia himself points to the enstoolment of men "who are Christian," in order to emphasize the significance of his central point that the institution of Chiefs is basically of a sacral nature. Furthermore, Dr. Busia was well known for his view that our churches must come to terms with the Akan understanding of the universe and the nature of society, particularly its religious aspects.

Since Busia wrote in the 1950s, the ambiguity that characterizes the relation of the Chief to the Christian community in our society has continued. It has remained as a crucial area of confrontation between the Christian faith as generally understood in our context and the religious traditions of Akan culture. When the Moderator of the Presbyterian Church of Ghana inaugurated, in March 1981, a committee charged with the specific responsibility of studying the relation of the Church to traditional culture, he drew attention to the persisting ambiguity of the Chief's position. According to the report, many Chiefs have been baptized and confirmed, but their positions prevent them from becoming

---

21. K. A. Busia, *The Position of the Chief in the Modern Political System of Ashanti* (A Study of the Influence of Contemporary Social Changes on Ashanti Political Institutions), (1951; reprint London: Frank Cass, 1968), 38.

full members of the Church. The question which he posed was: "What can bring these Chiefs and the Church together?"[22]

The Problem of the Chief's Authority

The Moderator was not the first to ask that question. Behind the decision to set up this committee lay the desire of some Chiefs, with their traditional Councils, to understand more fully how the Christian faith which they cannot now ignore relates to the cultural tradition in which they themselves stand. This is not the first instance of such an initiative by our Chiefs. In 1941 the Chiefs and Elders of the Akan state of Akim-Abuakwa sent a memorandum to the synod of the Presbyterian Church which was meeting in the Chief's capital, Kibi. The memorandum criticized the church on several counts, and particularly complained about what the state authorities saw as the disruptive effect of separating Christian converts into a community apart in each town in order to guard against what were considered to be "pagan" influences. This undermined the unified authority of the Chief over his natural subjects.[23]

Another state response to the Christian presence occurred in the same year, 1941, from Ashanti. The Ashanti Confederacy Council decreed that farming on Thursday, the natal day of the earth deity, Asaase Yaa, was to be regarded as an offence. Since the Christian community had, in the meantime, become quite a significant factor in the state, it is understandable that the traditional authorities were disturbed by evidence of increasing violation of this law, mainly on the part of Christians.

The Christian churches concerned responded to the state authorities on each of these points of state criticism. In the earlier case, the church pointed to the social and educational benefits of its work and stressed the Christians' loyalty to the state. In the second case, the Christian churches in Ashanti presented a memorandum to the Asantehene on the relations between Christians and the state. The memorandum asserted the rights of Christian conscience with regard to the law on grounds of Christian belief, and while protesting the loyalty of Christians to the state, attempted to secure a dispensation from the law for Christians.

---

22. *Christian Messenger*, Accra, Vol. IV, no. 4 (April, 1981): 3.
23. S. G. Williamson, *Akan Religion and the Christian Faith, A Comparative Study of the Impact of Two Religions* (Accra: Ghana Universities Press, 1965), 152–53.

The heart of the churches' argument for our purposes was found in paragraph 6:

> On the part of chiefs we would ask that they accept as a fact the existence of Christians as members of their state and lay down ways by which they can show their allegiance to their chiefs without at the same time offending their Christian conscience.[24]

I shall not discuss in detail the issues raised in these two instances of conflict between Akan traditional authorities and the Christian churches within their jurisdiction. But while the Christian faith was obviously attacking the institutions of sacral kingship as well as the position of the Chief in some of its most vital aspects, that is, its specifically religious dimensions, none of the Christian responses seem to have addressed themselves to these issues. The memorandum to the Asantehene tried to apply fully developed western Christian ideas on church and state to a sacred order which made no sharp distinctions between religious and political institutions. Busia's comment on this controversy provides a useful insight into the deeper issues at stake:

> In a society in which political and religious office are combined, the chiefs regard the request for the recognition of the existence of Christians and for the adaptation of native law as a request for the surrender of authority. As they see it, the Christian Church requests that they should not have power to legislate on certain things for certain members of the community, because the Church desires the right to legislate on these for those of the chief's subjects who have embraced the Christian Faith. Christianity challenges the traditional position of the chief as the religious as well as the political head of his tribe.[25]

The Factor of Christ and the Desacralization of Political Power

Behind this conflict between two authorities—the Christian church and the traditional state—lie two conceptions of power and differing views as to the source of power. In the religious view of the world underlying Akan social organization, the power of the reigning Chief as the channel through which cosmic forces operated for the well-being of the society, was based on his position as one "who sits on the stool of the ancestors." The power of the Chief among the living is therefore the power of the ancestors, sacral power, just as his title (Nana) is also

---

24. See K. A. Busia, *The Position of the Chief* . . . , 220–22; cf. 133–38.
25. K. A. Busia, *The Position of the Chief*, 137.

theirs. Consequently, presentations of Christ which fundamentally undermine and remove the power of the ancestors over the living at the same time undermine the sacred power of the reigning Chief. We may wonder how many of our Chiefs who now desire closer links with Christian churches realize how far their power as well as their own persons would need to be desacralized. Perhaps some of our natural rulers may rather be men among men. An understanding of Christ which alters so radically the nature and source of power carries, inevitably, immense implications for politics in our societies.

Here I mean politics in a wider sense than the political organization of our sacred states. Historically, biblical faith has had the effect of desacralizing societies,[26] and the story of Christianity in Africa has also demonstrated this quality in the Christian faith.[27] Much of the prestige associated with kingship in the past has been lost in the process of social change. New forms of political administration have been forged with the emergence of the new nation-states and their elected presidents. The natural ruler who sits on the stool of the ancestors is compelled now to seek ways of coming to terms with the new realities.

However, sacralization of political power is not confined to the "old" order. It can find its way into the new ideology of states as a secular parody of the old, genuinely religious social organism. Some modern African republics need to be understood from this angle. In so many of our modern nation-states, the leaders who achieved political independence often insisted on holding on to power even when they became unpopular. This may well reflect the role of the royal ancestor who never ceases to rule from the realm of spirit-power! Certainly praise-names and titles of some African presidents bear ancestral overtones. When Dr. Kwame Nkrumah accepted the title of "Osagyefo," he must have known what he was doing. Nkrumah was not concerned to promote the interests of the "old" sacral rulers and he was not from a royal house himself. But the title "Osagyefo" portrayed him as the "Saviour" from British colonial rule. Under his presidency, Ghana's coins bore his image and the inscription: *Civitatis Ghaniensis Conditor*, Founder of the State of Ghana. Nkrumah, for all practical purposes, became an ancestor

---

26. Cf. H. W. Turner, "The Place of Independent Religious Movements in the Modernization of Africa" in *Journal of Religion in Africa*, Vol. II (1969), 43–63, esp. 49ff.

27. A. F. Walls, "Towards Understanding Africa's Place in Christian History" in J. S. Pobee (ed.), *Religion in a Pluralistic Society: Essays Presented to C. G. Baeta* (Leiden: E. J. Brill, 1976), 180–89.

in the old sacral sense. It is not surprising that the Young Pioneers recited: Nkrumah never dies!

I have not drawn attention to the modern secular politics of African societies in order to lessen the significance of the old order. On the contrary, if we are to know how to deal as Christians with the problems of contemporary politics in our societies, we may need to find ways of coming to grips with the forces at work in the old order which have not yet been touched adequately by the Gospel. If there is to be a genuine encounter with the realities behind the traditional institutions at the level at which our people experience them, it is important that the Gospel of Jesus Christ be seen as *our* story also. If it is true that "the sovereignty of the world has passed to our Lord and his Christ, and he shall reign for ever and ever" (Rev. 11:15, NEB), this must find its meaning also in our context. In terms of the old sacred order, it is understandable that one Asantehene should say:

> I am the centre of this world around which everything revolves.
> And one of his subjects is reported to have said of him:
> Everything comes out of him, he is holding the source of power, force and generation.[28]

However, what happens when the spirit-fathers who ensure such power to the reigning Chief become subservient to Christ the Lord? What happens to the position of the Chief who "sits on the stool of the ancestors" when it becomes evident that Christ himself is the Great Ancestor of all mankind, the mediator of all divine blessing, the judge of all mankind, and that access to him is not dependent on inherited right through royal lineage, but through grace and faith, and repentance from the heart? Will the Chief be a man among men, respected and honored, but not venerated or worshipped?

All this goes to indicate that the Christian faith has a unique contribution to make towards the development of such forms of political life as ensure an adequate sharing by all persons in *real* power and so enhance stability in any society. The pointer to the Christian contribution is seen in Jesus' attitude toward power. When Jesus told Pontius Pilate that his (Jesus') kingdom was not of this world (John 18:36), he could not have meant that it had nothing to do with this world. If he had meant that, then his coming as *Saviour of the world* would have been

---

28. See Eva L. R. Meyerowitz, *The Sacred State of the Akan* (London: Faber and Faber, 1951), 57, note 1.

meaningless. His meaning could only have been that he held a conception of kingship and power which was fundamentally different from that which Pilate was used to and practiced.

The clue to, and the logic of, what our Lord meant are symbolized in the Cross which he willingly embraced—the symbol of his death which Pilate sanctioned. The Christian Scriptures are quite clear that Jesus won his way to preeminence and glory *not* by exalting himself, but rather by humbling himself, to the point of dying the shameful death on the Cross. In other words, by making himself of no account, everyone now must take account of him;

> All beings in heaven, or earth and in the world below will fall on their knees and will openly proclaim that Jesus Christ is Lord, to the glory of God the Father (Phil. 2:10–11, TEV)

The essential character of Jesus' conception of power is that of power as nondominating. This understanding of power will always remain one of the most significant Christian contributions to politics in any society, particularly those which are feeling their way towards a true and genuine open sharing in political power. Faith in Jesus Christ as alone Lord and Mediator of blessings and power, frees political leaders to become true human beings among fellow humans, and ennobles politics itself into a service of God in the service of our fellow human beings. Without such a conception of power as Jesus held, taught, and demonstrated by the Cross, the hope of achieving a real sharing of political power in any society will remain elusive.

The Relevance of Christian History

These problems are not peculiar to our context and are certainly not new in Christian history. The very early centuries of the Christian era are the most instructive for our purposes. Those early Christians were convinced that in the Good News about Jesus Christ and through Jesus Christ, they found access to the God beyond the gods, and that Jesus Christ met their spiritual needs and inspired higher hopes.

For this reason they were able to make a definite break with the cult of the emperor. However, many earnest men and women did not make that break even though they may have disapproved of much in the popular and state cults; they were not gripped by the Gospel. For such people the Gospel was alien, if not distasteful. But not so for the Christians; the Gospel assured them that the sovereignty of the world had indeed passed to their Lord and so all other claims to sovereignty paled into insignificance. And they won their victory, as John was shown on Patmos, " . . . by the blood of the Lamb and by the truth which they proclaimed; and they were willing to give up their lives and die" (Rev. 12:11 TEV).

The message is quite clear: the heart of the encounter of the Good News with our context is our understanding of Jesus Christ, how our faith in Jesus Christ, crucified and risen, relates to our existence and destiny in the world. With such faith comes a firm conviction that in and through Christ, we have found and been found by, ultimate truth, which is utterly dependable for interpreting our human experience. We also are bound to discover that we are involved in a struggle to the death. It is not with flesh and blood, but with more subtle powers and intelligences who would hinder men and women from perceiving the nearness of Christ as one who has opened for us a new way, a living way, into the presence of God, through his own body and as one of us! (cf. Heb. 10:20).

Bearing Witness to Christ . . . as Power Encounter

True witness to Christ, then, has to do with encounter, "pulling down strongholds," "destroying false arguments," leveling "every proud obstacle," taking every thought captive and making it obey Christ (cf. 1 Cor. 10:4–5). But this kind of encounter does not wait for the "specialists" and the "experts"; it takes place in the normal worshipping, witnessing life of the congregation, as the following incident reported a few years ago shows:

Drumbeat in Church

A sharp conflict recently erupted between the Christian churches and the traditional authorities in the Ghanaian town of Akim Tafo over the violation by the churches of a ban on drumming during a traditional religious festival. During the two weeks preceding the 'Ohum' religious festival, drumming, clapping of hands, wailing, firing of musketry and any other noises likely to disturb the gods is not permitted. But Christian churches in the town ignored the ban and continued to allow drumming during their worship services, arguing that drumming was an essential part of the Ghanaian form of worship.[29]

Obviously it is the fact of drumming in church which, in view of our missionary past, the reporter found most striking. I am more interested in the fact that the controversy took place in the context of wor-

---

29. *Voice Weekly* (Sept. 3–9, 1980), 6.

ship. We have here an encounter of experiences and of views of reality. We have a power encounter. It is equally interesting that the Christians claim their drumming in church to be "an essential part of the Ghanaian form of worship." They do not say *Christian* form of worship. However, since they are Christians, we have to assume that their worship has to do with Jesus Christ and not with the "gods" of the "traditional religious festival." So, we may ask, who is maintaining the authentic *Ghanaian* form of worship?

Our Christian brethren here have grasped the insight of the early Christians, that the issue at stake is not the confrontation of two religions or religious systems. The Gospel has to do with grace and personality, with God manifesting his love for us in and through Christ, touching our hearts and opening our eyes through his Spirit, so that we can respond to his love where he finds us, in our heritage of culture and religious tradition. Could it be that in their own way the Akan Christians of Akim-Tafo have understood that Christian identity (for salvation has to do also with identity—God calls us by name) has to do with the discovery of our true personality in Christ, touching both individual and social levels of our existence, and that this discovery, which is a gift of Christ, itself becomes the basis of confidence?

I doubt whether I have claimed too much for the theological awareness of the Christians of Akim-Tafo. Their attitude seems to have something of the understanding that I have described. This enabled them to confront the traditional authorities on the common ground of a belief in the value of worship and to challenge the devotees of the "old" gods (and ancestors) to recognize that their own *Christian* worship with the aid of drums, even though it might be in violation of a traditional religious ban, is in its own right authentic *Ghanaian* worship.

Such incidents and actions ought to give us hope. They show me that the approach which I have outlined above ties in with the Christian experience of those who share in the same cultural heritage.

The Epistle to the Hebrews as OUR Epistle!

Now I should like to return to what I indicated earlier about the importance for our situation of the *Epistle to the Hebrews*. It has often been assumed that the problem of theology in New Testament times was how to relate the Gospel to Gentile cultures and traditions. The meaning of Christ for Jewish religious tradition was thought to be relatively simple. The epistle to the Hebrews, however, corrects that error. The writer is aware that some Hebrews might be tempted to turn from the proclamation of the great salvation in Christ. His frequent warnings about the danger of falling away from Christ may sometimes sound theoretical. He balances them with assurances that his readers would not fall away from their Christian discipleship. Yet he is also conscious that he is seeking to give them "solid food" and that some of the readers might not be used to such heavy diet.

The clue to the epistle's teaching lies in its presentation of Christ. *Hebrews* is the one book in the New Testament in which Jesus Christ is understood and presented as High Priest. His priestly mediatorial role is fully explored and we are given one of the highest and most advanced understandings of Christ in the entire New Testament.

One of the most significant statements in the epistle must be chapter 8:4, "If he were on earth, he would not be a priest at all. . . ." And yet it is obvious that our Saviour does and did fulfill a High Priestly function in his redemptive work for us. The problem arises when one has to justify that insight on the basis of Old Testament prophecies and anticipations. The fact is, "he was born a member of the tribe of Judah; and Moses did not mention this tribe when he spoke of priests" (Heb. 7:14). Thus the view of Christ in Hebrews involves making room in the tradition of priestly mediation for one who, at the purely human level, was an outsider to it. How were the Hebrews to take this demonstration? "Why should an Akan relate to Jesus of Nazareth who does not belong to his clan, family, tribe, and nation?" My suggestion is that a similar question must have occurred to some Hebrews in time past, and the epistle to the Hebrews was written in part to answer that question.

The way the writer of the epistle to the Hebrews approaches the question we have indicated is to work *from* the achievement of Jesus—in the meaning of his death and resurrection—into the biblical tradition of sacrifice and high priestly mediation. In the process, the *universality* of the Lord from heaven, that is, his universal significance as the Saviour of all people everywhere, comes to form the basis of the call to Hebrew people to take him seriously as their Messiah. Even more strikingly, the writer shows that the High Priesthood of Jesus is not after the order of Aaron, the first Hebrew High Priest, but rather after that of the enigmatic non-Hebrew, and greater priest-king, Melchizedek (Heb. ch. 7–8). Therefore, the priesthood, mediation, and hence the salvation that Jesus Christ brings to *all* people everywhere, belong to an entirely different category from what people may claim for their clan, family, tribal and national priests and mediators. It is the *quality* of the achievement and ministry of Jesus Christ for and on behalf of *all* people, together

with who he is, that reveal his absolute supremacy. In other words, as
One who is fully divine, he nonetheless took on human nature in order
to offer himself in death as sacrifice for human sin. Jesus Christ is
unique not because he stands apart from us; rather he is unique because
no one has identified so profoundly with the human predicament as he
has done, in order to transform it. The uniqueness of Jesus Christ is
rooted in his radical and direct significance for *every* human person and
every human context and *every* human culture.

But the specific value for us of the presentation of Jesus in the epistle to the Hebrews stems from its relevance to a society like ours with its
long and deep tradition of (a) sacrifice, (b) priestly mediation, and (c)
ancestral function. In relation to each of these features of our religious
heritage the epistle to the Hebrews shows Jesus Christ to truly be the
answer to the spiritual longings and aspirations which our people have
sought to meet in the ways that our traditions have evolved.

(a) Sacrifice

Sacrifices as a means of ensuring a harmonious relationship
between the human community on the one hand, and the realm of divine
and mystical power on the other, is a regular event in Ghanaian society.
It is easy to assume that the mere performance of sacrifice is sufficient,
and yet the real problem with sacrifice is whether it achieves its purpose.
Hebrews gives us the fundamental insight that since it is *human* sin and
wrongdoing that sacrifice seeks to purge and atone for, in real terms, no
animal or subhuman victim can stand in for human beings. Nor can any
sinful human being stand in for fellow sinners. So it becomes clear that
the action of Jesus Christ, himself divine and sinless, yet taking on
human nature in order to willingly lay down his life for all humanity,
fulfills perfectly the end that all sacrifices seek to achieve:

> But when Christ came as a high priest of the good things that have
> come, then through the greater and perfect tent (not made with hands,
> that is, not of this creation), he entered once for all into the Holy
> Place, not with the blood of goats and calves, but with his own blood,
> thus obtaining eternal redemption. (Heb. 9:11, 12 NRSV)

No number of animal or other victims offered on any number of
shrines in the land can ever equal the one, perfect sacrifice made by
Jesus Christ of himself for all time and for all peoples everywhere. To
reject the worth of the achievement of Jesus Christ on the grounds of a
theory of race, ethnicity, and cultural tradition, as some would counsel,

is to act against better knowledge, distort religious truth, and walk into a blind alley. To choose such a path, in the words of the epistle to the Hebrews, is to court "the fearful prospect of judgment and the fierce fire which will destroy those who oppose God" (10:27). There is no need to arrive at such an end.

(b) Priestly Mediation

If the quality of Jesus' self-offering in death sets his sacrifice above all sacrifices and achieves perfect atonement, so also does his priestly mediation surpass all others. Since Jesus had no human hereditary claim to priesthood (Heb. 7:14; 8:4) the way is open for appreciating his priestly ministry for what it truly is. His taking of human nature in the Incarnation enabled him to share the human predicament and so qualified him to act for humanity. His divine origin ensures that he is able to mediate between the human community and the divine realm in a way that no mere human priest can ever do. As himself God-man, therefore, Jesus bridges the gulf between the Holy God and sinful human beings and so achieves for humanity the harmonious fellowship with God which all human priestly mediations seek to effect, but can only approximate.

And yet his priestly ministry takes place *not* in an earthly temple, at an earthly shrine (indeed it cannot, since no earthly temple or shrine can ever match the quality of his ministry). Rather, his priestly mediation takes place in the realm where it really matters, and where all issues are truly decided, namely in the divine presence. "For Christ did not go into a man-made Holy Place . . . He went into heaven itself, where he now appears on our behalf in the presence of God" (Heb. 9:24).

But the priestly mediation of Christ has done more than act "on our behalf." It actually brings priestly mediation to an end by bringing also into the divine presence all who by faith associate themselves with him. The meeting of the perfect sacrifice with the perfect priestly mediation in the same single person, Jesus Christ, is extraordinary, and it means that having identified with humanity in order to taste death *on behalf of* humanity (Heb. 2:14–15), he has opened the way for all who identify with him to be *with* him in the divine presence (Heb. 10:19–20).

This unique achievement of the priestly mediation of Christ renders therefore all other priestly mediations obsolete, so revealing their ineffectiveness. To disregard the surpassing worth of the priestly mediation of Jesus Christ for *all* people everywhere and to choose, instead, ethnic priesthoods in the name of cultural heritage, is to fail to recognize the true meaning and end of all priestly mediation, to abdicate from belonging within the one community of humanity and clutch at the shadow and miss the substance. The whole thrust of the epistle to the Hebrews is that such error is not only unredeemable, but also it is utterly unnecessary.

(c) Ancestral Function

Of the three features of our traditional heritage we are considering, ancestral function seems on the face of it to be the one to which Jesus Christ least easily answers. Although we have touched upon this subject briefly earlier, we can now treat it more thoroughly.

Ancestors are lineage or family ancestors and so belong to *us*; they are by nature *ours*. One might claim that whatever may be said in relation to sacrifice and priestly mediation, the cult of ancestors is beyond the reach of Christian argument. In other words, if the cult of ancestors is valid, then here is solid ground on which traditional religion can take a firm stand.

Yet it is precisely here that the problem lies. In what does the validity of the cult of the ancestors consist? Since not all become ancestors but only those who lived exemplary lives and from whom the community derived some benefit, are not ancestors in effect a projection into the transcendent realm of the social values and spiritual expectations of the living community? Since traditional society views existence as one integrated whole, linking the living and the departed in a common life, such a projection is understandable. However, the essential point is that ancestors have no independent existence from the community that produces them. The cult of ancestors provides the basis for locating in the transcendent realm the source of authority and power in the community. It is this that gives to leadership itself a sacred quality as we noted in our discussion of the religious aspects of kingship (chieftaincy) in Akan society.

Strictly speaking, therefore, the cult of ancestors, from the intellectual point of view, belongs to the category of myth, ancestors being the product of the myth-making imagination of the community. To characterize the cult of ancestors by the word "myth" is not to say that the cult is unworthy of serious attention. Rather, the term stresses the functional value of the cult of ancestors, for myth is sacred, enshrining, and expressing some of the most valued elements of a community's self-understanding. The cult of ancestors as myth, therefore, points to the role of the cult in ensuring social harmony by strengthening the ties which knit together all sections and generations of the community, the present with the past and with those as yet unborn. On each of the occasions of heightened feeling in the community—birth and presenting of infants, initiation into adulthood, marriage, death, as well as the installation into adulthood, marriage, death, as well as the installation of a Chief and celebration of harvests—the cult of ancestors forms an essential part of the ritual ceremonies which secure the conditions upon which the life and continuity of the community are believed to depend.

However, it is also important to realize that since ancestors do not originate, in the first place, from the transcendent realm, it is the myth-making imagination of the community itself which sacralizes them, conferring upon them the sacred authority which they exercise through those in the community, like Chiefs, who also expect to become ancestors. Earlier on we noted Prof. John Pobee's comment that "perhaps the most potent aspect of Akan (traditional) religion is the cult of the ancestors." Now we can state more clearly that the potency of the cult of ancestors is *not* the potency of ancestors themselves; the potency of the cult is the potency of myth.

Once the meaning of the cult of ancestors as myth is granted and its "function" is understood within the overall religious life of traditional society, then it begins to become clear how Jesus Christ fulfills our aspirations in relation to ancestral function too. Ancestors are considered worthy of honor for having "lived among us" and for having brought benefits to us; Jesus Christ has done infinitely more. They, originating from among us, had no choice but to live among us. But he, reflecting the brightness of God's glory and he, the exact likeness of God's own being (Heb. 1:3), took our flesh and blood, became like us, shared our human nature and underwent death for us to set us free from the fear of death (Heb. 2:14–15). He who has every reason to abandon sinful humans to their just deserts is not ashamed to call us his brethren (Heb. 2:11). Our natural ancestors had no barriers to cross to live among us and share our experience. His incarnation implies that he has achieved a far more profound identification with us in our humanity than the mere ethnic solidarity of lineage ancestors can ever do.

Jesus Christ surpasses our natural ancestors also by virtue of who he is in himself. Ancestors, even described as "ancestral spirits," nonetheless remain essentially *human* spirits; whatever benefit they may be said to bestow upon their communities is therefore effectively contained by the fact of their being human. Jesus Christ, on the other hand, took on human nature without loss to his divine nature. Belonging in the eternal realm—as Son of the Father (Heb. 1:1, 48; 9:14)—he has nonetheless taken human nature into himself (Heb. 10:19) and so, as God-man, he ensures an infinitely more effective ministry to human beings (Heb. 7:25) than can ever be said of merely *human* ancestral spirits.

The writer of the epistle to the Hebrews, confronted by the reality of the eternal nature of Jesus Christ, is at a loss for words and has to fall back on the enigmatic Melchizedek of Genesis 14:17–20 for analogy: without father or mother, without beginning or end, he (Melchizedek) is *like* the Son of God (Jesus Christ). The likeness is only in thought, for Jesus has actually demonstrated, through his resurrection from the dead, his possession of an indestructible life (Heb. 7:16). This can never be said of ancestors. The persistence of the cult of ancestors is owed, accordingly, not to their demonstrable power to act, but to the power of the myth that sustains them in the corporate mind of the community. This means that the presumption that ancestors *actually* function for the benefit of their communities can be seen to be part of the same myth-making imagination which projects departed human beings into the transcendent realm in the first place. We cannot in this study consider in detail the spiritual dynamics of the world of traditional religion, for indeed spiritual forces do operate here too. My point is that ancestral spirits as human spirits which have not demonstrated any power over death, the final enemy, cannot be presumed to act in the way tradition ascribes to them.

Since ancestral function as traditionally understood is now shown to have no basis in fact, the way is open for appreciating more fully how Jesus Christ is the only real and true Ancestor and Source of life for all mankind, fulfilling and transcending the benefits believed to be bestowed by lineage ancestors. By his unique achievement in perfect atonement through his own self sacrifice, and by effective eternal medi-ation and intercession as God-man in the divine presence, he has secured eternal redemption (Heb. 9:12) for all those who acknowledge who he is and what he has done for them, who abandon the blind alleys of merely human traditions and rituals and instead entrust themselves to him. As mediator of a new and better covenant between God and humanity (Heb. 8:6; 12:24), Jesus brings the redeemed into the experi-ence of a new identity in which he links their human destinies directly and consciously with the eternal gracious will and purpose of a loving and caring God (Heb. 12:22–24). No longer are human horizons bounded by lineage, clan, tribe, or nation. The redeemed now belong within the community of the living God, in the joyful company of the faithful of all ages and climes. They are united in a fellowship which through their union with Christ, is infinitely richer than the mere social bonds of lineage, clan, tribe, or nation, which exclude the "stranger" as a virtual "enemy."

Some Concluding Observations
Reading and Hearing the Word of God in Our Own Language

In the light of the significance of Jesus Christ as taught in the epistle to the Hebrews, it becomes clear that for the first readers of the epistle, as for us, there is no valid alternative to Jesus Christ. Once this discovery is made, the important question is no longer: why should we relate to Jesus of Nazareth who does not belong to our clan, family, tribe, and nation? Rather, the question becomes: how may we understand more fully this Jesus Christ who, in fact, relates to us most meaningfully and most profoundly in our clan, family, tribe, and nation? One of the helpful ways of growing in this understanding is to seriously read and listen to the Word of God in our own Ghanaian languages.

In matters of religion there is no language that speaks to the heart and mind and to our innermost feelings as does our mother tongue. The achievement of Christianity with regard to this all-important place of language in religion is truly unique. Christianity is, among all religions, the most culturally translatable, hence the most truly universal, being able to be at home in every cultural context without injury to its essential character. For a Scriptural religion that roots religious authority in a particular collection of sacred writings, this achievement is truly remarkable. The explanation for this must lie with Christianity's refusal of a "sacred" language. With the exception of the dominant role of Latin in the European phase of Christianity and in some sectors of Roman Catholicism, Christianity has, in the course of its expansion, developed generally as a "vernacular" religion. The significance of this fact has been most marked historically in Africa, where the early possession of the Scriptures in the mother tongue meant that many African peoples had access to the original sources of Christian teaching, on the authority of which they could, if need be, establish their *own* churches. The "mushrooming" of churches is *not* always evidence of the activity of foreign agents; in the majority of cases it indicates how fully at home we Africans have become in the Gospel of Jesus Christ. Each one of us, with access to the Bible in our mother tongue, can truly claim to hear God speaking to us in our own language!

The importance of this fact is a theological one. Unlike say, the Qur'an, which when translated, becomes less than its fullness in Arabic, the Bible in the vernacular remains in every respect the Word of God. This Christian belief has its basis in what took place at the very outset of the preaching of the Gospel on the Day of Pentecost. The Holy Spirit, through the first Christian witnesses, spoke at one and the same time to people "who had come from every country in the world" (Acts 2:5, TEV), each in his own language, causing them to hear the great things that God has done in Jesus Christ (Acts 2:1–12). Hearing the Word of God in our own language, therefore, is not to be sneered at and left to "illiterates"; rather it is what is required if we seriously seek growth in our understanding of Jesus Christ.

A final comment on the epistle to the Hebrews will clarify the point. The second part of Hebrews 1:3 in two popular English versions of the Bible reads as follows:

> When he had made purification for sins, he sat down at the right hand of the Majesty on high . . . (RSV)

> After achieving forgiveness for the sins of mankind, he sat down in heaven at the right had side of God, the Supreme Power . . ." (TEV)

The Akuapin Twi version of the same text reads as follows:

> Ode n'ankasa ne ho dwiraa yen bone no, okotraa anuonyam kese no nifa so osorosoro. (Apam Foforo)

If Akan speakers read their Bibles only in the English versions, neglecting the Word of God in their *own* language, it is conceivable that they would dutifully attend and participate in every annual *Odwira* Festival without every coming to the realization that the traditional purificatory rituals of *Odwira*, repeated year after year, have in fact been fulfilled and transcended by the one, perfect *Odwira*; that Jesus Christ has performed once and for all, and for *all* people everywhere, a perfect *Odwira* which has secured an eternal redemption for all who cease from their own works of purification and instead trust in him and in his perfect *Odwira*; that, (the Twi here being more expressive than the English versions), it is Jesus Christ in himself who has become our *Odwira (ode n'ankasa ne ho dwiraa yen bone no)*. The *Odwira* to end all *odwiras* has accordingly taken place.

What remains for us is to live to his praise, pray and seek for more understanding, and proclaim him to our people. There is perhaps no better way to bring this study to a close than to quote this simple, artless yet direct adoration of Jesus by Madam Afua Kuma. It expresses the refreshing sense of newness and fulfillment that comes from a real encounter with Jesus. (Her *Prayers and Praises,* both in the original Twi and in the English translation by Fr. John Kirby, are highly recommended.)

> Nkwagyesem afa yen kra nnommum
> de yen akotra asase foforo so.
> Ye ne asofo di nhyiam,
> adom ne nhyira nko
> na yen nsa aka.
>
> Yeaba wiase abebre yen ho,
> Yesu mu na yeako home.
>
> Salvation has taken our souls captive
> and carried us off to a new land.
> Along the way we met with *asofo*:
> grace and blessing alone have we received.
>
> We have come to this earth
> only to work and wear ourselves out.
> But in Jesus we find our rest.[30]

---

30. Afua Kuma, *Jesus of the Deep Forest: Prayers and Praises of Akua Kuma* (Accra: Asempa Publishers, 1981) (Twi and English), 25.

Asia

Introduction

Even more than the other two areas covered in this anthology, Asia's vast cultural and historical diversity defy generalization. It is true that Asia is marked by the presence of ancient and proud religious traditions that are still very much alive—Hinduism in India and Buddhism in Southeast Asia, Korea, and Japan. But at the same time there are pockets, such as Singapore and Hong Kong, that appear as secular and modern as any western country. While it was visited by missionaries long before either Africa or Latin America (India was said to be visited by the apostle Thomas, and missionaries apparently had great success in China during the Middle Ages), it has the smallest Christian population of any place in the world. Christians number barely two to three percent in most places; only in Indonesia, Korea, and the Philippines are the percentage of Christians significant.

Since Christianity represents such a small percentage of the population, the voices of those doing theological reflection have not been heard until relatively recently.[1] Even then evangelical voices have not been heard. If most of the reflection in Africa has come out of an evangelical context—and if, as Samuel Escobar points out, there is a protestant theological tradition in Latin America that goes back into the last century—Asia is unique in that early theological reflection came almost entirely from more liberal thinkers. There are a number of factors that account for this. Among them is the massive investment the theological education fund made in 1960s to train Asian leaders to the Ph.D. level in western universities, where a liberal theology was dominant and the fact that interdenominational evangelical seminary education has developed

---

1. See the interesting study of some of these areas in Daniel J. Adams, *Cross-Cultural Theology: Western Reflections in Asia* (Atlanta: John Knox, 1987). The most valuable collection of Asian theology is still the anthology of Douglas Elwood, ed., *Asian Christian Theology: Emerging Themes* (Philadelphia: Westminster, 1980). This collection shows the vitality that has existed in Asian theology at least since World War II.

only recently in Asia—the major institutions, e.g., China Graduate School of Theology (Hong Kong), China Evangelical Seminary (Taiwan), Asian Theological Seminary (Manila), and Union Biblical Seminary (India) are all little more than twenty-five years old.

I remember when Douglas Elwood visited our fledging seminary, the Asian Theological Seminary in Manila, in the early 1970s to ask if there was any evangelical theological writing that he could include in the collection of things he was working on. The twenty or so students at the time included David Lim, who writes an article for this volume, and others who have gone on to teach and make contributions. But that was all in the future when Elwood visited the small house in suburban Manila that we had converted to a seminary.[2]

But the situation is vastly different today. Churches exist in almost every country in Asia, and evangelical voices are to be found among their leadership. The few pieces we include here are a small, but signficant sampling of this emerging leadership. Many others could be included. Perhaps the most glaring omissions, are Japan, Korea, and Indonesia. The last of these especially is home to a growing number of Christians concerned to relate the Gospel to their context. Japan and Korea boast many highly trained theologians and biblical scholars, but for various reasons these have not produced significant indigenous theological reflection, at least from an evangelical perspective. But the essays that follow unwrap three very different themes vital to a contextual theology of Asia.

We have noted in the general introduction the need in the West for theological reflection on the earth and its processes. Ken Gnanakan, who has founded the Asian Center of Theological Studies in Bangalore, takes us some way toward filling that need. While his Indian setting makes him particularly sensitive to our mystical relationship to the earth and our interrelationship with all living things, that same setting has made him aware of the religious dangers of this interrelationship. This awareness makes him specially careful when he reads, for example, in

---

2. Interestingly there were two articles by evangelicals (Bong Ro and Saphir Athya) included in his collection in its Asian edition, *What Asian Christians Are Thinking* (Quezon City, Philippines, 1976), but one of these was deleted when the American edition appeared. The Asia Theological Association, now headed by Ken Gnanakan, is making a serious attempt to correct this situation. See Bong Rin Ro and Ruth Eshemaur, eds., *The Bible and Theology in Asian Contexts: An Evangelical Perspective* (Taichung, Taiwan: Asian Theological Association, 1984).

Jurgen Moltmann a tendency to blur the distinction between creature and creator.

Clearly, here is a discussion, only beginning in the West, to which Asians especially have much to contribute. While reading Dr. Gnanakan's paper I was struck by the various ways in which his argument and that of Cyril Okorocha intersect. While Okorocha takes as his starting point the holistic quest for a life that is viable in Africa, Gnanakan takes as his starting point the biblical teaching about creation, God's purposes, and our appropriate responses to this. In one sense Gnanakan in his Asian way is giving a biblical reading that answers the specially African questions that Okorocha raises, and he does this in a way that few western treatises could do. For both have an intuitive awareness of the interrelated nature of physical and spiritual realities and the way God's offer of life meets these expectations.

Another relation between the two essays is worth noting. Okorocha points out that, for the Igbo people, the danger is a kind of emphasis of the human pursuit of righteousness as the prerequisite for spiritual vitality. This makes it difficult for them to see the transcendent and gift character of God's righteousness. In one sense Gnanakan's setting suggests the opposite problem. For the Hindu world the transcendent character of reality discourages any moral effort on earth. In both settings the Gospel provides the antidote that is needed. For Africa redemption involves a concrete future hope which gives meaning to our present efforts; for Asia that same future solicits our best efforts to care for the earth and its goodness. In both cases the discussions enrich our sometimes sterile debate in the West over the relation between creation and redemption.

If anything, Evelyn Miranda-Feliciano, a well-known writer from the Philippines, has her roots even more deeply in her setting than anything else in this collection. I have never read anything by her which has failed to move me deeply—whether it is reflection on a traffic accident viewed from the back of a jeepney or, as in this case, a thoughtful reflection on the last days of Ferdinand Marcos. Her gut-level feelings about the abuse of power and the exhilaration of a people taking things into their own hands throws new light on the teaching of the New Testament about submitting to and honoring the emperor—a light which I suspect would be consistently lacking in our North American context.

Hermeneutically, this piece is also striking, for she is constantly moving between the poles of her Filipino situation and her reading of Scripture. Nor is she doing in this in the quiet of her study. Her reflection, and thus her reading of Scripture, is taking place in the context of what she sees as her Christian obedience—watching the polls as a volunteer to try to ensure a fair election, joining the stream of citizens protesting the elections and helping create—yes, that is the right word—one of the most amazing and bloodless revolutions in our century. As these calls to respond Christianly are the stuff of Christian obedience, so reflection on Scriptures in this context is the starting point of a contextual theology. Valuable as a record of this extraordinary event, it is even more precious as the first steps of theological reflection on an event which will forever be a benchmark for Filipino political theory.

David Lim, a Filipino who has studied at Fuller Seminary as well as in Manila and Seoul, turns his attention to the evangelical church inside and outside his own country. His article should forever put to rest the notion that listening in on Third World theologians will be a pleasant diversion for western theologians. As with any cross-cultural (or interpersonal) encounter, we should not begin a relationship if we are not prepared to learn something new and to act on that new information. As with any prophetic voice, his probings are not always easy to hear: Has the "success" of evangelicalism in the West (and one might add, elsewhere in the world) been achieved at the expense of neglecting critical parts of our spiritual heritage? Dr. Lim wants us to ask: what if we made "Christ and him crucified" actually central to our evangelistic and missiological strategies? What structures would result? Whatever we think of his criticisms of western evangelicalism, we cannot deny his contention that we are in desperate need of a new "Great Awakening."

Creation, New Creation
and Ecological Relationships

Ken Gnanakan

In a scathing attack on the "Christian doctrine of creation" Lynn White, Jr., dealing with "man's unnatural treatment of nature and its sad results," has blamed Christians for the devastation of the earth and its resources.[1] He traced the historical roots of the ecological problem to the "victory of Christianity over paganism," claiming that was the greatest psychic revolution in the history of western culture.[2]

White alleged that the climax of the biblical account of creation was the teaching that man and woman had "dominion" over everything. "God planned all this explicitly for man's benefit and rule. No item in the physical creation had any purpose save to serve man's purposes."[3] Therefore, for him "especially in its western form, Christianity is the most anthropocentric religion the world has seen," encouraging one to believe that it is "God's will that man exploit nature for his proper ends."[4]

While Bible-believing Christians, shocked by such accusations, have busied themselves pointing out what is mistaken in these attacks, the ecological crisis has taken such a global proportion that it is impossible for anyone to stand unconcerned and indifferent. The depletion of the earth's resources, the pollution of our environment, and the alarming consequences of the rapidly growing population poses a worldwide

---

1. Lynn White's lecture was delivered on December 26, 1966, in Washington, and is reproduced by Francis Schaeffer in his book *Pollution and the Death of Man: The Christian View of Ecology* (Hodder and Stoughton, London, 1970). Schaeffer deals with Lynn White's criticisms. Page references to White's article are from Schaeffer (Appendix, 70–85), 78.

2. Ibid., 78.

3. Ibid., 78f.

4. Ibid., 79.

threat that is far too real to be dismissed as merely the agenda for "environmentalists."

Undoubtedly, we will need to refute White's accusations, as well as the flood of others since his paper in 1967, but what we hear is not invitation to a debate, but a call for concerned action. The ecological crisis demands our attention as well as involvement, and such reminders have brought us to realize the enormous Christian responsibility. As a theologian, I see the urgent need for us to search for a biblical theology of creation that will relevantly address this situation, as well as clearly remind us of our responsibility.

Many attempts have been made to develop relevant theologies of creation. We need to heed these reminders, but we must also address some of the pressing present issues. We need to reiterate, or even correct, what has been said and dig deeper into the Bible in order to explore all that God has already revealed for his people and for his world. However, in doing so it is imperative that we move forward with some constructive attitudes, not merely defending ourselves, nor making affirmations that will have no relevance to the real issues that we face.

Developing Our Theology

We have recently been encouraged to develop theologies that will boldly, yet biblically address our present context. In developing a theology within any context, our first task is to affirm some axes around which we can coordinate our considerations. Let me briefly outline three axes that will assist me in this exercise of theologizing. These are not spelled out in any order of priority, as that will depend on each situation.

The Bible, the revealed Word of God, will be the first such axis. Biblical implications will be an essential foundation of such a theology, or else it will face the danger of dissolving into a humanistic effort with no firmly based convictions. The authority of the Word of God that declares the redemptive purposes of our Creator God will need to be affirmed afresh, even rediscovered, as we interact with our context.

Second, and not necessarily in this order, we will need to address this context. I am not particular how we start our theology. It may be either from the text to the context or vice versa. In fact, in our present case we are coming to the Bible from the context. But, wherever we start, there is an interaction between the two, an interaction aimed at developing a theology that will address crucial environmental issues crying for our attention today. Theology cannot exempt itself from making known the Word of God within the actuality of every outworking within God's world today.

Third, and just as important as the other two, we will look at some other theologies and theologians. One cannot write theology alone. It is a community effort—an interaction with the efforts of God's people all over the world, the community in its widest sense, as well as the interaction within each local situation. The efforts of God's people in the past must also be called upon. For a theology such as the one on hand, there is hardly any justification for me to confine myself to Indian or Asian theologians. For one thing, not many have written on the subject. Clearly these reflections will have to have local reference. Yet at the same time, a theology of creation in relation to ecological issues will need to be such a worldwide effort that one cannot restrict oneself to any local situation.

The recent Rio Summit[5] was a major step in seeing environmental concerns in truly global proportions with a view to global solutions. The delegates agreed that the earth had been inhabited by humanity as a whole, and therefore its problems had to be faced by one and all. It was not merely local, regional, or national, but a global concern. A biblical theology ought to be no less and therefore needs to have a worldwide interaction. And in so doing, the biblical God, revealed through the Lord Jesus Christ, will need to be seen to have universal relevance, as creator of no less than the whole heaven and earth.

God and Creation

We have been reminded that at the root of the environmental issue is the confused relationship between humankind and the rest of creation. Lynn White's accusation of Christianity being the most "anthropocentric" religion presupposes that what men and women acquired in God's making creation available to them was the attitude of "dominion" that led to "exploitation." It is imperative to take a fresh look at the Bible to review what God has really intended for his people.

In order to discover this relationship within its right context, it will be useful for us to get back to an even more fundamental relationship: the relationship of God to his creation. Here is an underlying factor for any theology that will address the ecological issue, and hence give some clear biblical direction. On the one hand, we will need to avoid any

_____

5. The United Nations Conference on Environment and Development (UNCED) called the Earth Summit in Rio de Janeiro, Brazil, in June 1992.

extreme dualism that will separate God from his creation with no vital link of any kind. Yet, on the other hand, we will need to avoid a monism or pantheism that will confuse the creator with his creation.

An assertion of God's Lordship over his creation will imply God's continuing relation to the world. However, the Bible not only speaks of the glorious creation of God, but also graphically depicts the sad rebellion of humankind resulting in a "fallenness" of creation. Yet the fact remains that God does not abandon his creation. He continues to be concerned and reveals his redemptive purposes, desiring to bring about a "new creation" as the prophets of the Old Testament so frequently declare.

The fact of God's Lordship, however, implies a distinction between God and his handiwork. The initiation that comes from God, who declares his will, "Let there be . . . ," is of primary significance for our theology today. Creation is no accident, but the result of God's deliberate and purposeful word demonstrated in the completion of the heavens and the earth "in all their vast array" (Gen. 2:1).

Gerhard von Rad points out that the idea of creation by the "word" preserves "first of all the most radical essential distinction between creator and creature."[6] What he tries to preserve is the distinction between creation accounts that make creation an emanation from God or even include God in the realm of nature, and the biblical implication of creation being "a product of his personal will."[7]

Enthusiastic environmentalists can confuse this distinction and set forth a pantheistic teaching that sees God and creation to be one. If creation is God, then, they would plead, we will need to respect and worship it, and on such grounds develop better attitudes toward nature. While the intentions are good, there is no justification for such a deification of creation, nor even the implied degradation of humanity subordinated to a divine creation.

Interestingly, the Sanskrit word *sristi* which is commonly used as the equivalent of "creation" literally means "emanation." Creation is seen as an emanation of God. This monistic understanding of God has found acceptance among environmentalists who advocate respect, even reverence, for creation. The popular Hindu monistic teaching maintains the idea of a Supreme Person (*Purusa*) who pervades the whole universe to the extent that all created objects are part of that one person. The

---

6. Gerhard von Rad, *Genesis* (London: SCM Press, 1961), 50.
7. Ibid.

Bible allows no room for such a confusion of the Creator and the created.

However, in underlining a distinction, we must not imply that God is not involved with his creation. Here von Rad points out that "the idea of creation by the word expresses the knowledge that the whole belongs to God. It is his creation, he is Lord."[8] This kind of corrective is needed to remedy totally immanentist ideas of God and creation that sublimate God into some impersonal power behind creation. If he is Lord, God stands apart from creation and continues to give it the direction towards the new creation he has personally purposed.

The ongoing relationship of God to creation is demonstrated powerfully through his ongoing involvement with his creation as its creator and redeemer. Very clearly the Bible depicts creation, both in the Old and New Testament in terms of God's redemptive activity within history, moving towards a newness he has purposed. On the basis of his covenant with his people he continues a relationship toward fulfilling his revealed purposes.

Almost every religion will have references to some kind of a relationship between their god and creation. Israel's God is not to be made out to be distinctive because of his ongoing relationship with creation. "What is distinctive of Israel's faith is the belief that God revealed his character in his activity, and that there was a moral purpose governing it."[9] God's creative activity has a purpose behind it, a redemptive mission which is unfolded through his covenant.

The Old Testament displays a very clear link between the doctrine of creation and the covenant. We will need to develop this link so that our theology will possess a firm foundation on the one hand, and yet is able to explore the fullest implications of creation for all that is outside the covenant on the other hand. This will also help free us from limits we have imposed on creation when we see it as primarily a religious affirmation of faith, purely for the believer and without any historical significance.

The covenant link is further clarified in the New Testament in its ultimate connection with Jesus Christ. This is consistent with the Old Testament. Jesus Christ clearly shows himself to be the fulfillment of all the promises of God in history and the one who ushers in the new covenant in continuity with the old. Even creation now takes on a newness as

---

8. Ibid.

9. H. G. Rowley, *The Faith of Israel* (London: SCM Press, 1956), 59.

Jesus Christ fulfills his promised relationship within the reality of the new creation.

Relationship: The Fundamental Issue

Our brief consideration of God's relationship to his creation has brought to light some crucial issues. First, criticisms of Christianity rest on a misunderstanding reflecting a faulty understanding of the fundamental relationship between God and his creation. This confusion entails a wrong understanding of the relationship of human beings to the created order. This misrepresented relationship gives rise to criticisms from ecologists of various persuasions. It is the heartless exploitation of creation by humankind. We are told, as if humans alone mattered, that this exploitation lies at the heart of the crisis. But if we truly recognize our relationship to the Creator, then all ensuing relationships will fall within their right perspective.

Second, we will note that it is impossible to rectify our attitude to the earth and its resources without first acknowledging the reality of a God-intended relationship between humans and creation. When we speak of a relationship we speak in terms of mutual privileges and responsibilities. Is ours only a one-sided relationship with all the privileges weighted on the side of human beings? Or, does creation possess similar privileges?

If our relationships are restored to the kind that God originally purposed for his creation—just, righteous, and loving—the whole created order will begin to reflect order, meaning, and significance. This emphasis on relationships in the doctrine of reconciliation must be given far more importance in communicating the salvific work of the Lord Jesus Christ. The Gospel brings together parties that have had their relationship marred and strained by sin and rebellion.

Exploitation within relationships is an evil that has been brought to our attention frequently in recent times. This has prevailed particularly in relationships where parties are "unequally yoked," as in relationships between the rich and the poor. The rich have often exploited the powerlessness of the other party, while over the years we have begun to see the poor exploit the rich because of their poverty. If this is the case with relationships within the human community, it is hardly surprising that we see exploitative tendencies in human relationships to the created order. Human beings desire to be Lords over creation.

A very challenging study on the subject has come from Jurgen Moltmann, who points out that the basic problem starts from our considering God to be the "absolute subject." Therefore when human beings had to take over control, they too endeavored "to become the Lord and owner of the earth." He notes this attitude resulted in "hierarchical doctrines of sovereignty."

> Our standpoint is a different one. We have begun to understand God, in the awareness of his Spirit, for Christ's sake, as the triune God, the God who in himself constitutes the unique and perfect fellowship of the Father and the Son and the Holy Spirit. If we cease to understand God monotheistically as the one, absolute subject, but instead see him in a trinitarian sense as the unity of the Father, the Son and the Spirit, we can then no longer, either, conceive his relationship to the world he has created as the one-sided relationship of dominion."[10]

This kind of a one-sided relationship of domination is all too familiar to us not only in the environmental scene but in the history of missions. Whether it be the conquering spirit of the colonial powers or the manipulative tendencies of the caste system, lopsided relationships have resulted in a powerful minority manipulating the weaker majority. It is to be noted that many such evils have been justified on grounds of God's mandate, just as even the Indian caste system is justified as a religious necessity.

But perhaps Moltmann is incorrect in thinking of human domination purely on the basis that because God is seen as absolute Lord, men and women want to become lords. In most cases, an exalted image of a transcendent God would lead a devotee to demonstrate fear and dependence rather than display domination. In this sense, if one accepts the proper perspective of God as absolute Lord over humanity and creation, we will all the more develop a proper sense of accountability to God in terms of our utilization of creation and its resources, rather than be led to an exploitation to fulfill our own selfish needs. This must lead us to developing a better understanding of the Lordship of our Creator God, rather than abandoning it.

James Houston reminds us that "to know the Creator is to be dependent upon him for everything, and our self-sufficient technological society, and our crass materialism, insulate us from needing, and therefore from knowing, God."[11] Calling us to "living wisely before the Creator," Houston points to the need of a fear and reverence within which "con-

---

10. Jurgen Moltmann, *God in Creation: An Ecological Doctrine of Creation* (SCM Press, 1985), 1f.

11. James Houston, *I Believe in the Creation* (London: Hodder and Stoughton), 191.

cern, favour, grace, intimacy, gratitude and praise" will all be demonstrated.[12] It remains true that a wrong understanding of the nature of God and his relationship to humanity will lead to wrong attitudes to the world and all that there is in it.

Here Moltmann makes an interesting point. If a doctrine of creation is to be ecological, then it must get away from analytical thinking, with its distinctions between "subject" and "object." Instead it must "strive to learn a new, communicative and integrative way of thought."[13] He criticizes the aim of the "exact" sciences to reduce an object to its smallest possible components which are no longer divisible. This eventually leads to the domination of these objects. There was an emphasis on the parts rather than the whole. On the contrary, "objects can be known and understood very much better if they are seen in their relationships and coordinations with their particular environments and surroundings."[14]

This is what ecology is all about. At the heart of ecological studies in their earlier biological context was very much the study of plants and animals within their particular interlocking systems. In this sense, there is a God-intended network of relationships, within which meaning and purpose are discovered. This will ensure that things are integrated, not isolated, perceived in their totality, not split up. "To be alive means existing in relationship with other people and things. Life is communication in communion."[15]

Moltmann's contention is that as long as the subject-object relationship exists between humanity and the rest of creation there is bound to be an exploitative result. However, his corrective sounds pantheistic, more akin to Hindu monism than to biblical revelation, suggesting that for an ecological doctrine of creation there should no longer be the distinction between God and the world. The centre of such thinking is "the recognition of the presence of God in the world and the presence of the world in God."[16] He claims that this does not depart from the biblical traditions, but rather returns to them "God and creator of heaven and earth is present in each of his creatures and in the fellowship of creation which they share."[17] In this way he wishes to explore "the pluralism" of the Trinitarian concept of Godhead.

---

12. Ibid., 170.
13. Moltmann, op. cit. 2.
14. Ibid., 3.
15. Ibid.
16. Ibid., 13.
17. Ibid., 14.

To be fair, Moltmann wants to maintain both the transcendence and the immanence of God, but he is particularly burdened to demonstrate the much needed immanence of God within creation. "The God who is transcendent in relation to the world, and the God who is immanent in that world are one and the same God."[18] He draws our attention to the Christian doctrine of the Trinity.

> In the free, overflowing rapture of his love the eternal God goes out of himself and makes a creation, a reality, which is there as he is there, and is yet different from himself. Through the Son, God creates, reconciles, and redeems his creation. In the power of the Spirit, God is himself present in his creation—present in his reconciliation and his redemption of that creation.[19]

Here Moltmann makes a valid point: the more we see God distanced from his creation, the more easily we can develop self-centered attitudes towards the world that result in exploitation and ultimate disaster. The Hindu tradition of monism provides strong arguments that the universe and all its constituent elements- -the three worlds of the physical, psychological, and the spiritual —are all one integrated, interrelated whole. And it is this kind of interrelatedness that we must underline as long as the distinction between God and the world is maintained.

If the fundamental issue behind the ecological crisis has to do with relationships, then the fundamental relationship between God and his creation will need first to be put right. We will need to explore this relationship both in order to show the intimate relationship as well as the distinction. In order to maintain the distinctness of God apart from his creation, Hindu monism's most well-known exponent, Sankara, held that although there was one reality, the world was not real creation, but *maya*—an illusion or appearance only.

Believing that this implication of unreality would hinder Hinduism from truly being concerned for ethics and historical actualities, S. Radhakrishnan attempted to reinterpret the concept of *maya* in more concrete terms. "While this doctrine suggests that the world may not be worthy of being lived in, it holds that life in it is worth living only if we have faith in a transcendent goal. Mere morality without spiritual conviction or *jnana* is incapable of giving satisfaction."[20] The emphasis is

---

18. Ibid., 15.

19. Ibid.

20. S. Radhakrishnan, *Eastern Religious and Western Thought* (Oxford University Press, 1992), 93.

shown to be on the reality of God rather than on the unreality of his creation.

Although we dismiss the concept of an illusion, we must appreciate the heavy emphasis put on an understanding of God to the extent that all else finds its meaning and significance only through him. It is this kind of a relationship in its biblical sense that we will need to underline, yet without diminishing the reality of creation. Let us spell out some implications of our relationship to God's creation.

First we note that the creation of human beings is set very much within the context of the totality of God's creative process. God created us, just as he has created all the rest of his creation. Therefore, there is a contingency that is part of every created element. Langdon Gilkey writes—"Finite things are contingent: they 'have' existence as a gift from beyond. They 'are not' existence . . ."[21] Human beings along with every other created element are dependent upon God for their existence. We stand equal at that level.

However, this must not imply that there is no difference between humans and all else in creation. The creation accounts certainly give to man and woman a privilege and responsibility over and above all else that God has made. Created in the image of God, they are to exercise a responsibility implied within this distinction. It is primarily in this sense that we are the crown of God's creation, not in any sense of honored position to be claimed. Clearly, this has to do with roles and responsibilities. And in fulfilling these, human beings discover the intricacy of God-planned relationships, and the interdependence of God, humans, and all creation that is essential for discovering meaning and purpose.

Jesus Christ and Creation

Although there is not as much reference to creation in the New Testament as there is in the Old, we are not to conclude that it is an unimportant doctrine for the Christian. Some may even point to the fact that because of sin the doctrine of creation is abandoned in favor of the new creation that is anticipated. On the other hand, scanty reference to the doctrine of creation should be taken only to imply that the early Church was a Jewish congregation, and these fundamental facts were accepted without question. Timothy declares, "Everything God created is good" (1 Tim. 4:4).

---

21. Langdon Gilkey, *Maker of Heaven and Earth: The Christian Doctrine of Creation in the Light of Modern Knowledge* (Anchor Books, 1965), 87.

Also, the New Testament writers were far more concerned with the spelling out of the ministry of redemption and reconciliation that was anticipated by the Old Testament believers. Their Creator-God was now made available in Jesus Christ. This redemption is seen in terms of its all-inclusive reconciling ministry of bringing everything under God's control and thereby to the originally intended purposes. "For God was pleased to have all his fullness dwell in him [Jesus Christ], and through him to reconcile to himself all things, whether things on earth or things in heaven, by making peace through his blood, shed on the cross" (Col. 1:19f.).

Standing within the New Covenant instituted by Jesus Christ, we will inevitably have to look at our theology in terms of Jesus Christ and his relationship to creation. A biblical theology of ecology will have to be Christological. If Jesus Christ is the Lord of history, and the one through whom all things are to be made new and are to be actualized in the new heaven and the new earth, he must undoubtedly have a crucial part to play in creation even now. It is by Jesus Christ that all things "hold together" (Col. 1:17), and it is through him that "all things in heaven and on earth" will be united (Eph. 1:9, 10). He is the one who upholds the universe (Heb. 1:3 KJV).

Moreover, it is not just for the present that the lordship of Jesus Christ over creation is to be seen. His role has to be recognized in the initial creative process itself. John gives to Jesus the very creative power itself. "Through him all things were made" (John 1:3). This is the same idea as in Colossians 1:16, 1 Corinthians 8:6, and Hebrews 1:2. Jesus was always with God, and everything that God did, he did through Jesus Christ.

Such a Christological foundation to creation is essential, or else our understanding of creation could be abandoned to abstract philosophizing or accidental evolutionary acts in the name of God. It is through Jesus that the Creator and Redeemer is revealed. Our theology must inevitably be founded firmly upon a Christology that considers Jesus Christ to be the one through whom we know our Creator-God, the Lord of Heaven and Earth.

Moreover, creation is also seen in the New Testament from the future perspective under Christ's ultimate lordship. The picture of the creator enthroned in majesty and splendor, as painted by John in his depiction of the new creation, clearly captures the total sovereignty of God over all creation and over all history. He is not merely Lord at that moment but ". . . the Lord God Almighty who was, and is, and is to come" (Rev. 4:8).

We note that for the New Testament, underlying the theme of creation is the strong Christological emphasis. The doctrine that underlines and validates the truth is that all of history is under the sovereign purpose of God as revealed in Jesus Christ. He is the "Alpha and the Omega," "the First and the Last," "the Beginning and the End" (Rev. 1:17; 22:13; cf. 3:14). "The whole sweep of history, from creation to the new heaven and the new earth, has its fulcrum in him."[22]

Jesus and the "World"

Apart from dealing with Jesus' role in creation, we will do well to spell out some aspects of his attitude to the "world"—the realm of God's creation. We have asserted that the solution to the ecological crisis is to restore a right relationship between humanity and the created order, one that will be based on the fundamental relationship between God and human beings on the one hand, and God and creation on the other. What kind of an attitude did the earthly Jesus display?

This could be an important aspect for us. Some Christians display negative attitudes to the world, purely on grounds that Jesus' wanted us to withdraw. Derogatory references are made to "worldliness," and consequently the ecological issue itself seems outside of the scope of biblical spirituality. Some reminders are necessary to restore a more biblical concern.

We pick up some aspects of Jesus' relationship to the "world" particularly with reference to John's gospel. The term "world" is used in the sense of the orderliness of the universe as in John 1:10, "The world was made through him." The basic meaning of the word *cosmos* refers to an ornament, something beautifully built and artistically arranged, from which we get the English word "cosmetic." Jesus refers to this meaning of the world when he prays (in 17:5): "Glorify me in your presence with the glory I had with you before the world began." There is a glory to the creative significance of Jesus for the entire universe in all its orderliness and not merely for the earth.

Also, the "world" in Johannine usage refers to the human inhabitants in the sense of mankind and the human race. It is this "world" that John refers to as being the object of God's love (3:16). God loved man-

---

22. *Interpreter's Dictionary of the Bible*, ed. George Arthur Buttrick (Abingdon Press 1962) Vol. I, 731.

kind, and the environment within which he had placed them, so much that he sent his Son to live amongst them in that same environment. Yet, in all our attempts to emphasize the importance of creation we must not forget that there is clearly an emphasis on the centrality of men and women in God's plans and purposes.

It is not in keeping with God's redemptive purposes if we totally concentrate on ecological issues, without reference to people in God's world. God's redemption is directed primarily at humanity, and his salvific blessings are first for "whoever believes on him." Moreover, it is through the salvation of men and women that everything else will receive God's redemptive benefits. Neither the one-sided emphasis on salvation purely for humanity nor the emphasis on a kind of concern dealing abstractly with creation can be biblically justified. The biblical emphasis is on the concreteness of God's concern for a people within a particular world all of which needs to be redeemed.

Having emphasized the positive sense, we must not neglect the clear reference to the negativeness of the world as the realm of evil in enmity with God. In Johannine writings this receives emphatic treatment (7:7; 8:23; 12:31; 14:30; 15:18; 17:9, 14; 1 John 2:15). This is the new meaning that the term acquires in the New Testament usage which brings out the sharp contrast between the beauty of God's creation and the ugliness of human sin. Sinful humans and consequently a decaying creation around us confront the perfection of Christ.

There is also another important fact we will need to underline and that is the reality of the influence of Satan on creation. John makes it very clear that the "whole world is under the control of the evil one" (1 John 5:19). While this could be primarily spoken of in terms of Satan's influence on people, the biblical fact of the curse on creation will need to be reckoned with in all our discussions about God's relationship to the world he has created.

In fact, it is only through a proper understanding of sin and the curse that we will be able to explain some of the ecological problems that confront us. For one thing, we are able to understand the fact of greed and selfishness of humans only in terms of our fallenness. Moreover, we are confronted by the pests and decay, factors right within creation that bring about devastation of the earth and its resources. Did God create these? If he did, and creation is supposed to be "good" why does this form of evil exist? We will have to explain these only from the perspective of sin, the curse and fallenness.

The Earth and Our Responsibility

However, despite fallenness, God's continued dealings with human-kind are clearly depicted in the Old Testament. He is still Lord of creation. If the earth and all that is in it belongs to God, then there ought to be some way in which we who are God's people must be responsible for this earth. What is our attitude?

We consider Leviticus 25:1–7 for some insight into our relationship to the earth. The selfish human tendency is to think that the earth and all its resources are in our possession to use as we wish to. It is this kind of a misuse that is behind ecological disaster. God's command points towards a more responsible utilization. Natural resources have a claim to dignity in their existence and we are accountable to God for the use to which we put them.

The endless plundering of the earth to reap maximum benefits is wrong. Even the earth has been shown to need its rest. We have had no problems accepting that the Sabbath was a divine institution for human beings. But, interestingly, the year of Jubilee extends the privilege of the sabbath rest of even to the land. That is why even "The land is to have a year of rest" (Lev. 25:5). The whole network of relationships depicted, perhaps even idealized, in the Jubilee year are the restored relationships that foreshadow ultimate New Creation relationships. Men and women must take care to recognize that even the created order, which they could so easily exploit for their own ends, has some claims of its own. God commands us to take note. While God wants the best for humankind and therefore has placed it in charge of his creation, he also desires that his nonhuman creation be treated with care.

God has created the heavens and earth in a harmonious networking of interlinked elements. Economic interests must be carried out within ecological concerns. And that is why Moses reminds the people, "Do not take advantage of each other, but fear your God, I am the LORD your God" (25:17). And undoubtedly taking "advantage" is even to be questioned in relation to the humanity's dealing with the earth. Righteous relationships are demanded of the redeemed community, and these relationships are to be demonstrated not only within the community but in relationship to all that is God's.

Israel's history sounds a warning to us today. "The story begins in a land flowing with milk and honey: it ends in barrenness."[23] Here is the

---

23. Ron Elsdon, *Green House Theology: Biblical Perspectives on Creation* (Monarch: Tunbridge Wells, 1992), 113.

consequence of disobedience. "The people refused to obey God, and the price to be paid involved not only political ruin but also a despoiled environment."[24] Israel knew God's command and yet rebelled. If they had truly been the witness that God had wanted them to be, perhaps the world would have heeded God's word more responsively.

Refusing to obey God, humankind have set up their own gods, their idols. Science and technology, the idols of today that have taken control of everything said and done, must be restored to their right place. They need to be under our control, and not control us. "The danger sets in when science and technology replace the ultimate ground of our hope, and their white-coated practitioners become the priests of the present age. In the specific context of environmental issues, idolatry is then our expectation that science and technology alone can solve our problems"[25] as Ron Elsdon reminds us.

Idolatry is disobedience. The ecological devastation is a consequence of human disobedience, the unwillingness of human beings to give heed to the Creator-God and to his commands. God reminded his people throughout their history that it was through his grace that they were chosen. If that is so, then "his grace has the last word, and the fundamental goodness of creation is gloriously reaffirmed."[26] And because of his grace, God does not abandon his creation even though his people refuse to care for it. He will renew it.

Restoration of Creation

Whatever relationships we strive to build on earth are only shadows of the perfect relationships that are to come in future. There is a clear reminder of the ultimate purposes of God through the powerful theme of restoration of all creation to its original perfection. Beginning with creation and ending with the new creation, the Bible bares the compassionate heart of a God who continues to reveal his concern for creation despite the rebellion of humankind.

Whether it is the prophetic voices or the apocalyptic visions, the Old Testament clearly directs our attention towards the fulfillment of God's purposes in and through the created order. Evil will not prevail any longer and the righteousness of God shall reign over all heaven and

---

24. Ibid.
25. Ibid., 125.
26. Ibid.

earth. Sin has broken God-intended relationships, but God's righteousness will restore them to ultimate harmony.

An outline of God's plans is explicitly made available in the unfolding of his covenant with his people in the Old Testament. Of particular interest to the student of an ecologically oriented theology of creation is God's covenant with Noah. In fact, explicit reference to the concept of the covenant first appears only in God's dealings with Noah. In Genesis 6:18, when God says "I will establish my covenant with you . . . ," this becomes the first of the biblical covenants where God's promise for his people is explicitly unfolded.

An examination of this covenant reveals a clear reference to the everlasting covenant between God and all flesh upon the earth. If we look closely at Genesis 9:11, 12 as well as v. 16, we note the universal implications of this covenant, which in fact is a covenant between God and "the earth" (v. 13). And then later, after the rainbow which is to be "the sign of the covenant between [God] and the earth" (v. 13), God says—"I will remember my covenant between me and you and all living creatures of every kind" (v. 15). It is a "covenant between God and all living creatures of every kind on the earth" (v. 16).

The emphatic reference here to all creation within God's redemptive and reconciliatory purposes, is not merely a passing reference. If it is a divine covenant, it has eternal significance, and every part of God's creation has a part within this covenantal significance. We have often restricted ourselves to personalized and individualized implications of God's redemptive purposes, seeing them only in terms of their effects on men and women. This is not wrong, provided it is placed in the context of God's covenantal concern for all of his creation.

However, it is in God's calling Abraham that we begin to see a dramatic unfolding of the long term purposes of God for his world. The blessings of the covenant are to be extended to all of God's creation. God clearly tells Abraham ". . . all peoples on earth will be blessed through you" (Gen. 12:3). Once God has established his relationship on the right basis with Abraham, the potential extends to similar relationships among all peoples of the earth. God's reconciliatory program has been set in motion and the impact is going to be universal.

Lest we once again confine ourselves only to human salvation, one of the promises specifically given to Abraham relates to a land that God has ordained for his people. That which was intended in Eden will in a limited way now be made available on earth before its ultimate availability in the New Creation. Canaan was not the end in itself. It was only a very earthly picture of the ultimate promised land—the new heaven and the new earth.

Bede Griffiths reminds us of the three calls issued to Abraham. The first was the call to follow God. The second was that he would become a great nation and be a blessing to all the earth. The third was that he was promised a place to dwell. Griffiths comments

> These three callings represent the call of humanity to return to its origin and to rediscover its ultimate destiny. Humanity is to be reconciled with God by going out from its present state of civilization and venturing into the unknown. To bring this about it has to be formed into a new people will be reconciled with the earth, with the world of nature by being given a land in which to dwell.[27]

Clearly then, God is concerned for the ultimate restoration of right relationships in the broadest sense. Whether it be the several emerging forces that are threatening to disintegrate humanity from within itself or the ecological disaster that threatens the survival of the whole created order, remedial measures cannot be brought about by power or wealth, or by the many manifestations of these cravings of humanity. The very roots of broken relationship must be remedied. "Human liberation is always seen as reconciliation with God and with nature in a renewed humanity."[28]

Resurrection and the Future

We obtain the clearest glimpse of renewed humanity in the resurrection of the Lord Jesus Christ. Creation, rather than being sublimated by other New Testament doctrines, is powerfully juxtaposed beside the doctrine of resurrection. The new life of the new creation community has its rationale in the resurrection. As Moltmann reminds us, "the New Testament testimony about creation is to be found in the resurrection kerygma and in the experience of the Holy spirit, who is the energy of the new creation."[29]

---

27. Bede Griffiths, *A New Vision of Reality: Western Science, Eastern Mysticism and Christian Faith* (Harper Collins, India), 84.

28. Ibid., 85.

29. Moltmann, op. cit., 65. We must not minimize the role of the Holy Spirit in all of God's plans for creation and new creation. The Spirit is depicted both in his activity at creation as well as in the inauguration of the new creation community, the church. However, I choose to emphasize the Christological aspect solely to emphasize the reconciliatory work that is so vital in bringing about right relationships urgently called for. But it is the Holy Spirit who actualizes all the influence of Jesus Christ both for the new creation community and the creation community, as well as for the whole created order.

Paul is explicit about the implications of the resurrection for the ultimate blessings for humanity in 1 Corinthians 15. Jesus Christ is the "first fruits" of the new creation, of which we are all to be part in the *eschaton*. Our bodies are to be raised "imperishable," "in glory," and in "power" (1 Cor. 15:42ff.). It is the resurrection that will provide for us the perspective of the new creation in the eschatological sense.

Theologians have underlined the priority of the resurrection within the new creation. Wolfhart Pannenberg, consistent with his theology written from the end-perspective, proposes that the creation of all things as mediated through Jesus Christ should not be thought of in terms of a temporal beginning of the world, but rather in terms of the *eschaton* (or end event).

> It is rather to be understood in terms of the whole of the world process that receives its unity and meaning in the light of its end that has appeared in advance in the history of Jesus, so that the essence of every individual occurrence, whose meaning is relative to the whole to which it belongs, is first decided in the light of this end. To be sure, the cosmos with which we are familiar can be supposed to have had a temporal beginning, but to speak of the creation of the world does not refer just to this beginning but to the world process as a whole. This is conceivable, because the creation must be understood as an act of God's eternity, even though what is created by this eternal act has a temporal beginning and a temporal becoming. However, God's eternal act of creation will be entirely unfolded in time first in the *eschaton*. Only at the *eschaton* will what is created out of God's eternity be consummated in the accomplishment of its own temporal becoming.[30]

Pannenberg is right to remind us that the temporal acts of creation can only be properly understood from the perspective of their eschatological fulfillment and not from the perspective of the beginning. But in reality this becomes more a matter of an abstract theology rather than a factual foundation on which theological considerations can be founded. There is no doubt that the eschatological dimension gives meaning and significance to creation. But to insist that even Jesus Christ's role in creation is only "in retrospect" could make Jesus Christ an afterthought, or merely matter of a perspective rather than a reality. History must have a continuity, and Jesus Christ's role in creation history must not be stripped of this continuity.

---

30. Wolfhart Pannenberg, *Jesus, God and Man* (London: SCM Press, 1968), 391.

There is no doubt that with the resurrection, a future has been ushered in, a future that has an overwhelming influence on creation even in the present. That is why creation is seen to "groan" in anticipation (Rom. 8:22). It is only in this sense that we look back on the entire creation process and see God's hand all along, despite the obvious decay and degradation of God's handiwork. The ecological crisis is only temporal and is to be expected if the biblical definition of sin is to be accepted as a fact. Placed in the exploitative and manipulative hands of sinful humankind it is not surprising that such should be the fate of creation. Marred relationships will foster greed, selfishness, and callous nonconcern and will bring about devastating consequences.

However, in the Cross and Resurrection God's eternal work has been revealed in the temporal realm. The vision of the new creation that had been revealed to the prophets Isaiah and Ezekiel has been demonstrated before us in its firstfruits in Jesus Christ. These give the new creation community the encouragement to move forward in hope and confidence. Temporality is inescapable but God's future is certain.

Creation and the New Creation

The more we consider the implications of the revelation of God within history, the more we come to realize that God's purposes are demonstrated to his creation in its entirety. Any theology that abandons God's desires for the present creation will diminish the significance of God's activity in the present, which points to the fulfillment of his ultimate purposes.

Fallenness and disobedience must not be glossed over. But in affirming this, the fundamental relationship between the old fallen creation and the new creation must not be minimized. All that we see within the goodness of creation and its longings for perfection are an anticipation of all it will experience in the *eschaton*. This means that it is not possible to speak of creation except in the eschatological sense of where it is headed.

Is there a connection between the present fallen creation and the future new creation? Some biblical insights can be noted. The OT prophets imply a newness in the new creation which does not totally obliterate the old (Isa. 66:22). The fact of God's present lordship in history is emphasized along with a constant reminder of his power and wisdom in relation to this creation, and it is upon this that the assurance of the future is built. Isaiah's eschatological depictions of end times are painted in terms of pictures of the first things. "Creation anticipates the consummation, and the consummation is the fulfillment of the beginning."[31]

The fact that emerges is God's creative involvement in the world. If present creation is such a glorious act of his handiwork, planned and purposed, the question arises as to whether God will abandon it altogether. Despite creation at present not being what it was intended to be, Isaiah does not allow for God's withdrawal. The new creation returns to God's original perfect and purposeful designs.

Redemption primarily is about reconciliation, the restoring of new creation relationships. The fundamental relationship between God and humankind is set right, and from there all other relationships are seen to be restored to a justice and righteousness that will anticipate the perfect relationships of the new Creation.

Justice has become a very common theme in spelling out the implications of God's mission for the world. The call for justice is issued whether it be social action or even ecological consciousness. ". . . justice is actualized in just relationships. Unequal partnerships and patterns of dominations are unjust. It is obvious that today human relationship with nature is not that of equal partners, but of domination and exploitation. Unjust treatment of the planet by humans is one of the principal causes of the ecological crisis."[32] It is on these grounds that "eco-justice" is demanded.

"Justice" is an appropriate word. It is a strong Pauline image and has been much in use in recent times. "Justice, Peace, and the Integrity of Creation" is the title of the program of the World Council of Churches which is aimed at arousing an ecological consciousness and related concerns to human life itself, and aptly sums up some of the crucial issues. However, the word "justice" is strongly legalistic and does not have the best of connotations within the context of relationships.

Interestingly, the word "ecology" carries with it the prefix *eco* which is derived from the Greek *oikos* or the home. To "legalize" such a familial relationship can deprive the whole family of God of relationships built on love, grace, compassion, and concern. One is not to discard the whole image of "justification" which so clearly describes the work of Christ that brings about reconciliation. But to stop at "justice" and not move on to the wonder of reconciliation is not to see the entire

---

31. *The Interpreter's Dictionary of the Bible*, op. cit., 731.
32. K. C. Abraham, *Eco-Justice: A New Agenda for Church's Mission* (Bombay: Build Publications), 7.

work of God for his family. We are "God's people and members of God's household" (Eph. 2:19).

The New Testament abounds with illustrations of this familial relationship that comes from God's ultimate reconciliatory purposes. John's apocalyptic vision in the book of Revelation beautifully illustrates this fulfillment of God's familial relationships—God and his people will enjoy a perfect relationship. There is definitely a continuity implied. In other words, the kind of God-intended relationships include those between people and their God, among people, as well as between people and the rest of creation. Whatever be the new creation, it is definitely going to be marked by a community characterized by new relationships. "The dwelling place of God is with men" (Rev. 21:3).

Not only does the environmental issue need urgent attention today, but there is also the growing threat from religious fundamentalism. This, too, is a matter of relationships. If we recognize that beyond our differences there is the wider community of human beings where trans-cultural and trans-religious relationships are possible, we will face our common future in a much more mature manner. The widening chasm that threatens humanity with fears of ultimate fragmentation will disintegrate society into narrow fundamental units which will eventually become a threat to our corporate human existence. The threat of fundamentalism does not stop with the forming of one homogeneous unit. It naturally degenerates into the narrowest form of individualism that eventually threatens its existence.

The New Creation Community

What is urgently needed alongside the call to relationships is basically a call to accepting one another's *creation-ness*—a humanness that is God-given—to build relationships on purely a creational and human level. Set within the whole ecological framework, this is a call to discovering and demonstrating our *creationality*. I use the word *creationality* instead of "creatureliness" as it refers to the privilege we are given, rather than to subservience within the environment of God's creation.

But then, how do we distinguish this level of relationships from the level made possible through the reconciliatory work of Jesus Christ? It is here that we speak of the community of those reconciled by Jesus Christ to God living within the community of those composing the widest circle of God's creation. The relationship between the new and the old creation brings to light this important connection between the people of God and those people within the creation of God.

Jurgen Moltmann speaks of the "eucharistic community of creation" . . . "In perceiving the world as creation, the human being discerns and enters into a community of creation."[33] "This community becomes a dialogue before the common Creator. Knowledge of the world as creation is in its primal form thanksgiving for the gift of creation and for the community found in it, and adoring praise of the Creator."[34] There ought to be a very real "dialogue before the common Creator," on a level that is not related to salvation, redemption, or reconciliation. It is certainly this kind of a creational relatedness that could resolve a number of tensions the world community faces today.

Moltmann prefers to call man a "eucharistic being," one who is able to "discern the world in full awareness as God's creation, to understand it as God's hidden presence, and to apprehend it as a communication of God's fellowship."[35] The proposition is a bit too idealistic. It does not take into account the fact of human fallenness. We could refer to a "Creation" community and a "New Creation" community. The New Creation community consists of those who are able to express a genuine creational relationship with each other within the realm of God's creation, without diminishing the distinctiveness of the redeemed community of Jesus Christ. The Creation community is one which has access to all the gifts of creation but is still under the bondage of sin which restricts it from fully knowing the Creator, and thereby from enjoying its full creationality.

We will need to underline the reality of sin and the ongoing influence of Satan if we want to fully understand all that is happening in God's creation over against the desires of humankind. In fact, it is the blinding through Satan and our bondage to sin that hinders human beings from looking beyond creation to the Creator-God. Being blessed with the image of God that gives to men and women a desire for God, but being blinded by Satan, they direct their worship to creation as the solution to the ecological crisis. Creation itself stands in need of reconciliation, and no amount of worship will satisfy its longings for ultimate redemption.

However, within this wider creation community is the New Creation community, those in Jesus Christ who discover real creationality (2 Cor. 5:17). They are able to experience the "firstfuits" of ultimate rec-

---

33. Moltmann, op. cit., 70.
34. Ibid.
35. Ibid.

onciliation here and now. Men and women in Christ are not transported into another realm distant from the Creation community. They discover their complete creationality even more as they dwell alongside those who still are outside the reconciliatory work of Jesus Christ.

What are the distinctives of this community? First, the New Creation community that God creates is a community that cares. This is a key word for the *oikos* of God who enjoy and need to demonstrate the privileges of the family relationship of God. The bondage of sin has diminished the joys of caring within the widest network of all that God has created. The ecological crisis intensifies because of the selfishness and greed that characterizes the creation community. The community of the New Creation begins to see its need to transcend such limitations and moves towards caring as a tangible expression of their new creationality. Caring for one another and caring for God's earth are essential elements that bring us closer to solutions within the ecological tensions that have assumed worldwide proportions.

There is also a sense of responsibility. The New Creation community conducts itself within the Creation community with a renewed sense of responsibility as stewards of all that God has entrusted to us. Exploitation is sin. Responsible relationships are characteristic of God's New Creation community and such relationships are to be established at every level in God's creation.

Further, the community of the New Creation, the body of Christ, begins to experience the joy of createdness once again. What was lost through human rebellion soon after creation and what is missing in fallen creation becomes possible. Human beings made in the image of God are created with an individuality within community. This individuality was characterized by dignity and freedom to "be" all that God intended us to be. God's work in redeeming his creation must be seen in restoring "worth" and value—re-"deeming"—so we can all be restored to relationships of dignity within the network of creational relationships. Joy is the outcome of good relationships.

Freedom within creation does not mean the liberty to do what one desires. Freedom within relationships has its boundaries at the best interests of all concerned. It is the wrong understanding of freedom that has resulted in chaos. True freedom is that which is set alongside responsibility, and therefore is conducted within the context and function of fulfillment.

The creation community is crippled under the bondage of sin, and this is clearly manifested before our eyes in all kinds of seen and unseen shackles. The dehumanization of men and women by exploiters and oppressors, the alienation of humans from humans by racist discriminations, the devastation of the earth's resources by those in power, and other ills are far too obvious. But the New Creation community will demonstrate to the world the care, responsibility, dignity, and freedom which characterizes the joyful relationships that Christ restores.

Interdependence within Relationships

The ecological crisis is characterized by the fact of broken relationships within the Creation community and within the New Creation community. But the power of Christ convicts and compels us towards truer relationships. Whether the problem be the exploitative tendencies of the rich West in their relationship to the poorer nations, or the exploiter landlord and the poor laborer, there is the need for us to restore proper relationships that are based on values that are accessible to the new community of creation through its relationship to Jesus Christ.

Apart from the reminder to establish right relationships, the ecological disaster has brought us face to face with the interdependence within our relationships. Recent global conferences have all underlined the need for global cooperation that could ease the crisis. It isn't a matter of individual concern, but something for the whole Creation community to be actively involved in. The very fact that the New Creation community is placed within this Creation community compels it to act along with the rest of the world to demonstrate the healing effects of true interdependence.

This situation has brought to our attention what we might call *eco-relationships*. Ecology in its earliest biological form studied intricate networkings of plants and animals within their environment. It was the disregard for such interlocking relationships that brought chaos and disaster. The interrelatedness of the constitutive elements of God's creation is a powerful picture of interlocking eco-relationships that need to be restored. This is not necessarily a relationship on equal terms, but one built on the fact of interdependence within the right perspective.

When God created Adam and Eve it was precisely a relationship based on interdependence that he was ordering. Each needs the other and it is within such a relationship that fulfillment is experienced. It was not equality in the fullest sense. They certainly were equal in the context of their relationship to God, but they were given varying roles and responsibilities within their interdependence. The problem of sin has basically left humankind seeking independence rather than interdependence. Even the "equal rights" movements have the tendency to get carried away by this quest. Relationships imply interdependence and interdependence implies appropriate place of respect for each party involved.

Heaven must be characterized by such eco-relationships. The whole emphasis on the "new creation" in the New Testament starts with the fact of a new relationship between the Creator and the created one. The central fact of salvation in all its images—redemption, justification, and propitiation—is therefore a reconciling of broken relationships. All else is an outcome of this restored relationship.

The ultimate goal of human history is not merely a peace and prosperity within a utopian environment, but one of righteous relationships based on the redeemed relationship that God intends for his people. The ultimate vision of redeemed humanity in Jesus Christ is that of a dwelling place where God will dwell with his people in a redeemed created order where love and righteousness reigns. Love and righteousness will characterize the relationships of the New Community of creation.

Actual relationships must be a very important fact of God's creative act, or else there is not much point speaking about a personal creator instead of an evolutionary accident that resulted in a world compelled to mechanical movement. In a sense, the reality of all other relationships is gauged by the tangibility of human relationships. One *feels* the reality of such earthly bonds. We are *hurt* by the selfishness of some, and are *healed* by the caring of others. It is through an experience of human relationships that we are able to value the necessity, and indeed the reality, of a right relationship with God, and thereby a responsible relationship towards creation. Ultimately, we see an intricate interdependence of all relationships within God's beautifully multifaceted creation.

Our Relationship to Future Generations

There is another level of human relationships that comes to the surface with the world's resources being depleted. In reminding present generations to exercise greater stewardship of resources, concerned voices are calling for a sensitivity towards future generations and their ability to meet their own "needs." The greed that is at the centre of the crisis is primarily a manifestation of selfishness that seeks the best only for oneself.

The concern is not just that others presently may not have enough, but that our selfishness will prevent future generations from meeting their basic "needs." Development has begun to pay attention not only to the sustainability of resources in all countries whether developed or underdeveloped, but also in terms of sustainability "that meets the needs of the present without compromising the ability of future generations to meet their own needs."[36]

At the heart of sustainable development is "common interest."[37] And this is undoubtedly the hardest attitude to achieve in a sinful, rebellious, self-centered world. It is the Spirit-filled New Creation community that is to be characterized by common interest (1 Cor. 12:3). "Conflict is recognized as one real cause of unsustainable development."[38] Although seen primarily in terms of armed conflict, we must also accept this in terms of human power and exploitation. The imbalance of power is the cause of great conflict today.

Returning to the Noahic covenant, we do well to note that the covenant established between God and "the earth," and "between God and all living creatures of every kind on the earth" (Gen. 9:16) was also "a covenant for all generations to come" (v. 12). God's reconciliatory purposes contain both universal and eternal aspects in the sense of a continuation of his purpose for generations to come. Caring that restricts one to the present generation is selfishness in God's total community of his people. Eco-relationships have a multidimensional interaction that truly harmonizes with God's convenantal concern for his world.

Everything that makes men and women think of themselves with no sense of their interdependence on others, whether in the present or for future generations, is sin. Eco-relationships characterized by selflessness are overwhelmingly influenced by God's covenantal concern for common interests. Unless and until such a common interest is demonstrated we are unable to speak in terms of the kind of relationships that will bring about an alleviation of ecological calamity.

There is hardly any doubt that the community of Creation, men and women still within the sanctity of God's creation, are capable of such concern. But it is ultimately the responsibility of the New Creation community to demonstrate this attitude of caring and sharing within the creation community.

---

36. *Our Common Future* (The World Commission on Environment and Development, 1987), 43.

37. Ibid., 46.

38. Ibid., 294.

Global Thinking

The recent Rio Summit was history's biggest summit and, even more significantly, the first world gathering to address the basic issue of humanity's survival on earth. Not only did it bring about awareness of earth's deteriorating resources, but it highlighted the necessity of right relationships between the rich North and the poorer South. The North feared that with the rapid industrialization of the South, atmospheric pollution would increase at uncontrolled rates. The South rightly issued a rejoinder that it was in fact the industrialized Europe and American that had been polluting the globe for over two centuries.

Eventually, they all agreed that the earth had been inherited by humanity as a whole, and therefore its problems had to be faced by one and all. Perhaps the biggest achievement of the Rio Summit was creating an awareness among the major powers that economic growth will need to seriously take into account ecological factors. Environmental concerns do not simply have to do with pollution of our environment but with the survival of earth and all its forms. There was an interlocking of the economic and ecological issues that made interdependence an even more crucial factor than had been earlier acknowledged.

The crisis we face ultimately boils down to the issue of proper eco-relationships within the widest expression of the *oikos* of God's creation. The North-South relationship and the way in which this interdependence is actualized is a matter of urgent concern, since it is on this interlinking that the very survival of the earth and humanity as a whole depends. Sustainable development in terms of the future may become a moot point unless proper relationships between the developed North and the rapidly developing South are realized at present.

The community of creation is in urgent need of recognizing its reality as a people bound together in Jesus Christ and demonstrating God-intended eco-relationships. The Creation community, while still possessing a potential for righteous relationships, cannot actualize these relationships. It is the New Creation community that will need to discover its potential more and more, its dynamic reality in Jesus Christ within the Creation community. And it is in doing this that it will actualize the purposes of God in anticipation of the New Creation to come.

Conclusion

The discussion above has aimed to emphasize not only the intensity of the ecological crisis, but also the urgency of the need for Christian involvement. Ample biblical undergirding, although limited in this discussion, is available and we will need to develop it further. However, what must follow is action. Let me summarize some of my propositions.

1. The Bible clearly authorizes Christians to be ecologically conscious of their relationship to creation and to the Creator. Ours is a role of responsible stewardship, not selfish exploitation.

2. Although creation has been marred by human sin, God has not abandoned his plans for it. Integral to his plans for the redemption of humanity are his plans for redemption of the created order. God has already revealed his plans for a New Creation.

3. All our considerations of a theology that will address current ecological issues will have to be Christological. It is Jesus Christ who plays a pivotal part both in creation and the new creation.

4. The central issue in resolving the ecological crisis is that of relationships. God's creation is held together by an intricate network of relationships, what we have called eco-relationships within the widest framework of the family of God. The reconciliatory work of Christ is directed towards the setting right of these broken relationships.

5. The "New Creation" community, placed firmly within the context of the "Creation" community has the responsibility to discover and demonstrate eco-relationships in the world today. However, these are only an anticipation of the perfect relationships to follow in the New Creation that God has planned for his people and for his creation.

Dictatorship and Revolution: Our Philippine Experience

Evelyn Miranda-Feliciano

Wrestling with the Apostle Peter

"Be subject for the Lord's sake to every human institution, whether it be to the emperor as supreme, or to governors as sent by him to punish those who do wrong and to praise those who do right. For it is God's will that by doing right you should put to silence the ignorance of foolish men . . . Honor all men. Love the brotherhood. Fear God. Honor the emperor." (1 Peter 2:13–17, RSV)

Just after the Election of February 7, 1986[1]

My "quiet time" meditating on the apostle Peter's letter these days is far from quiet. I carry on a running argument with him and, I suppose, with God himself—especially about that part on submission to and honoring the emperor.

How do I apply this passage to our Philippine situation today, where the incumbent president of twenty years again became the self-proclaimed winner of the recent hotly-contested election? How do I submit myself to a leadership which I and several million others perceive as corrupt, unjust, and self-serving? How can any Filipino honor a government which rewards wrongdoings if they serve its end, and brutalizes good intentions and actions if they impede partisan or personal interests?

Where will a conscientious Christian citizen situate herself or himself in a system in which money, power, and force (plus a number of religious superstitions) make people do its bidding, consciously or unconsciously?

---

1. The first part of this chapter is as it appeared in *Together* (July–September 1986). *Together* is a publication of World Vision International.

I was comforted by studying the background of St. Peter's epistles. When he said "Be subject . . . to the emperor," I learned he was actually addressing vast numbers of slaves, many of whom were Christians, living under an autocratic monarch. Under this political set-up, there was no other choice but to submit, to obey, to come on bended knee.

But this is not the situation in my country. Since early childhood I have been taught that we are a republic, a democracy. Even the Marcos dispensation mouthed these words before the world, styling our kind of government as "constitutional authoritarianism," whatever that meant.

In a democratic state, according to C. B. E. Cranfield, an eminent Bible commentator, the keynote must not be *subjection* but *cooperation*, for the duty of the citizen is not only to submit to being ruled but to take a necessary share in the ruling. Hence, if the Christian is to fulfill his duty to the state, he must take his part in its government. This explanation came as a relief to me.

When I take my seat as a poll "watchdog volunteer" to help minimize election frauds and electioneering right inside the voting place, I recognize that I am within my Christian duty. When I march to the National Parliament to show my solidarity with the many other thousands of citizens who demand a clean canvassing of election returns, I am simply being a Christian. And when I write protests and criticism against unethical acts of the government and government officials, that is still within the purview of my faith.

Not that these are grand actions. In fact, I feel they are just innocuous and hesitating steps. Other countrymen—braver and stronger than I—have already laid down their lives for doing what they believe is their Christian duty and moral responsibility. I am proud of them.

Yet, there is no denying the fact that when Peter wrote his letter, the emperor was Nero, the maniacal monarch who fiddled in his palace while Rome was burning. And to escape suspicion that it was he himself who engineered the fire, he laid it on the Christians. It was Nero who allegedly made torches out of Christ-believers to light his parties, who threw them to the Coliseum to be torn and eaten by beasts, who hounded them to the catacombs. It was to this mad leader that Peter was referring when he admonished the Christians to "Submit to the emperor . . . Honor the emperor."

William Barclay, in his commentary, makes this devastating statement: "It is the teaching of the New Testament that the ruler is sent by God to preserve order among men and that he must be respected, even when he is a Nero."

The statement is hard to swallow. Maybe in an imperial system of government, yes. But my country is a democracy. What if this ruler sits on a stolen seat of power? What if he has used massive frauds and force to gain a questionable majority? What if the order he tries to establish is not the order for the entire nation but only for his own interests and those who are close to him? What if criminals are allowed to go free because they are useful in intimidating the populace while conscientious political objectors languish in jails—many of them not charged with any crime? Does that ruler deserve my obedience, my cooperation, my respect?

My whole being cries out "No!" This leader has already lost his legitimacy to lead. He has sabotaged the people's will. Before God, he stands condemned for repudiating the divine mandate of government as God's instrument to punish the wrongdoers and reward the good. As he repudiated divine laws, and as he repudiated justice, truth, and freedom for his people, he deserves rejection—both personally and collectively. As a citizen and a Christian I will not have any part in his rule.

This is good as far as my intellectual resolve goes. But do I have the moral courage to express this protest in action? What options do I have for demonstrating my grievances against a discredited government? As a Christian activist, I cannot accept the facile dictum commonly heard in Protestant circles about passively letting God's will be done. As if it were God's intention that there should be methodical disenfranchisement of millions of voters, goons terrorizing the voters, people's votes being bought with money and few kilos of rice!

Is it God's will that there be an "indecent haste" in the proclamation of winners over loud and valid protests from the opposition party? I am sure God was not privy to any other underhanded methods that claimed a number of precious human lives. God is truth. He is just and fair. He cannot condone sin. To let things stand as they are, and to accept them as God's will—in order that I can get on with my life—is a gross insult and an irreverence to his name.

Surely, I can do something more than just be a passive observer of the unfolding events in this unhappy land. I can claim my constitutional rights—freedom of dissent, liberty of expression and movement—to air my grievances to the government while the already-mangled constitution still holds. Options like marches and demonstrations and other expressions of civil "disobedience" are still open for me.

I can help form public opinion by writing letters and articles for publication. I can form a movement among friends of kindred mind to articulate our thoughts, feelings, and observations about the government we have and want to have. I can be a member of a movement that shares the same dreams and ideals that grip my will.

There are many "I cans." But there are many voices that advise prudence. Most evangelical Christians in this country look sourly on fellow Christians who rally at the Rizal Park (unless it is a harmless prayer rally) or who march down Makati or EDSA avenues. To them, these actions show a lack of faith in prayer and in what God can do.

Others warn of future reprisals. And this is more valid. Those in authority have become more and more inconsistent and erratic. What is tolerated today may be prohibited and severely punished tomorrow. And, of course, one has to consider one's family—sons, daughters, husband, wife, and elderly parents. Retaliation is effectively carried out through them, as many protesters in the past have experienced. Nor can one ignore one's own solid, human fear of the sordidness of imprisonment and of torture or death.

To be a genuinely involved Christian and to be a true Filipino citizen has been extremely difficult during the past years, but more so during these unpredictable, incendiary days through which we are passing. How much easier it is to look indifferently at the contemporary scene and get on with "the Lord's work" of preaching Christ as the answer to all our problems—conducting evangelistic campaigns to save souls from hell. How much easier it is to write about safe topics such as love, courtship, and marriage, rather than spend sleepless nights pounding the typewriter, writing about events and incidents that grip one's soul.

How tempting just to be quiet, and to rationalize that a Christian must not indulge in partisan politics—which in reality means being a wishy-washy, spineless individual when confronted with the moral and ethical issues ravaging our society. Any of these—or even all of these postures—cannot satisfy.

What, then, is the Christian stance?

After the Revolution of February 22–25

My question on where to situate myself as a Filipino Christian in the context of what was happening in my country was answered dramatically. It was at Gate 2 of Camp Aguinaldo, fronting Camp Crame, the two camps which became the center of the four-day revolution against the dictatorial regime of Marcos.

Philippine Military Defense Minister Juan Ponce Enrile and Armed Forces of the Philippines Vice Chief of Staff Fidel Ramos led a rebel group against Marcos and announced their revolt in an international press conference. With the support of the powerful Catholic Church, appeals were made from people to ring the two camps to prevent attacks from Marcos' soldiers.

That fateful Monday, the 24th, my husband and I heeded the call. We took the 45-kilometer bus trip to Quezon City, hiking the last four kilometers, as important entry points were already barricaded. We joined the now famous "people's power revolution."

It was bizarre and awesome.

Bizarre, because nowhere can one find a revolution with a very gracious and festive atmosphere. Except here! People streamed towards the camps with baskets of food and water jugs, flowers, drinks, and pennants, their persons bedecked with yellow ribbons, caps or Cory's buttons. Flags, posters, and tents—mostly yellow, the oppositions's color—mushroomed along the way. Groups marching up and down the length of the avenue drew cheers and applause. Everybody was smiling and flashing the famous "L" sign (using thumb and index finger) and chanting the revolution mantra "Cory! Cory! Cory!" in reference to the woman who became president. Even the vehicles took up the chant by blowing "*toot*-toot" in time with the shouting.

As we neared the two camps, we became merely two infinitesimal points in a sea of humanity extending five or more miles both ways. The cacophony of sound was beyond description. Every other person carried a transistor radio, tuned to Radio Veritas, which gave us instructions on what to do and reported on the latest developments inside the camp, and on the movement of Marcos' troops.

This babel of tongues clashed with the martial music which came from different public sound systems placed at various points. Two helicopters continuously buzzed the whole area, serving as look-outs against the military forces of the embattled president in Malacanang, the seat of power. Further upward, two jet fighters swooped above us in graceful loops—whether enemies or not, we were not sure.

The awesomeness lay not only in the numbers—estimated to be 2.5 million by noontime that day—but in the unity of spirit and the concern for one another. It seemed that in fighting for a just cause, people turned to one another in common humanity. The sophisticated rich gladly held the shoulders of the grimy, rubber-sandaled poor to form one endless line to make human traffic possible.

It was as if, to a man, the entire Filipino nation had stood up to say decisively: "We can do it together—through prayer, by our collective presence and our willingness to die. We will bring this dictatorship to its knees—not by arms, but by reconciliation; not by violence, but in peace."

In those fearsome but glorious days, people of all religions, classes and kinds drank from the same plastic cups, slept on the same cold streets, hushed each other's fears and apprehensions and inspired each other to heroism. Never the like has been seen before.

At very crucial moments when tanks wanted to ram through the human barricades, there were nuns and priests, boys and girls, poor and rich who shoved their bodies against steel, planted flowers on cannons' mouths, handed food, flowers, cigarettes to the soldiers—all the while making appeals for peace and defection to the people's camp. Tanks, manned by gunners with tears in their eyes, had to backtrack—unable to carry out Marcos' order of carnage. Air force officers commanded to bomb the camps refused to do so and instead defected. By the morning of the third day, a huge percentage of the military force had already sided with the people, and everybody knew that the Marcos era was ending.

Prayer, presence, and winsomeness toppled a dictatorship and ushered in an almost bloodless revolution. God, I believe, caused his face to shine upon the Filipino people during those special days, sparing our nation from a protracted war of blood and gore, of hunger and pestilence and death, as is occurring in many lands today.

I also see myself in a better light. I am both a citizen of heaven and of my country. While still here, I have to commit myself to the working out of Kingdom values—truth, peace, freedom, human dignity, and others. I should couple my prayers with involvement, my piety with presence, my devotion with action.

No Christian should remain nonpartisan when basic moral and biblical values are at stake. Never should a Christian be passive in the midst of persecution or corruption by those in power. Never should a Christian be indifferent to any form of debasement of another fellow human being. Never should a Christian stay in church when he could challenge evil powers by being in the streets. The evangelical church should not sleep when it is time to awake and be vigilant.

God's power was manifested through the common solidarity of the Filipino people in the four historic days of February. As for my personal argument with the apostle Peter, I find my peace in doing right in the context of the recent situation of my country. I sought for peace through nonviolence and pursued it to the very gates of military camps, together in locked arms and in much prayer with other peace-loving Filipinos like myself.

Never have I experienced so glorious a moment. Never have I been prouder to be a Filipino.

Seven years have come and gone. The "people power revolution" started by the Filipino people became the inspiration of many other nations which were struggling from oppressive regimes and governments. However, among sensitive Filipinos, we realized that toppling a dictatorship was much easier than building structures that are truly democratic and responsive to the needs of the country. True, the democratic system of government was restored to our relief and thankfulness but the Aquino government in its six years in power, did nothing much else but maintain the traditional institutions and frame of mind popularly held prior to the Marcos regime.

The removal of the United States Bases from Philippine soil, for instance, was a result of years and years of stubborn protests and lobbying by concerned Filipino nationalists more than of a presidency inclined for their removal. In fact, the President put on line her whole personal charisma to persuade Congress to vote against it but the will of the people prevailed. She lost. On the whole, however, the kind of democracy we have (despite the change of personalities in the government recently) remains the "democracy of the elite." The poor who compromise the majority of the population are powerless, manipulated or manipulable, and oppressed.

No longer do I engage in a running argument with apostle Peter. I am now reflecting on Hosea 4:1–3 where the prophet describes the Israel of his times. He could have been describing the Philippines now when he says:

> "Hear the word of the LORD, O people of Israel; for the LORD has a controversy with the inhabitants of the land. There is no faithfulness or kindness; and no knowledge of God in the land; there is swearing, lying, killing, stealing, and committing of adultery; they break all bounds and murder follows murder.

> Therefore the land mourns, and all who dwell in it languish, and also the beasts of the fields, and the birds of the air; and even the fish of the sea are taken away." (RSV)

Here, I am silent. The whole Philippine landscape looks bleak from whichever side one looks. Coup d'etats from both "rightist" and "leftist" military rebels plagued the Aquino administration during its whole tenure. Kidnappings for ransom running into millions of pesos ushered in President Fidel Ramos' ascendancy to power. It scared investors and drove many native Chinese business people to less hostile countries. Nature itself has risen in protest. Volcanic eruptions, floods, typhoons, droughts have stalked our land more frequently now than I could remember. Peace talks with rebel groups are wobbling. Saddled with paying a gargantuan foreign debt of some 30 billion dollars, the government has hardly any money left for basic services. Graft and corruption has become a way of life in many governmental bureaus. No wonder, the Philippines has been labeled as "the basket case in Asia."

In the midst of all these, reports say, the evangelical church is growing phenomenally, making the Philippines the third fastest growing church in the world. The charismatic movement is the engine that causes this growth. Catholic renewals are also flourishing within the Catholic church. And of late, there has been a spate of Catholic miracles—weeping images and dancing sun and a number of young visionaries bringing messages from the virgin Mary and the infant Jesus.

I rejoice over this upsurge of interest in the biblical faith, spiritually, and the numerical growth it brings to the evangelical fold. It encourages me, too, that God's Spirit is moving within the Catholic church bringing about renewal that focuses more and more on the Lord Jesus Christ. The abundance of signs and wonders and miracles I regard with excitement and caution.

Excitement because God's power is bursting forth in most unlikely places affirming His almightiness. He empowers the powerless and the Spirit traffics with anyone He chooses.

However, my skeptical side tells me that some of these reported divine interventions and revelations could just be the result of helplessness and hopelessness. As one wag commented on the alleged miracles of virgin Mary's image crying and the sun dancing, "where people are hungry, they see visions."

Which leads me back to Hosea. I discovered that God's contention was as much as with the priest as with the people (Hos. 4:4). More on the former, I believe. The guardian of God's law, the priest, represented by the house of Levi in the Jewish structure had failed to translate the law into practical terms. It did not bring about a high morality in the interpersonal and national life of the Israelites. It did not result in peace, justice, equality or sufficiency for all. Neither did it bring about thankfulness to nature nor humility and obedience to God who created.

I fear a similar situation is happening in our society today. What influence has the proliferation of evangelical churches and charismatic Christians on the institutional habit of bribery and graft and corruption in our government offices? What do visions and dreams have to say to the senseless killings and kidnappings? To a bloating military force against straggling and surrendering rebels? How do the divine messages bear on the issue of land reform now mutilated by our own Congress to serve the landed and the rich, many of whom are sitting in that august body? What is our Christian stand on the foreign debt that automatically siphons sixty percent of our national budget? What Christian action are we taking to halt the rapid diminution of our national resources by corrupt politicians and multinationals? How have Christians as institutions or groups or individuals helped in the empowerment of the poor?

The answers to these questions are important because they are God's priests; we are his people (1 Peter 2:5, 9). And his controversy is with us.

I have no concrete answers myself. My own questions could have overwhelmed me to immobility and hopelessness if not for the small mercies of our God, who at his beautiful moment provides pinlights of hope.

Two months ago, I traveled up north of our country for fifteen hours through winding, mostly dusty roads, impassable during the rainy season. There, in a remote village clinging to a cliff, lives a cultural community called the Tingguian. The Institute for Studies in Asian Church and Culture has helped them organize and put up a multipurpose cooperative store, and the three-hundred strong populace is celebrating its first anniversary. Ani Gagriel, ISACC project director, has lived with the Tingguians for the last two years hazarding his own life—organizing and conducting seminars, sharing his faith and motivating them until they were able to do what they thought was impossible to do on their own.

The cooperative store stands by the roadside with its name proudly carved on a first-class wood. Residents from distant barrios come to buy their basic commodities here. During the rainy season, this store will be the lifeline of thousands of people in this mountainous region.

Our coming was heralded with the clashing of gongs and cymbals, and mountain singing and indigenous dancing went far into the night. The coop leaders, mostly women, shared their dreams of doubling their profit, of enlarging their capital and expanding projects to help more people to become independent and more self-sufficient. I dreamt with them. "With God's help, nothing is impossible," I said, as we prayed together to ask for the impossible.

Traversing the same dusty road back, I imagined if we could have more communities rising on their feet like this Tingguian village—our Christian effort would not be in vain. Our faith would have been rooted in the elemental needs of our people and we need not fear about becoming irrelevant, or Christianity being accused as an opium that deadens the senses, making people forget how to live more humanly with dignity. I and the whole Institute feel that this is the way He wants us to obey him in this time.

From wrestling with dictatorship to people empowerment is just an aspect in my constant struggle to make my biblical faith speak to my context as a Filipino. There are many others. My constant prayer is to be kept from becoming numbed to the events around me so I could pursue my personal agenda. Or to be overcome with hopelessness to the point of despair. Or, to become so cold and dispassionate that I could no longer laugh, cry or rage.

Or hope.

Prophet Hosea kindly strengthens me in this. Further on, he says:

> "So you, by the help of your God, return,
> hold fast to love and justice,
> and wait continually for your God."
>
> Hosea 12:6 (RSV)

Beyond Success:
Another "Great Awakening"
through U.S. Evangelicalism Soon?

David Lim

Introduction

This essay is a revised version of the author's critique of U.S. evangelicalism published in *Evangelicalism: Surviving Its Success* edited by David A. Fraser in 1987 by Princeton University Press. It is primarily a prescriptive article that interacts with the agenda raised in the Evangelical Round Table (E.R.T.) that was held at Eastern College and the Eastern Baptist Theological Seminary at St. Davids, Philadelphia last June, 1986. After reflecting on the papers and delineating the points of consensus and tensions in the conference as a whole, it tries to suggest some directions on how U.S. evangelicalism can survive its success.

The writer self-consciously recognizes that he writes as a westernized Asian evangelical. He is "westernized" because he thinks, speaks, makes decisions, and acts more like a westerner than most of his Asian contemporaries, and he feels comfortable conversing with western terms and categories.[1] He is "Asian" because he is a Chinese Filipino who can claim to represent Asians, since he was nurtured and did serve as a minister of the Gospel in various Asian contexts. He is an "evangelical" because he has categorized himself and has been recognized by others

---

1. He has learned to prefer English with its "strange" words, grammar and sentence construction and has adapted to western ways, e.g., in assertiveness, individual initiative, secularized worldview, etc. This is not necessarily unfortunate, for the western churches would be much poorer if it were not for "westernized" Two Thirds World (T.T.W.) evangelicals like him to help translate and communicate our perspectives to them in understandable terms. However, it may take two or three more generations for truly indigenous theologies to rise in T.T.W. evangelical Protestantism. Though one would like to be more optimistic, this seems to be realistic mainly due to the traditionally strong conservative *ethos* of evangelicalism, in contrast to that of the ecumenical Protestant and recent Roman Catholic circles.

as one; he has been discipled in the Philippine evangelical tradition (which has been greatly influenced by U.S. evangelicalism); and he received his theological training and also taught in evangelical seminaries. It is therefore without difficulty that he uses the first person plural in the following references to "U.S. evangelicalism."[2]

Definitions

Evangelicalism. Mainstream "U.S. evangelicalism"[3] circumscribes all the individuals and groups who are amenable to the doctrinal, devotional, evangelistic, ethical, social, and ecclesiastical ethos of the National Association of Evangelicals. The narrower use of the term "evangelical" refers to the Protestantism modified after the Reformation by European movements (such as Pietism, Puritanism, and Wesleyan/ Methodism), and North American movements (such as Revivalism, Fundamentalism, and Pentecostalism).[4]

Those who gathered at the E.R.T. belonged primarily to the "inclusive fundamentalist" stream. Historically, this stream is a post-World War II phenomenon, located mainly but not exclusively in the fundamentalist side of the Fundamentalism Modernist controversy of the early twentieth century,[5] and have recently been liberated from the separatism and ultraconservatism of its past.[6]

Success. Has U.S. evangelicalism experienced "success?" Most cer-

---

2. Even if he is a Filipino citizen, "we" comes very naturally in the author's Asian usage, especially as he recognizes the strong linkages between his Philippine evangelicalism and U.S. evangelicalism not just in the past and present but also in the future.

3. This paper hesitates to use "*American* evangelicalism" for the discussion does not include the realities of Canada, the Caribbean, Mexico, and other Central and South American nations.

4. The broader use would embrace "evangelical" elements in the other major streams of Christianity, i.e., the Roman Catholic, Eastern Orthodox, and ecumenical Protestant streams.

5. The two-party paradigm of U.S. evangelicalism continues to predominate in popular usage: (1) the right-wing fundamentalist churches with their more conservative constituencies (who prefer to be called "evangelicals"), loosely associated with National Association of Evangelicals (N.A.E.) and the World Evangelical Fellowship (W.E.F.); and (2) the left wing "mainline" or ecumenical churches with their less- or non-liberal constituencies (who have just started to feel comfortable being called "evangelicals") affiliated with the National Council of Churches (N.C.C.) and the World Council of Churches (W.C.C.). Isn't a "third party" paradigm emerging? See below. Also cf. G. Marsden, "Introduction," and Joel A. Carpenter, "From Fundamentalism to the New Evangelical Coalition" in G. Marsden (ed.), *Evangelicalism and Modern America* (Eerdmans, 1984), vii, xix, 3–16.

tainly, if "success" refers to numerical growth and heightened prestige in terms of greater popularity, social privileges and political power. U.S. evangelicals have also accumulated great assets and have replaced the mainline or "ecumenical" churches in their high visibility in the media. This "success" is also seen in its private school enrollments, media networks and infrastructure, businessmen's associations, and prayer breakfasts, to mention only a few of its institutions.

However, questions have been raised whether or not such a materialistic measure of success means actual success (i.e., spiritual authority and moral power) in terms of God's priorities for his church. Has "success" also enhanced its "salt and light" impact on the national conscience and the personal morality of its culture? We should note the tragedy of the loss of the Christian mind, the lapse to cultural captivity and the junkie spirit in the grassroots in which even the world-denying fundamentalists have become the worldliest Christians. It seems that instead of the church transforming the world, the reverse has happened: mainstream U.S. evangelicalism may have lost its distinctive nature and message in its sociocultural milieu.

Growing church membership rolls have *not* significantly lowered the crime statistics, lessened the public acceptance of divorce and abortion on demand, or discouraged the materialistic and hedonistic lifestyles even of its members. Christianity had devolved into a "consumer religion" or "hedonistic spirituality" that teaches that those who follow Jesus will succeed in any venture they enter (e.g., business, athletics, beauty contests, parking spaces, prayers for healing, etc.).[7]

Such "seduction by success" and development of its own isolated subculture point to a very qualified definition of "success": in gaining the world we may have lost our soul. This critique hopes to show some directions for "godly success" (called an "awakening") in which the

---

6. Modern "far right" fundamentalism is still generally known for its suspicion of advanced "secular" education, rejection of biblical higher criticism *per se*, judgmental attitudes towards those in ecumenically related denominations, uncritical political conservatism (Christianity equated with anticommunism and laissez-faire capitalism) which deplores politicizing the Gospel on the left but politicizes it to the right, and a polemical approach to theological discussion. Recently biblical "total inerrancy" has become its *shibboleth* by which it measures orthodoxy.

7. Cf. Os Guinness, "The American Hour, the Evangelical Moment," in David A. Fraser (ed.), *Evangelicalism: Surviving to Success* (Princeton: Princeton University Press, 1987), 192–97.

increasing popularity of religiosity will also turn into a positive influence in morality.

Survival. The dialogue in this E.R.T. takes "survival" to mean not only the preservation of the existence of evangelicalism on U.S. soil, but also the enhancement of its positive impact in its context. We were reminded that there is no holding operation; like an airplane in flight, we cannot stand still. We must keep the momentum. Indeed new wineskins have to be constantly developed for the ever new wine of the Evangel.

A clearer challenge was given: we need to *mature* beyond childish infatuation with "success." We need to grow up and out of our defensiveness, parochialism, and superficiality. Rather than getting stuck with our culture's "success mentality" and its American dream to become "rich and famous," we have to reach out for the right ends (and so be true signs of the kingdom) with the right means (with spiritual and not worldly "weapons").

The uniqueness of this *kairos* (opportune moment) in world history must be highlighted. The great experiment in the U.S., constituted by its two supreme root faiths of Enlightenment liberalism and Reformation Protestantism, has resulted in a "spiritual sun-belt" in a superpower nation of the world today,[8] and has reached a very critical juncture, especially since the 1960s. This essay will proceed with the optimistic view: even though we are already on a downward slump,[9] there is hope that we can be renewed by God's Spirit, perhaps even against our will, because humanly speaking, it seems that too much of God's kingdom is at stake.[10]

The real hope is that U.S. evangelicalism can more than survive its success, that we can be renewed "in our minds" (cf. Rom. 12:2) and take up godly leadership to establish a world-transforming movement. Rather than continuing to console people who feel personal alienation and apocalyptic anxieties, we may move to another "Awakening"[11] to regenerate our national life and pose cultural and religious challenges

---

8. Such important *kairoi* occurred in the days of Calvin, Wesley, Lincoln, Kuyper, and Kagawa (among others), but their contexts did not have such a large potential for universal visible and powerful impact as U.S. evangelicals have today.

9. We are perhaps in the same sad condition as the early church in Laodicea (Rev. 3:14–22), and thus in humility, we need to repent and do what pleases our Lord. To take our Lord's temptations (Matt. 4; Luke 4) as our analogy, we have been offered the glory of the earthly kingdoms, and sadly, we have begun to worship the tempter to "gain the world"; but we can still repent and say, "It is written, you shall worship the Lord your God, and him only shall you serve."

for Christians worldwide. Using the E.R.T.'s basic framework, this article discusses some of the aspects of a genuine spiritual revival[12] which U.S. evangelicalism can (and should) aspire for—to the glory of God.

On Our Common Call:
Proper Understanding of Historical Roots

There is a consensus among historians that the U.S. has always been a highly pluralistic and largely secular nation rather than a "Christian" or "godly" nation as claimed by some.[13] Though its culture has the benefit of many relatively good Judeo-Christian traditions, it includes substantial non-Christian influences, especially Enlightenment humanist views about democracy, freedom, justice, and progress.

Yet U.S. evangelicalism has had a higher degree of influence upon its society, far more than its proportion of the population because of its previous dominant commitment to Reformed and millennial (later labeled postmillennial) and transformist views of the role of the church

---

10. Of course, the disestablishment of the churches in Europe shows that no church is guaranteed protection from losing its "saltiness." So what must be emphasized is *"humanly* speaking" i.e., from earthly perspective, in a world where all peoples are becoming more closely interrelated and linked (in communications, economics, politics, and even lifestyles), how crucial it is that the Christian resources (talents, finances, institutions and personnel) in a modern superpower nation can serve as the instruments in God's hands to finish the task of world evangelization and world transformation, in proper coordination with the rest of the body of Christ.

11. It seems customary to refer to two previous "Great Awakenings" in U.S. history: the first *circa* 1725–69 and the second *circa* 1787–1825. See articles in J. D. Douglas (ed.), *The New International Dictionary of the Christian Church* (Grand Rapids: Zondervan, 1974), 428f., 894; and J. C. Brauer (ed.). *The Westminster Dictionary of the Church History* (Philadelphia: Westminster, 1971), 370f., 758f. T. L. Smith, *Revivalism and Social Reform* (Baltimore: John Hopkins University Press, 1980) writes in his afterword (following R. Baird) that revivals have become a constituent part of religious life after the second awakening in the U.S. W. G. McLoughlin adds a third (ca. 1890–1920) and a fourth (1960–90) in *Revivals: Awakenings and Reform* (Chicago: Chicago University Press, 1978). However, this critique considers the recent U.S. religiosity as superficial and only a potential awakening at best.

12. Some other ingredients of Awakening include: movement for corporate prayer (and fasting), emphasis on "spiritual warfare" and spiritual gifts, mobilization for the world mission, etc. These are not elaborated here because they were not included in the E.R.T.'s main agenda.

13. Among such evangelical works are: T. L. Smith, op. cit.; R. Lovelace, *Dynamics of Spiritual Life* (Downers Grove, Ill.: InterVarsity Press, 1979); and M. A. Noll, N. O. Hatch, and G. M. Marsden, *Search for Christian America* (Westchester, IL: Crossway Books, 1984); contra F. Schaeffer, *A Christian Manifesto* (Crossway Books, 1982).

in the world.[14] The First and Second Great Awakenings brought tremendous advances in sociocultural mores in U.S. society. Such reforms, coupled with humanist humanitarian (not necessarily "secular humanist") influences, overshadowed U.S. culture and were assimilated into its mainstream.

Evangelical influence diminished in the 1920s and 1930s (often called the "Great Reversal") as Fundamentalism withdrew from post-millennarian eschatology. The culture clash did not occur until the 1960s revealed evangelical Protestantism's dependence on the general social consensus for its guidelines. Having gotten used to accepting the government's moral judgments uncritically as God's will to be obeyed (based on Romans 13), we were caught unprepared to check sub-biblical standards of personal morality (divorce and remarriage, abortion on demand, pornographic proliferation), violence in the media, sexual, and social injustice (only our black churches and feminist activists kept us in touch with the mainstream civil rights movements), economic order, the cold war and nuclear arms race, etc. But until now, unlike our forebears, our churches generally have not learned how to serve as prophetic countercultures rather than merely preaching halls and social clubs.

Thus, for genuine renewal, we have to learn to be salt and light in our contexts in each generation. We can never sit back and assume that the state or public consensus would make evangelism and social transformation easy for us. If, in fact, the teachings of our Lord and the New Testament are culturally relevant for us, then we have clearly failed to be his faithful witnesses in our world (cf. Matt. 5:10–12; John 16:33; Phil. 1:29; 2 Tim. 3:12, etc.). We have become too uncritical of the world (even the world within ourselves and our churches) and so are dulled in our understanding of God's will for our role in history-making for his kingdom.[15] May we recover from this historical lapse as soon as possible and not repeat this same mistake (and sin) again.

On Our Common Call:
Effective Media or Authentic Evangelism

Undeniably a significant part of our evangelical identity (and a sig-

---

14. Cf. D. Brown, *Understanding Pietism* (Grand Rapids: Eerdmans, 1978); D. Dayton, *Discovering An Evangelical Heritage* (N.Y.: Harper and Row, 1976); N. Magnuson, *Salvation in the Slums* (Metuchen, N.J.: Scarecrow Press, 1977); G. Marsden, *Fundamentalism and American Culture* (Oxford University Press, 1980); J. Rifkin, *The Emerging Order* (N.Y.: Putman, 1979); and T. L. Smith, op. cit.

15. Further discussion below in "On Our Common Objective . . ."

nificant reason for our "success") is our prioritization of and ardent zeal for evangelism. However we also need to submit our practice to Christ's lordship, especially to reflect on what our Lord meant when he rebuked his contemporary religious teachers for an eager evangelization that made their converts worse than before (Matt. 23:15). We need to ask: What are the right ways of presenting the Gospel so that "Christ and him crucified" is the *only* stumbling-block to the unbelievers?[16]

The Right Personnel. The primary channel of the Gospel is through the lips and lifestyles of the people of God. Youth for Christ discovered that to reach unchurched youths, committed and caring young adults are the best "evangelists." This calls into question the confrontational approach in our traditional practice of evangelism, as well as the quality of membership demands in our congregations. How can we expect self-centered, self-seeking, self-righteous, temperamental, mediocre and immature believers to be good evangelists even after attending "personal evangelism seminars?" Can the gospel of "costly grace" be conveyed through lives which do not live it out? This leads to the next question about the right institutions for Christian nurture.

The Right Church Structures. The contemporary church and para-church problems grow out of the vague conflict between charisma and order, dynamism and conservatism in church structures.[17] Missiologists know of Ralph Winters' sodality-modality model and the homogeneity of church membership.[18] But these just underscore the lack of a Protestant "theology of the visible church,"[19] especially in its renewed form and in contrast to the Catholic hierarchical model. What visible norm(s) should the churches militant take if indeed they are Spirit-filled, especially if freed from the shackles of ethnocentrism, nationalism, mammonism, and "successism" or "triumphalism"?

---

16. This paper assumes that our main problem is less on the *what* but more on the *how* of evangelicalism. Our wineskins often dilute or destroy the wine. The Gospel we share is often made to fit the media we use, rather than having our fixed message shape our media. The rhetorical "the medium is the message" may be taken to mean "the medium greatly affects the message."

17. S. Escobar, "The Church: Help or Hindrance to Evangelism?" in Fraser (ed.), *Evangelicalism*, 68–76.

18. Are parachurches not "*churches* in mission" (not just in frontier situations)? Are there not sodalities in modalities, and modalities in sodalities? Cf. Howard Snyder's paper in Lausanne, 1974.

19. This problem seems to have been originally defined in this way by Indian evangelical theologian Saphir Athyal.

We need to outgrow our self-satisfaction with "functional cooperation" and "doctrinal unity" as a basis for our evangelistic work and
ecclesiastical relations. We need to reflect on the necessity and proper
use of institutional forms to serve God's kingdom as his churches on
earth. Can we not break the historical cycles of revival-institutionaliza-
tion-organization-institutionalism-revival (breakaway)? Can there not
be constantly renewed churches in mission?

Perhaps instead of the present paradigm or vision of a renewed
Christendom, which imbues society with Christian vision by means of
visible Christian sociopolitical participation and media saturation, we
can envision a loose network of small servant-communities, organized
as simple local churches or house groups which live out their commitment to the Gospel in the context of the missionary and liberation movements of their respective contexts on the local, national, and global
level. This nonhierarchical, nonpaternalistic and micro-institutional
model may just be the ecclesiology which moves beyond the denominational, super-church and antiecumenical structures found among evangelical Protestants. A local church would thus be any community of
believers which claims to have a clear Christian identity, built upon a
base-community (e.g., a neighborhood, ethnic ghetto, village, school,
factory, church or parachurch structure, social movement, etc.), and
organized to live out, confess, communicate, reflect upon and celebrate
their faith together on some regular basis.[20]

The task of evangelism and world mission would thus be "returned"
to the laity rather than remain with a few experts. The grassroots laity
would be mobilized to do evangelism and good works in nonthreaten-

---

20. Such autonomous local fellowships, especially in homes, across the social spec-
trum affirm their unity in Christ through simple regular meetings, and show their interdependence with other local fellowships through some form of local cooperative structure
and simple ad hoc mass meetings held by itinerant revivalist-pastors and evangelists—like
in the N.T., the Awakenings, and other revivals. This just requires a more consistent reflection on Protestant ecclesiology to check our current ecclesiastical tendency to become
more Catholic (a Christendom with top heavy hierarchical denominational and super-
church structures) rather than truly Protestant evangelical (a kingdom movement with
"powerless," simple grassroots communities of more disciplined believers). Too many
resources are being channeled to amass Christian institutional assets rather than to extend
Christian missionary and liberation work. It would be very enlightening to see what results
from the "new reformation" happenings in the Basic Christian Communities (B.C.C.s) and
"the popular churches" of the Roman Catholic Church. Cf. R. Shaull, *Heralds of a New
Reformation* (Maryknoll, N.Y.: Orbis, 1984), and G. Cook, *The Expectation of the Poor*
(Orbis, 1985).

ing, nonmanipulative and nontriumphalistic ways, rather than giving funds to finance superstars and their huge and expensive ecclesiastical structures.

Right Modern Media. We need to keep seeking more effective and authentic ways to use modern media for evangelism. We need to beware of idols (1 John 5:21)—we need to recognize the problem of the idol-making phenomenon of modern mass media: Can evangelicals communicate the Gospel *authentically* and effectively through radio, television, and video cassettes? Hopefully we can, but how? We seem to have been broadcasting and telecasting packaged answers (and also packaged messages even in personal evangelism) from our cultural ghettos without engaging people in intelligent discourse about the faith. Should so much Christian resources be put into such evangelistic ventures that seem primarily to target Christian audiences? If the ecclesiastical model suggested above is accepted, then it seems that we should emphasize face-to-face and communal nurture as well as life-to-life personal friendships for evangelism and preevangelism.

Television in particular (more so than radio) has promoted cultural decadence by implicitly, if not explicitly, commending moral permissiveness and relativism. Though it appears to show diversity, in fact it enhances uniformity: the variety of fashions and opinions are modified towards materialistic similarities. It appeals to human weaknesses and discourages reflection and deep thinking;[21] it presents trivialities; and worst, it routinely robs too much time which could better be given to prayer, serious reading, and Bible meditation.

Hence, it may be very difficult to deliver authentic messages effectively on television. Whatever we produce would be primarily for Christian consumption rather than for evangelism. Perhaps we should encourage and equip our laity-in-the-media to be "media-ministers," to change television's materialistic idol-making ethos and secularist disregard of religion, and to use "secular" television to convey Christian virtues and morality, instead of developing our own evangelical media

---

21. It really propagates the materialist "American dream" which creates high expectations and raises false hopes of the "good life" characterized by endless leisure and entertainment in paradises on *earth* (like Las Vegas, Hawaii, Disneyland, etc.). The brain stays idle while the eyes are stimulated to crave for more and more. Even religious programming, especially those which focus on faith-healing, seem to cater to the self-seeking longings for security of salvation (and from suffering), instead of the search for "signs of the kingdom" to the glory of God. In this writer's judgment, the best spiritual television show in recent years is "The Little House on the Prairie" series.

subculture. Such a subculture hardly speaks to the materialistic television audiences who misinterpret our programs to be hard-sell religious propaganda.[22] Perhaps we can use the media effectively and authentically, not by pouring our resources into setting up parallel media ministries, but by subverting the secular media from within.

On Our Common World:
Biblical Authority for Evangelical Vitality

For an awakening to occur, we need to be rooted constantly in God's authoritative revelation in his word, the Holy Scriptures. However, U.S. evangelicals have been divided over "the Battle for the Bible," which actually means fighting over the usage of the term "biblical inerrancy" and over the attitude towards "higher criticism," specifically redaction criticism.

Concerning the "inerrancy" issue, we must "let the Bible be the Bible." Instead of imposing our presuppositions on how we wish (or need) its inspiration to have happened, we must let the Bible's self-understanding about its nature and intention be studied and expounded in such a way that we do not re-create the "phenomena of Scripture" in our image. What is most important is that, as evangelicals, we believe that in the Scriptures we have revelation, the authoritative and infallible witness to God's gracious self-revelation, the authentic and trustworthy record which teaches us how to live in restored relationship with God and with his creation (as stated in the Lausanne Covenant).[23] It is a question whether those *theologians* who insist on "inerrancy" have really wrestled with the text itself as *exegetes*.[24] Perhaps we can use the incarnation as a paradigm to understand the relation between the divine and the human in bibliology: should human errors be considered as sins

---

22. Using modern media also seems to be an effective shortcut to saturate the world with the Gospel, but in reality it has drained away too much work-hours and resources from face to face evangelism and personal discipling.

23. Since 1974 world evangelicalism has been greatly impacted by the Lausanne Covenant, especially for defining our evangelical identity and unity, but U.S. evangelicalism hardly seems to be so affected. In its creative uniqueness, has U.S. evangelicalism not become an aberrant development in mainstream world evangelicalism? How seriously does it listen to evangelicals of other contexts, especially the non-English-speaking ones?

24. If proper exegesis is done, the Bible texts would cause "inerrancy" to be qualified in so many ways, that it becomes a question whether it is really helpful to use the term at all, in spite of the seeming necessity to use it for apologetic purposes vis-à-vis modern non-Christians who understand the Bible to be full of errors. The term "infallible" seems to be more than adequate.

or as limitations? This paper thinks that further discussion and more study on the phenomenon of language would tend towards the view that errors are just limitations.

It has also been suggested that such longing for full certainty in an "inerrant" text is walking by sight, not by faith, i.e., longing for "a little post-parousial vision in our pre-parousial world of faith." We need not press too far for absolute certainty about biblical authority by using unverified theories about the nature and composition of the "original texts," for biblical research is finding that our present canonical forms have come to us through a series of editings or redactions.

In the author's view, this debate in U.S. evangelicalism is the result of its capitulation to the use of a post-Enlightenment secularist framework which seeks for absolute or objective statements (or propositional truths) to describe absolute Truth or "facts."[25] Without denying the existence of the Absolute(s), can we not accept the fact that on this side of eternity, especially with fallen humanity, all creaturely descriptions of the Absolute(s) are relative? It should be hoped that the twentieth-century Einsteinian paradigm used in the modern physical sciences may soon be used by evangelicalism in expounding Christian theology.[26] The Enlightenment framework (which claims to give *naturalistic* expressions to human existence, social life and history, excluding the supernatural from the natural and emphasizing empirical and precise ways of thinking) has also caused the defenders of faith to define "faith" more as *beliefs* in more precise confessional forms[27] than as personal *trust* (as understood by the Reformers). With the later romanticism that entered through the Pietistic and revival movements, faith was further defined as *emotional* enthusiasm to adhere to such *beliefs*, i.e., to believe in "faith," instead of in God.[28]

25. Roman Catholics have sought such earthly certainty in the church (the Papacy and the sacraments), Reformed Protestants in the Scriptures, manual labor, and material prosperity, Wesleyans in the "second work of grace," and the Pentecostals/Charismatics in supernatural "spiritual gifts" all trapped in the materialistic, scientific search (or obsession?) for observable and repeatable "proof," even of one's salvation.

26. Then, as in most Eastern thought, relative propositions about the Absolute(s) may be accepted as valid and as logical as others, each from a different perspective or even from a different framework. Cf. "centered sets" and "fuzzy sets."

27. This is mainly because Enlightenment thought has bred a growing uncertainty over basic Christian doctrines.

28. Cf. J. Turner, *Without God, Without Creed: The Origin of Unbelief in America* (Baltimore: Johns Hopkins University Press, 1985).

The "higher criticism" of the Bible arose historically out of the desire to learn the literary and historical backgrounds of the Scriptures, thereby freeing biblical studies from its imprisonment to the proof-texting theological systems of post-Reformation Protestant Scholasticism. Its use is presently of greater importance since it protects the text from our (mis)interpretations, and especially from our various cultural temptations to read too much of our times into the text, and often to justify our own thoughts and behavior. This seems the best, if not the only way to take the Biblical text seriously.

The real problem is not so much one's "high" or "low" view of Scriptures, but one's hermeneutics: with what methodology does one properly interpret the biblical data, and then apply its teachings authoritatively to particular historical contexts? We must recognize that each of us has prior conditioning in coming to the text (with varied questions arising out of our respective histories). Yet we must let our serious study of the ideals and development of the personal piety and social institutions of the people of God in both the Old and New Testament reshape our own thoughts and actions. Our thinking must be truly shaped by the Scriptures rather than by our cultures.[29] This also requires a humility which recognizes that what we can see is "behind our eyes." We need a "hermeneutic of distrust" which issues in an internal, self-criticism of the ideologies, sociocultural influences, and rhetorical inaccuracies of many of our recent biblical interpretations.[30] Unless we use a more critical approach in our biblical exegesis and theological formulation, our "scholarly" productions will continue to be based on data and categories that may be historically untrue, theologically inaccurate, and worse, spiritually bankrupt.

For a true revival, we must let the Bible be freed from its ideological bondage to the immature aspects of U.S. evangelical biblical schol-

---

29. E.g., is the Jesus of our gospel (U.S. version) the same as the Jesus of the Gospels, or has he been re-created in the image molded by our culture of success and prosperity? The people he rebuked the most were not the "dirty sinners" (in fact he was quite comfortable in their company), but the "clean saints" who seemed to take a very high view of the Torah by interpreting its contents as literally as possible, and who were most sure of their salvation.

30. Our low "ambivalence tolerance" has blinded us to the fact that ideologies and other factors color the way we read and understand the Word and the world, or that even "objective" or scientific scholarly works often serve ideologies. If this fact is raised, it goes unheeded because it upsets our fundamental assumptions about how the Word and our world make sense to ourselves. Hence our creativity is often limited by our hermeneutical naiveté and conservatism.

arship. We may begin first by destroying the rigid Enlightenment paradigm which we often adopt in concert with our society in conceptualizing and interpreting what the Bible says about religion and culture.[31] Rather than simply fighting verbal battles over "inerrancy," we will get serious about studying and obeying the Bible in its prophetic call to break down our idols. We will let God's Word prophesy against the decadence, ambiguity, and loss of radical dynamism in our churches, and the dehumanization, demoralization, and secularism of our society.[32] And we will be open for God to guide us by his Spirit into a deeper understanding and better application of his Word for our generation.

On Our Competing Present:
Creative Sophistication in Evangelical Theologizing

In awakenings, theologies arise which do not simply reflect the culture, but which transcend and transform the culture. They often raise us to new levels of awareness and reveal reality in terms of greater metaphysics. D. Elton Trueblood rightly characterizes the greatest challenge of our times: we need evangelicals who can outthink the world and whose intellectual sharpness will be used to transform the mind of a generation and even of whole cultures.

Though we are more concerned for "sound doctrines" than other Christians, we have expended most of our efforts battling among ourselves over nonessentials, instead of challenging unbiblical or sub-biblical worldviews. We have done too much work on the formal questions about biblical authority rather than derive comprehensive biblical, theological, and philosophical works so desperately needed at this critical point in the life and thought of this nation and the world.[33]

---

31. E.g., Jubilee (Lev. 25) will then be seen as the basis for *economic* liberty for the poor, a divine plan for the redistribution of wealth for God's people, even if this goes against our "success theology."

32. Most of us have grown fat and lazy in our Mammon-worship. E.g., we are proud of superstars rather than of prophets, who would most probably be excluded from speaking in our conferences. Cf. J. White, *Golden Cow* (Downers Grove, Ill.: InterVarsity Press, 1979); and D. B. Kraybill, *Upside-Down Kingdom* (Scottdate. PA: Herald Press, 1978).

33. Those who want to continue the current level of debate must consider the following: if theological orthodoxy is safeguarded by affirmation of biblical inerrancy, why have conservative evangelicals hardly produced any significant exegetical and theological works? If making relevant worldviews is guaranteed by emphasizing the Reformation view of revelation, why is there a great lack of philosophical works on Christian theism and holism which speak to our times?

We have enough solid foundation to launch into creative theologizing. However, we have not been able to construct integrative and culture-shaping theologies, mainly because of the naive empiricism of U.S. intellectual traditions that lead to superficiality and not to depth. We have become dominated by a worldview which is foreign to both our spiritual roots in the Bible and our historical experience of "the faith of our fathers." Thus, instead of effectively giving creative leadership to our society, we have developed a kind of authoritarianism in which almost every church leader can claim to have "the Bible alone as guide" and impose his or her form of biblical interpretation on his followers who likewise profess to be led by "the Bible alone as guide."[34]

Our creativity has also been hindered by our conservative concern for orthodoxy, which often means using predictable clichés, and which has considered new ideas and new formulations to be controversial if not subversive to the Gospel. There is a high risk of creative thinkers being marginalized since new ideas invite cruel counterattacks rather than careful counterarguments. Theological maturity means recognizing that reality involves mysteries and paradoxes, and it does not exist as closed and logically consistent system. Moreover, theologizing is also existential, especially as spiritual reflection in crisis experiences. Our theologies are always *theologia viatorum*, not *theologia comprehensorum*. Our orthodox traditions are our starting points, not our stopping points.

For great thinking to occur, we need to raise an intellectually competent generation which is both literate in the humanities (not just in engineering or computer sciences) and articulate about its "Christian mind." We must set it free to find previously unnoticed biblical motifs and design new concepts and new paradigms that can better express the full truth of the glorious Christ.[35] This would let the Bible raise its own agenda, as well as address as many issues as the world would throw at

---

34. Cf. M. A. Noll, "Evangelicals and the Study of the Bible," in Marsden (ed.), *Evangelicalism*, 103–21.

35. We have been building our theologies on philosophical paradigms and analyses which were not produced by evangelicals at all. Perhaps we can interpret biblical data with Jesus Christ as the center of two major concentric circles, the inner circle the redeemed and the outer circle all humanity, etc.; cf. R. J. Mouw, *Politics and the Biblical Drama* (Eerdmans, 1976), chap. 4. New models must emerge, especially those of mutual submission, interdependence and partnership to replace those of self-sufficiency, superior inferior relations, and extreme dualism.

us, even if this prospect may be frightening for typical evangelicals who prefer to stay "safe."

Perhaps more important is that we must learn to listen and relate to those who are outside our evangelical "bounded sets" in the entire Christian movement. Evangelical black theology has not only introduced unique theological language (e.g., the *"Holiness"* of Jesus), but also helped us to be more orthodox, especially in our understanding of the social dimensions of biblical faith.[36]

We also need to always remember that theologizing must be primarily seen in our doing rather than in our publishing. Ministering together in open dialogue between different traditions in the U.S. setting is necessary and helpful for creative sophistication to surface.[37] And interaction with those from other contexts, especially from our Two Thirds world (T.T.W.) contemporaries, may even be more necessary and helpful for the world-shaking theologizing we are talking about.

Obviously to get ahead of our times for another "Awakening," we will need to put demands on ourselves, especially on our minds. May we constantly remember this ancient Hebrew prayer:

> From the conscience that shrinks from new truth,
> From the laziness that is content with half-truth,
> From the arrogance that thinks it knows all truth,
> Oh, God of truth, deliver us.

On Our Competing Present:
Integrative Vision for Christian Unity

One of the major issues we have to face is our problem of unity and love. No awakening can be realized unless we are able to maintain the bond of peace that is given by his Spirit to his church (cf. Eph. 4:1–16). Thus it is very pertinent for us to have Romans 14 to check our attitudes and behavior in this area.

Among the main reasons for our present disunity are our low "ambiguity tolerance," especially concerning varied theological pet issues; our inherited fundamentalist tendency to separatism; and our narrow vision of the church which goes together with our lack of a theology of the visible church. All these are influenced by the strong U.S.

---

36. Black evangelicals have also been interacting with non-evangelical and non-Christian worldviews and lifestyles, especially in their ministries in the cities in U.S.

37. This seems to mean that our best minds must be "incarnated" and involved in the "secular world," especially in the academy, the media, and the government.

cultural strands of individualism, egalitarianism, antitraditionalism, pragmatism, ideological extremism, and unrestrained demagoguery, as well as by the evangelical subcultural disregard for the corporate solidarity of the church and our poor sense of history and tradition.

The threat of censorship and the practice of labeling and name calling are tragic symptoms of our spiritual immaturity, if not of our sinful pride. We need the humility to recognize that our understanding is subject to error, that even evangelicals do not possess the final truth nor should we claim to be the sole possessor of all truth. We need to be more self-critical and break out of our ideological blindness. We need to listen to each other's biblical exegesis and take each other seriously, and learn even to agree to disagree.[38] We must have the faith to believe that eventually truth will win over error.

At the same time, we must find a new synthesis in the broader horizons of the kingdom of God.[39] We can then welcome all Christians, even non-evangelicals who differ from us on matters of belief and practice, as we outgrow our mania for "distinctives" in nonessentials so that we can emphasize our "commonalities" in essentials.[40] In highlighting the central core of essentials, we evangelicals can most probably forge a comprehensive ecumenical movement which would first draw evangelicals together and gradually all other Christ-honoring believers from different denominations and traditions.[41] This visible unity of the church must adopt a nonhierarchical and nonpaternalistic model in which the proliferation of smaller groups[42] will be combined with the ministries of

---

38. This means granting others the right to be wrong, and learning to persuade patiently rather than judging their motives. Though we may disagree, we must defend the right of others to express their opinions openly even if they are opposed to ours. May we have warm hearts and cool minds.

39. Our new synthesis can not be in theological, mission program, or institutional terms. If evangelical unity is guaranteed by doctrinal unity, why is there more divisiveness among us who have much more in common theologically than do the ecumenicals? If God is satisfied with functional cooperation between Christians, why is unity-in-diversity still not perceptible by us, much less by others?

40. Besides learning how to differentiate essentials from nonessentials, we also need to learn to have weaker convictions on the nonessentials as our group's "distinctives."

41. Can we not have a broader view that sees evangelicalism as only a segment of the whole Christian movement, and thus consider any man, woman or organization that calls upon the name of Jesus Christ to be part of us? It is theologically unsound to deny any evangelical the right to be affiliated and to work in nonevangelical institutions, like the World Council of Churches.

itinerant self-supporting personnel[43] who network and coordinate local evangelical initiatives at larger regional levels.

Thus, for an "awakening" work of the Spirit, we must put to death our old nature of exclusivism, sectarianism, and attributing guilt by association. Let us become like our Lord who transformed all the relationships and structures he came in touch with, bringing love and reconciliation among believers, and inviting hatred and persecution from unbelievers (yet responding with patience and forgiving nonviolence). May every evangelical (and Christian) in sincerity and eagerness submit our ongoing differences to honest and humble dialogue on the basis of God's word. Taking small steps towards such unity would significantly help bring about another "Awakening."

On Our Common Objective:
Biblical Justice for Social Involvement

This paper hopes that there will be no more uncertainties and objections in mainstream U.S. evangelicalism to the view that doing justice is at the very heart of biblical spirituality.[44] May the Spirit move us to produce "sample-signs" of God's shalom through our prayers and labors for

---

42. We must learn to build and multiply local Bible study and Christ centered groups (not necessarily as legal entities) to implement ministry programs with some localized foci, to release some gifted members as leaders for cross-communal ministries, to merge for strategic reasons, or even to let some groups die (regardless of how God used them in the past) to devote more resources to more God-glorifying ventures of faith. Most U.S. evangelical groups are simply too big, with hierarchical models. We have to learn to decentralize and also adopt the recent Catholic principle of subsidiarity which delegates decision making to the lowest possible unit of the organization.

43. We have to trust the Spirit to raise *ad hoc* integrative structures, publications, or leadership quote spontaneously that can coordinate and enhance cooperation through loose fellowships of informal fora, resident and itinerant leaders, and community-wide ministry projects. Love requires that we cooperate with the most conservative or the most liberal as much as possible.

44. It was euphemistically (and rightly) asked why this issue was raised at all so that we still needed such an "apology" in this E.R.T. What happened to the Chicago Declaration of Evangelical Social Concern (1973), Lausanne Covenant (1974), Evangelical Fellowship of India's Madras Declaration (1979), An Evangelical Commitment of Simple Life-style (1980), A Statement of Intent (1980), Grand Rapids Report: Relationship of Evangelism and Social Responsibility (1982), and Track III of Wheaton 1983, "The Church in Response to Human Need"? We need to humbly recognize that we need to catch up quickly with the U.S. Roman Catholic bishops and mainline denominations with firmer biblical underpinnings and better Christian mindsets.

appropriate applications of the kingdom ideals revealed in the Scriptures.

Awakenings will surely bring forth more social justice. It seems clear that great revivals were accompanied by great social reform movements.[45] However, their effects were usually short-lived or marginalized for lack of comprehensive and workable social ethic.[46] We need to forge a new kingdom vision based on the prophets and the New Testament. We must reject the Enlightenment notion that modern civilization must be built on secular foundations. Rather, if God is indeed Lord over all, then even social foundations must be religious.[47] God calls us to fight against the spiritual "powers and principalities" (both "secular" and religious) which reign over the nations and other social institutions including the churches.[48] We should then be able to work towards a biblically spiritual vision of peoples and nations truly "under God" in pluralistic societies.

U.S. evangelicalism still suffers from its social withdrawal since the "Great Reversal," its ideological polarity and the right's concern for political freedom and family values. Apathy towards social issues has grown because of the government's assumption of responsibility for the elderly, poor, handicapped, etc., and for health care, retirement provisions and medical decisions, and perhaps to a larger extent, because of

---

45. It seems clear that the two U.S. awakenings contributed to the early resistance to the British Crown, to the definition of the Constitutional form of government, to the abolitionist movement which led to the emancipation of slaves, and to the movements for public education and feminism. That such history has been obscured from social memory testifies to the dominant secularized state of U.S. society and the departure of modern evangelical Protestantism from its radical past.

46. E.g., in spite of the postmillenialist vision in the Civil war and subsequent emancipation, the evangelicals in the North had their social consciousness impaired by their preoccupation with "self-reliant individualism," while those in the South understood their social ethics to be restricted to personal conversion and private conduct. Without an "awakening social ethic," our present "successes" will continue to impede us from stopping militarism, racism, sexism, economic exploitation, and especially the nuclear arms build up and ecological destruction.

47. Both major worldviews (western and Marxist) have been founded on secularist and humanist philosophies; one is capitalist materialism and the other is dialectical materialism. We may restore our understanding of "Covenant Community" by studying the Reformers' views (especially Calvin's) more closely, or even learn from the Hindu concept of "*swaraz*" or Islam's concept of "*ummah*"; cf. I. Jesudacan, *A Gandhian Theology of Liberation* (Orbis, 1984), and P. Parshall, *Beyond the Mosque* (Baker, 1985), esp. 117–227. Also cf. D. Chilton, *Paradise Restored* (Tyler, TX: Reconstruction Press, 1985).

48. Cf. W. Wink, *Naming the Powers* (Fortress, 1984).

the comfortable middle-class lifestyle of the majority.[49] It is therefore very difficult to develop a comprehensive social ethic which can prophetically critique the cultural bondage to individualism, separatism, hedonism, and materialism and at the same time become acceptable in the modern U.S. context.

But, for a true awakening to occur, this prophetic social ethic must be developed, proclaimed, and lived out.[50] Such an ethic would put priority upon the survival needs of the poor rather than the alienation problems of those pursuing the "American Dream."[51] It would advocate austerity and simplicity in all things and more times of corporate prayer (and fasting) and ministry to others. Besides calling for a more equitable society, it would also call for a more ecological society, with less obsession for a technological progress that pollutes and rapes nature. This would lead further to direct criticism of the "consumer culture" created by our economic system.[52] Maybe we can learn from the Lakota Indians in South Dakota: a family, now poor, would soon receive gifts from others in the village. This tradition provides for a constant flow of goods from those who have enough or more to those who have little or nothing.[53]

A comprehensive Christian social ethic will be able to differentiate

---

49. The cultural ethos is therefore politically conservative (for this protects their lifestyles) and socially liberal (which gives freedom to do whatever they please).

50. Perhaps our success points rather starkly to our lack of being prophetic?

51. We must understand that God inquires about our treatment of the weakest members of society, more than our religious rituals or private experiences of piety (cf. Isa. 58; Amos 5:21-24; Matt. 25; James 2; 5:1-6). Our ethics seem hardly to grapple with the problems of the inner cities, single-parent homes and racial discrimination. Even worse, we have been largely unconcerned for the small rural farmers here and the rural poor worldwide who form the base of human subsistence.

52. Urbanized technological development financed mainly by big economic institutions has been presupposed as normative. The naked greed for profit central to this model has seldom been condemned as idolatrous and antithetical to the gospel itself by evangelicals. We have failed to think and work with the nonmaterialistic goals and motivations to build a just society according to God's kingdom ideals. Gandhi said, "The world has enough for everyone's need, but not enough for everyone's greed." Acts 4:32–35 presents us with an ideal to strive for (cf. 2 Cor. 8:1–15).

53. Mentioned in a recent newsletter of Jubilee Crafts, Philadelphia, Pennsylvania. Actually the American Indians are the only genuine U.S. natives. Perhaps justice requires that they must have a share in the governance of this land? Regrettably they did not even have a say in the drafting of the U.S. Constitution. The writer knows of only two evangelical groups which are working for Indian rights: The *Other Side*/Jubilee and the Friends Committee on National Legislation.

between church and state without isolating politics from religion. Our faith should be useful to humanize politics (and all spheres of life) and enrich them with Christian morality without fanatically imposing our agenda on the nation nor misusing the Bible for our narrow political purposes. Being blessed to live in a land of freedom with the opportunity to develop to our full potential and to share our opinions openly, we must also learn to destroy vestiges of evil in our society. Each generation has to apply the judgment of God's Word in order to dismantle evils, a few at a time, to make our world a better place to live in, create alternative politics, or even organize a political movement consistent with the biblical vision.[54] Let freedom mean the right to do what is just rather than to do what one pleases.

Doing social justice while belonging to the most powerful nation on earth (which claims to be the "policeman" or main defender of democracy worldwide) entails bigger responsibilities and difficulties. Basically, we need to prophesy against our "civil religion," and to differentiate between faith and ideology. We must criticize our national security manual which has put our first-line defenses in other parts of the world and stockpiled megatons of super-nuclear weapons. Unless we repent, our success will continue to blind us from the militaristic and technological ways of thinking in our local and foreign policies. We need to transform our "power politics" to "non-power politics" where there is the rejection of competition, coercion, and manipulation, and the development of processes and institutions which are essentially non-hierarchical and cooperative.

This wholistic ethic will help us recognize that our country is just one among many nations, and that we should be a "servant (not a master) to the nations."[55] We need to realize that we are those whose bless-

---

54. A. Kuyper's achievement has been suggested as a model. The present two U.S. political parties do not differ much from each other, and have hardly any clear political ideology. Popular movements which introduced new political ideas seldom swept the land. The antislavery and civil rights movements were two of the best, but the former alone created an actual political party which gained power in 1861. But ten years later it deviated from its intent, and what might have been the start of a golden age for the U.S. became a lost opportunity. The present nuclear freeze movement (which presents an alternative to the biggest chunk in the federal budget) shows some potential of becoming a real political force, but the recent conservative trend makes it relatively remote.

55. Many non-evangelicals have heard the cries of South African blacks better than most of us. How refreshing to hear apartheid denounced theologically in this E.R.T. As Carlos Fuentes (Mexican author) quipped, "what the U.S. does best is to understand itself; what it does worst is to understand others" (Time, June 16, 1986, 52).

edness came out of the dream of the religiously persecuted, politically oppressed, socially marginalized, and racially discriminated;[56] that the "American dream" can only be fulfilled by humanity as a whole, that all internationalization of the "American Dream" would make the U.S. a blessing to other peoples, while the Americanization of this dream makes the U.S. a burden for others.[57]

Above all, justice-ethics has important implications for our task of world evangelization: our concern for the needy and the oppressed should be similar to our concern for the lost. This means we should be sending the best of our youths who will struggle with "hard and dirty" issues like totalitarian governments, urbanization, mass unemployment, exploitation of natural resources, profit-making of big U.S.-based business, etc. Such integrative missioners will act in close coordination with national churches instead of being under highly centralized control of U.S.-based agencies.[58] We need more exchanges of less affluent personnel[59] instead of simple infusion of dollars.[60] We need more efforts and resources to check our nation's foreign policies,[61] and assail the oppressive international economic structures which impoverish T.T.W. economies and thus cripple our T.T.W. brethren from supporting their own ministries.

---

56. To be more exact, it was dreamt by Europeans and transplanted from Europe; cf. J. Moltmann, "American as Dream," *On Human Dignity* (Fortress, 1984), 147–61.

57. This dream has all too often been Americanized to justify the ideological self-righteousness of the U.S. "Empire," and the free enterprise of its transnational corporations and its mission-enterprises. The Americanization of this dream has made the human impossible. Cf. ibid., 149.

58. It is hoped that the new phenomenon of short-term missions would help U.S. churches to be better informed of the basic issues involved in present mission context which seem to have often been misrepresented by U.S. fund-raising mechanisms.

59. It is poor stewardship to send highly expensive (and often less effective) church-planters or institutional staff to do what nationals can do better. Besides, mission is best done in solidarity by incarnational living rather than at a distance by affluent patronizing.

60. There are less visible ways to serve as partners with our T.T.W. brethren (and help return the profits transferred here by U.S.-based transnational corporations from their "investments"). E.g., we can trade with T.T.W. Christian entrepreneurs, grant scholarships for locally owned, locally produced and locally managed situations or similar projects, etc. The fact stands that for most T.T.W. evangelicals to receive help from outside (often very visibly) gives a bad impression before their Muslim, Hindu, Buddhist and Communist neighbors who hardly receive any help from outside. Cf. R. Stanley, et al., "The Curse of Money on Missions to India," *Evangelical Missions Quarterly* (July, 1986): 294–302.

61. E.g., the U.S.'s uncritical support for Israel's policies and its attacks on Libya and Iraq has made it very difficult for us to evangelize Muslims and Arabs worldwide.

Indeed an awakening will result in a greater commitment to do justice, utilizing an integrative social ethic, acting in the spirit of love and humility. Such action will hopefully be better than the efforts of present secular movements (which, in many areas, are more effective than we are today). Our obsession for success will be overshadowed by our concern for the suffering;[62] our truimphalist spirit will turn to humble servanthood.

On our Compelling Future:
Bright Prospects for the Next Awakening

Having discussed some of the major areas that require reflection, maturation, and reformation in the theology and life of U.S. evangelicalism, this article concludes with the prospect of them being fulfilled in the near future. As mentioned above, this critique has a cautious yet optimistic outlook on the breaking forth of another "Awakening," perhaps even in our own generation.

Challenge for Radical Discipleship. Though the recent trends of evangelical Protestant handling of "success" leave much to be desired, there is hope that we can meet the great demands of becoming faithful kingdom-witnesses to the secularized and pluralistic world in which we live. There is hope we can achieve our God-given and God-empowered mission "beyond success" in the manner by which God wants us to carry it out.

We can start changing our messages of "easy believism" to those of "radical discipleship." We can call people to help build a "spiritual civilization" with eternal glory rather than earthly prosperity as goal. We can shift mainstream evangelical thought from its defensive and conservative posture of "self-satisfied piety" to a daring and radical outlook of "suffering servanthood" in order to share what we have in Christ with the world that waits to know God's love. We can amend our present tendencies to follow the "way of the cross" rather than the "ways of the world." We can emphasize the call for "inner discipline" and hard work to energize us out of our spiritual anemia and powerlessness to transform society according to God's Word. We can call for radical commitment to Christ, a call to take his teachings seriously even with all their costly *consequences.*[63]

---

62. We would less be asking, "What is God's will for my life?" and more, "What is God's will?" (or "What is God's program on earth and where do I fit in?"); adapted from John Perkins, *Quiet Revolution* (Word Books, 1976).

Demand for Voluntary Nonsuccess. Another "Awakening" must involve fresh obedience to our Lord's costly *demands* (not just *counsels*) to become voluntarily poor or voluntarily unsuccessful in the world's eyes (esp. Luke 9:57–62; 14:25–33).[64] Christ's words are not just to be applauded, but to be followed. Just as our Lord became a "suffering servant" to fulfill his mission to save the world (esp. Isa. 53; 2 Cor. 4:21; 8:8; Phil. 2:5–8), so we are called to imitate his example to do his mission to save others (esp. 2 Cor. 4:7–18; 6:3–10; Col. 1:24–25; 1 Peter 2:21–25).

Our success has obscured the Gospel, for it seems clear that many who claim to be evangelicals have believed primarily for superficial, material motives rather than deep spiritual ones. Though our service in Christ's name should have pushed us out of ourselves to make us identify more with the poor and the lost, our success (with its affluence, prestige, and power) has isolated and separated us from the poverty and lostness of many.[65] Our success has made us too fearful to venture out of our middle-class shelters (such as cozy sanctuaries and suburban homes) with their assuring sense of earthly security, so that the visionary ingenuity and missionary fervor which the Spirit works within us have been overpowered.[66]

This means that we should stop emphasizing personal success (including self-fulfillment, financial prosperity, and freedom from suffering) and institutional success (e.g., big churches, big budgets, slick ministries), and rather emphasize the choice of unpretentious vocations and lowly ministries which fit the priorities of God's kingdom. Further, this should also mean that we must consciously choose not to make full use of our success, as our Lord himself turned down the temptations to use worldly means to accomplish his divine redemptive mission.

---

63. Often our calls for moderation or balance in Christian living have led to lukewarmness, superficiality and mediocrity. Rather than seeking to avoid failure and death, we should seek to risk failure and death for Christ's sake.

64. The Scriptures seem clear that repentance must include renunciation of the world and its ways (cf. 1 John 2:15–17; James 4:1–10).

65. Success has made us oblivious (unintentionally?) to the "Go" of the Great Commission. For us, it now means "go among," or even "go down" to be in touch with and to reach out to the lost and needy, risking personal discomfort, damage to our reputation, and even *loss* of our success.

66. In concrete terms, an awakening would effect the sending forth of at least one-tenth among us to serve as Christian "Peace Corps" (without C.I.A. ties) and holistic missionaries here and everywhere.

Instead, he consistently lived and suffered as a poor servant so as to minister (and ultimately die) among those whom he came to save.

Such detachment from success would take away our crusading and truimphalist spirit of paternalism. We have talked about servant-leadership for too long, yet we continue to cling to our positions and the structures of prestige and power which perpetuate dehumanizing relationships. Most of our "spiritual leaders" perpetuate hierarchical elitism with biblical or theological platitudes that are actually cover-ups for their own insecurities and anxieties. It is only by our renunciation of elegance, affluence, or prestige (which we use to impose ourselves on others, especially to hasten their conversion or discipleship) that we can truly become God's ambassadors for reconciliation; to give his invitation persuasively, yet also wait patiently for people's response *alongside* them, as equals, as friends, as copilgrims, as servants.

Demand for Incarnational Counter-Success. Obedience to Christ's call for voluntary nonsuccess should lead further to counterculture communal lifestyles and incarnational witness. In our success-oriented materialistic society, we need the support of counter communities with considerable vitality and maturity. Collectively, we can turn away from the model of Christendom where Christian authority in earthly affairs is asserted through the social and political power of elitist hierarchies, while our churches are organized as super-churches according to the same model of domination.[67] Rather, we can adopt the servant-church model where our authority in society is expressed through the "powerless power" of little nobodies and disenfranchised groups, while our churches are based on personal relationships marked by solidarity, equality, and mutual service.[68] Such grassroots churches will develop committed Christians and equip them to address both concrete community concerns (as starting points for heightening social consciousness) and to broaden their concern to national and global issues.

Church authority would then be primarily based on spiritual gifts and moral character (especially whether one lives and serves among the

---

67. Such a top-down model is seen in our fascination for more traditional forms of church life, like highly educated clergy, more elaborate liturgies, establishment values, and elitist evangelical-owned and operated institutions.

68. Such bottom-up model will be shown in more spontaneous, egalitarian, lay-oriented and highly innovative forms of community life, focusing on culturally marginalized and economically impoverished communities. This nonpaternalistic and transideological model is necessary to discern which trends are humanizing and liberating and which are not.

poor) rather than on "success" credentials and charismatic personalities (with ostentatious lifestyles). Our heroes and superstars would live more like the early apostles who left all they had in order to serve and die as self-sacrificing ministers among the poor. These pastor-teachers would dare to preach unpopular views,[69] even if their congregations would dwindle. Churches may have to become "little flocks" once again, but they will act as real salt and light to the worldly culture (however American or success-dominated it may be)—as nonretreating, courageous, incarnated counter-communities.

Such awakening will also reverse the present trends toward giant power formations (political, economic, media, ecclesiastical, etc.). It will diffuse these centers of power (and oppression) into stewpots[70] of *smaller* community units.[71] Social institutions will be organized for the fulfillment of each one's self-sufficiency or one's isolated nuclear family. This does not mean the rejection of the use of power, but the limitation of the abuse (or misuse) of power. Hence, it seems best for us to try to humanize institutions by seeking to decentralize and distribute power from within[72]—as incarnational agents of renewal with our distinctly different values and "counter-success" lifestyles.

Reasons for Prudent Optimism. Francis Schaeffer was quite pessimistic,[73] and we have many reasons to be pessimistic, too. It is almost

---

69. Our Bible expositions would not only critique secular and non-Christian idolatries, but also the defects of biblical faith itself where our theologies, structures and rituals have become idolatries of success, social oppression and elitist privileges, as well as those which ignore God's agenda of doing mission and justice for, with and by the poor.

70. *Stewpots* make tasty brews in which each ingredient retains its identity (a picture of unity in diversity), whereas *melting pots* dissolve the elements into indistinct entities.

71. "Small" is not only beautiful, but also more humane. Structures are managed by humans who (no matter how godly) can not be fully trusted to be persistently incorruptible by the power of power, and who always tend to become paternalistic, self-aggrandizing, and arrogant. Thus, scaling them down helps set limits or controls on human and institutional abuses of power. Smaller institutions are less concerned about who gets the credit (or the profit or the harvest). Cf. E. F. Schumacher, *Small is Beautiful* (Harper and Row, 1973); G. McRobie, *Small is Possible* (Harper and Row, 1981), and T. Sine, *The Mustard Seed Conspiracy* (Word, 1981).

72. This means a reformation of our separatist tendency to start "evangelical institution" to try to impact the institutions from without (usually to avoid persecution it seems). Incarnational witness within institutions seems to fit the biblical imageries of salt in meat, light in darkness, seed in soil, leaven in bread, and sheep among wolves.

73. Though Schaeffer was pessimistic on the whole, he also believed in "substantial healing" of human problems as signs of the kingdom; cf. *True Spirituality* (Tyndale House, 1972), chapter 11.

impossible to break out of our "middle-class captivity" to the dominant culturally materialistic, politically conservative, socially liberal atmosphere. Our success has all too often made us blind or silent against the many unchristian behaviors and policies, as long as our comfortable and luxurious lifestyles (and private piety) are not threatened. The picture of the Babylon-to-fall (Rev. 18) depicts twentieth-century U.S. more than any other nation on earth.

However, there are six good reasons to believe that another "Awakening" can occur in and through U.S. evangelicalism soon—not in naive optimism, but in confident biblical realism.[74] First, revivals or awakenings have happened before—especially when the rediscovering grows from our root orthodoxy and orthopraxy than from a call to revolutionary innovation or rebellion.

Secondly, there are "radical disciples" and radical communities in U.S. evangelicalism who have already chosen the way of the cross, voluntary nonsuccess and incarnational counter-success. They are already enabling the marginalized to witness in a pluralistic and materialistic society. They are networking individuals, churches, parachurch groups, and secular service agencies to help expedite the church's holistic mission. They are already showing that faithfulness to the Gospel is worth the price—any price, including imprisonment or even martyrdom. Not many—but these few "mustard seeds" could very well be the sparks which will spread spiritual "forest fires" across the U.S. and even around the world.

Third, the U.S. provides one of the best cultural contexts for the free explosion of Christian religiosity. Its political freedom,[75] press freedom, economic semi-equality (relatively small gap between the rich and the poor), democratic structures, and religious pluralism are better than social conditions found in most of the rest of the world. Thus, "to whom much is given, much is required" means that God has given U.S.-based evangelicals the greater responsibility to lead in the fulfillment of his plan for the world.[76]

---

74. Cf. J. R. W. Stott, *Involvement. Vol. II* (Revell, 1984), 247–64.

75. The U.S. has allowed a healthy proliferation of issue-oriented groups. Though some have grown too big, they can easily be decentralized if given just a bit of political vision and political will.

76. Of course, God can surprise us by giving the task of actually effecting his awakenings among other Christians who live in more difficult nonsuccess situations (like China perhaps?).

Fourth, most people in the U.S. are vigorously self-critical people of conscience and compassion, with a strong sense of responsibility. More and more U.S. evangelicals (probably more so than non-evangelicals) are realizing that recent trends are a cause for deep concern, and are willing to consider the reversal of the cultural values of a success-dominated and success-plagued society. This sense of dissatisfaction will hopefully result in shifts of worldviews,[77] which will in turn lead to the recognition of the problem's roots (i.e., the love of money and success) and the problem's *spiritual solution* which is the open future of the kingdom of the nonsuccess oriented and the unsuccessful "suffering servant." This one has called us to "follow his footsteps" (cf. 1 Peter 2:21) faithfully till he comes again to reward his counter-success servants.

Fifth, we can also count on the adventurous, frontier spirit of most U.S. residents. They dare to try new and risky things, and have strong ambitions to excel and succeed. If they know what is best for themselves and for the world in God's sight, they may risk even their all to give it their best shot. The U.S. is still a young nation, growing out of its turbulent adolescence. Hopefully, guided by a revived biblical vision (which was part of its former national self-consciousness), and tempered by a Christian conscience, we can see another "Awakening" as it matures to venturesome adulthood.

And above all, theologically, our understanding of God's kingdom tells us that God desires that all peoples will be saved, and thus intends his people to be effective witnesses of love and concern for the physical, psychological, social, and spiritual well-being of all humankind. The period between the first and second comings of Christ is one of struggle and warfare between the kingdoms. But, of course, the outcome is never in doubt: Satan and his forces were already defeated at the Cross. God, in his sovereign wisdom, has chosen to give us the privilege of participating in the sure victory by actively planting the seeds which represent his kingdom on earth.[78] Our weak (and even sinful) efforts toward

---

77. Culture outlooks on the meanings of society and life must change as people get tired of superficial remedies which have not only aggravated the disease, but also brought world civilization to the brink of total destruction and annihilation.

78. These are real seeds; our historical "good works" are prototypes of what is to come, and God will accept them up into his future kingdom (Rev. 21:24–26; cf. 2 Cor. 5:10, etc.). Historical events are of eternal significance, although God's kingdom will not simply be the result of what humans do in history. Such anticipations of the kingdom-on-earth tomorrow (though never perfect) is justification enough for our serious and courageous action for it today—even if we do not experience success today or tomorrow.

effecting an awakening are not insignificant; they are works of faith, hope, and love, the "already" signs of the "not yet" kingdom, which sometimes have exploded (and may explode again and again) in dramatic social transformation to the glory of God. In fact, even in many instances, others have already become part of his kingdom's advance. We may join this success not so much by the voluntary obedience of God's people, but primarily by the force of his actions through various counter-success movements happening even outside our circles.

May this critique challenge all of us who are concerned about the glory and the kingdom of God to take small (and some giant) steps of faith into becoming nonsuccess volunteers and counter-success incarnational servants of God to bring his church to full maturity beyond success. May we see another "Awakening" in our generation, as God moves us to follows Jesus in the way of the cross with his resurrection power.

Latin America

Introduction

Even a superficial reading of the history of Christianity in Latin America yields an important paradox. In no part of the world has modern history been more intertwined with the spread of Christianity; in no part of the world do Christians feel more estranged from their own history. Part of this lies in the unique circumstances associated with the coming of Christianity, just over five hundred years ago. What might be euphemistically called "evangelization" was really a conquest, a "just war" waged against infidels by divine right and based on pontifical bulls. As a result, until very recently, Christianity has often been viewed as an alien and oppressive influence, and the Church has been seen as allied with the reigning political powers. Holders of both religious and political power have excluded the vast majority of the populace from meaningful participation.

So that while most Latin Americans would call themselves Christians, the people, as Enrique Dussel has put it, have always felt outside their own history.[1] Not only has her history been written by others, it has been dominated by a Greek conception in which reality lies beyond the historical world in the eternal realm. The form of Constantinian Christianity which came to Latin America was the earthly shadow of this divine reality, indifferent to the vast suffering and powerlessness it inflicted on the people of the continent.

But in the recent history of the region, two realities have dramatically changed the nature of Christianity in Latin America: One is the rise of Liberation theology and the other is the explosive growth of Protestant—primarily Pentecostal—Christianity. Inevitably, theological reflection coming from the region must interact with these two realities. But even these recent developments must always be read against the

---

1. See *The History of the Church in Latin America: An Interpretation* (San Antonio: Mexican-American Cultural Center, 1974), 3.

backdrop of the centuries of alienation from oppressive government and a Church insensitive to the needs of her people.

Liberation theology is a theological movement, primarily in the Catholic Church, that arose in response to the political and economic realities of the region. The massive poverty of the people of Latin America came to the attention of the world just after the Second World War. The Ango-American-sponsored Alliance for Progress was initiated to respond to the continent's economic situation. But by 1960 it was clear that the program had failed miserably—to this day the whole notion of "development" (or "desarrollo") has a negative connotation to many people in Latin America. In the early 1960s the unrest was evident particularly on university campuses. The Second Vatican Council (1960-1965) called by Pope John XXIII to "bring the Church up to date" became the ecclesial context for the rise of liberation themes. Liberation theologians asked, in the light of the suffering of Latin peoples and the Second Vatican's emphasis on the Church as the People of God, how the Bible might be read from the situation of poverty in Latin America. Many began to wonder: What if we used the idea of God's liberation as the dominant metaphor for salvation rather than, say, forgiveness of sins?[2]

One of the values of Samuel Escobar's chapter below is that it puts this critical movement in its theological and historical context. On the one hand it can be argued that Liberation theology has returned to theology in Latin America (and elsewhere) certain biblical emphases that had been lost, and that to a certain extent had been anticipated by the Protestant movement of the 19th century.[3] At least two of these themes might be briefly mentioned.

First, Liberation theologians restored to the theological conversation the central role played by the practice of Christian obedience. Dussel and others have pointed out convincingly that our western captivity to Greek categories has made us feel that knowing about God (and thus right knowledge) is for many in the West the part of theology that really mattered. Doing the truth, or obeying God, was something of lesser importance, a matter of applying what is true. Latin American theolo-

---

2. The classic expression of this theology is Gustavo Gutierrez' *Theology of Liberation* (ET: Orbis, 1974; Second Edition, 1989). Though this book appeared in the Spanish edition in 1971, Gutierrez had given the outline of the book in an important speech in Switzerland in 1969.

3. Professor Escobar makes the case for this view in his recent book *La Fe Evangelica y las Teologias de la Libercion* (El Paso, Texas: Casa Bautista, 1987).

gians realized that this overlooked important sociological and biblical realities. Liberationists pointed out that people are immersed in practices that precede (and in many ways inform) their formal reflection on theology. The fact that these practices have theological significance suggests that there is another way of describing the movement in theology, that moves from practice to reflection, and that can be seen as an important supplement to the usual movement from theory to application.[4]

A second lesson that many have learned from Liberation theology is what is sometimes called the "preferential option for the poor." What if theology, rather than being a learned discussion among the educated elite, was a movement among the people themselves, who had for so long been excluded from theological significance? What would happen if Scriptures were read again from the point of view of those outside of power, rather than by those in power? Did not the redemptive work of God in Scripture from the beginning have a special consideration for those who are at the margins of power as the world sees it? Many people have come to believe that, when this is carefully distinguished from the Marxist notion of class conflict, the "option for the poor" is an important biblical insight that the Church has sometimes overlooked. In its official statement about Liberation theology, the Vatican went so far as to agree that Scripture gives "preference to the poor, without exclusion, whatever their form of poverty, because they are preferred by God."[5]

These lessons, and others we might mention, have been helpful to many, but that is not the whole story. Some have seen in the emphasis on practice a pelagian tendency to believe human efforts could bring in the kingdom; and the special interest in the poor has led many to see the shape of that kingdom solely in terms of political socialism. This has led many evangelicals to be wary of Liberation theology. And it is from this segment of the Church that the major, if implicit, criticism of the emphases of Liberation theologians has come.

The explosive growth of the (primarily) Pentecostal Protestant churches, as we have noted, is one of the most striking characteristics of recent Latin American history. While there has been relatively little seri-

---

4. In hermeneutics this dual movement has come to be called the hermeneutical circle, or spiral. See Anthony Thiselton's important recent study *New Horizons in Hermeneutics: The Theory and Practice of Transforming Biblical Reading* (Grand Rapids: Zondervan, 1992).

5. Joseph Ratzinger, *Instruction on Certain Aspects of the Theology of Liberation* (Rome: Sacred Congregation for the Doctrine of the Faith, 1984), 24.

ous theological reflection on these issues from the Pentecostal side,[6] many observers have pointed out that the liberationist emphasis on practice and political reform (or even revolution) has neglected the level of spirituality.[7] In spite of liberationists' claim to attend to the real needs of the region, the pentecostal emphasis on a personal relationship with Christ in the context of a lively worship experience has appealed more immediately to the people of Latin America than the theological and worship reforms represented by Liberation theology.

Whatever its causes, the Protestant explosion raises critical questions about the future of theology in the region and calls for close study from the evangelical perspective. Our two articles explore this situation from two different points of view. Since the Protestant churches are the fastest growing churches in Latin America, it is critical to know their historical roots, and, more to the point, why these roots have been inimical to the development of an indigenous theology.

Antonio Barro from Brazil asks why there has been so little theological reflection among Protestants in Latin America. The article makes an important connection between theological and cultural identity. It could be, he points out, that Protestants have not found their theological voice because they have not been sufficiently rooted in their own history and culture. The zeal and enthusiasm of the missionaries, even their honest motivation to serve God and their neighbor, could not make up for their inability to understand the historical and social situation of the people. This weakness, coupled with the individualism and other-worldliness of the theology they brought from North America, pre-determined that the churches they planted would be theologically impotent in the Latin American context.

Samuel Escobar's chapter brings the discussion up to the present. In many ways continuing the theme of his earlier work, he notes that a Protestant voice has been present for some time. This voice, represented largely by members of the Latin American Theological Fraternity, while appreciating some of the themes of liberationists, was biblically critical

---

6. The relevant literature is cited in the valuable issue of *Pneuma: The Journal of the Society for Pentecostal Studies* 13 (1991), see especially Manuel J. Gaxiola-Gaxiola, "Latin American Pentecostalism: A Mosaic within a Mosaic," 123-27.

7. The weakness of Liberation theology in the area of spirituality has been widely recognized and, to a certain extent, it has been addressed in the later so-called pastoral writings of Liberation theologians. See, e.g., Eduarod Bonnin, ed. *Espiritualidad y Liberacion en America Latina* (San Jose, Costa Rica: DEI, 1982), and G. Gutierrez, *We Drink From Our Own Wells* (Maryknoll, NY: Orbis, 1984).

of the movement from the beginning. While he would not disagree with Barro's negative assessment of evangelical theology in Latin America, he helpfully points out that articulate voices were being raised already in the 1960s. His discussion not only serves as an important history of recent evangelical theology (his notes provide what is probably the best recent bibiography of evangelical writing on Latin America), but he points out the direction that this theology will be likely to take. Justice, poverty, oppression, and liberation, he notes, are not incidental themes which liberationists have discovered, but they are themes that "cannot be separated from the core of God's self-revelation in Jesus Christ." And they will be central to the task that Escobar calls us to: the development of a missiological Christology.

The Search for a Missiological Christology in Latin America

Samuel Escobar

Evangelical theology in Latin America emerges from churches that are relatively young and fast-growing within the general decline of Christendom. This means that evangelical theologians find themselves at the margins of the cultural establishments of their countries but at the center of the missionary action of their churches. Their interlocutor has been more frequently the evangelical activist with whom they sit in the pew or march on the streets on Sunday, than the academician crossing the "t's" and dotting the "i's" of the history of western ideas. They are part of communities that see the world as a territory to be "conquered for Christ," and the Gospel as a transforming message that will bring forth a new spiritual, social, and political creation. For the time being they find themselves in Galilee but they are surely committed to taking the transforming gospel to Judea, Samaria, and even unto the ends of the earth.

Approaching the task of doing theology from this missionary stance, we come to experience the end of the twentieth century as a transitional moment, one of those periods in which theologizing becomes at the same time painful and fertile. Remembrance of the fifth centennial of the Iberian conquest and Christianization of the Americas brought back to the missiological debate the old question of the relationship between mission and empire, evangelization and civilization, gospel and culture—especially within the frame of transcultural mission. Controversies around it reflect clearly that thinking Christians everywhere question the centuries-old assumption that "Christianity is inescapably associated with the dynamic character of western civilization."[1] The question of how God acts in history, within the ambiguities of the rise

---

1. Max Warren, *Social History and Christian Mission* (London: SCM Press, 1967), 84.

and fall of empires, has been posed again with new relevancy. The urgency of the question is also determined by the need for a radical departure from the Constantinian pattern of a missionary enterprise that relied on military power, economic conquest, and technological prowess. This demands a search for a fresh look at the biblical pattern.

On the other hand, around the world today there is a growing awareness that Europe and North America, the strongholds of Christianity at the beginning of the century, are rapidly becoming pagan territories where the Christian presence must take again a missionary stance. In the northern world, this involves a perplexing assignment, "Christians are now in the odd position of trying to destroy, or at least critique, the very culture we created so that we can be more nearly faithful."[2] Latin America was precisely the first part of the world where this kind of critical appraisal of Christendom took place. The Protestant missionary presence at the beginning of this century forced upon Catholicism the question of its nominalism, its institutionalism without spirit.[3] Only in the sixties, with the coming of Vatican II and the rise of Liberation theologies, did Catholics themselves develop a self-critical stance that questioned the cherished assumptions of Christendom in Latin America.[4]

A growing number of evangelical pastors, missionaries, and theological educators are involved in the search for answers to these questions within the Latin American context. For us neither the Geneva style ecumenical dialogue, nor the Liberation theologies born in Roman Catholic soil could offer adequate answers.[5] Ecumenical theology from Geneva was shaped by a mood and a stance that reflected the uncertainties and the fatigue of a declining Protestantism in Europe. Liberation theology from Catholic sources was heavily dependent on the assump-

---

2. Stanley Hauerwas and Will Willimon, "Why *Resident Aliens* Struck a Chord," *Missiology* 19 (4): 422.

3. In this regard the meeting of the International Missionary Council in Jerusalem 1928 was one of the first instances in which awareness of the need to consider Europe and North America mission fields became public. This fact was not unrelated to the fact that it was also in this meeting that the validity of Protestant missionary work in Latin America was acknowledged by the ecumenical movement. See Gonzalo Báez-Camargo, "Mexico: A Long Stretch from Edinburgh," *The Ecumenical Review* 16:266–73.

4. I have studied the missionary origins of this theological development in the article "Missions and Renewal in Latin American Catholicism," *Missiology* 15(2):33–46.

5. Samuel Escobar, "The Kingdom of God, Eschatology of Social and Political Ethics in Latin America," *Theological Fraternity Bulletin (TFB)* Buenos Aires 1 (1975): 1–42; *Christian Mission and Social Justice* (Scottsdale: Herald Press, 1978).

tion that Latin America was "a Christian continent." In such a predicament evangelical theologians became engaged in the development of a contextual theology which aimed to be "forged in the heat of evangelical reality in Latin America, in faithfulness to the Word of God."[6] That theology was not to be "an adaptation of an existing theology of universal validity of a particular situation . . . aided by benevolent missionary paternalism."[7] Rather, its aim was to offer

> A new open-ended reading of Scripture with a hermeneutic in which the biblical text and the historical situation become mutually engaged in a dialogue whose purpose is to place the Church under the Lordship of Jesus Christ in its particular context.[8]

Within the evangelical world, the Lausanne movement after 1974 came to accept that there is a new global missionary situation which includes growing and vigorous Third World churches. This made possible a new reading of Scripture as a communal exercise involving the multicultural and international fellowship of believers around the planet. Latin Americans made an important contribution to the discussions about "Gospel and Culture" in Willowbank 1978, sharing the conviction that there was an urgent need to develop a fresh reading of the Bible as a dynamic interplay between text and interpreter.[9] This contribution was incorporated in the *Willowbank Report* which sets an agenda for evangelical mission theology. Protestantism can only be enriched and revitalized by it, being ready to accept the consequences of this new dialogical situation:

> Today's readers cannot come to the text in a personal vacuum, and should not try to. Instead, they should come with an awareness of concerns stemming from their cultural background, personal situation, and responsibility to others. These concerns will influence the questions which are put to the Scriptures. What is received back, however, will not be answers only, but more questions. As we address Scripture, Scripture addresses us. We find that our culturally conditioned presup-

6. Samuel Escobar, "Biblical Content and Anglo-Saxon Trappings in Latin American Theology," *Occasional Bulletin*, Latin American Theological Fraternity 3 (Oct. 1972): 2.

7. C. René Padilla, "Biblical Foundations: A Latin American Study" *Evangelical Review of Theology* 7(1): 86.

8. Ibid.

9. See especially the contributions of Orlando Costas and René Padilla in J. R. W. Stott and R. Coote, eds., *Down to Earth* (Grand Rapids: Eerdmans, 1980).

positions are being challenged and our questions corrected. In fact, we are compelled to reformulate our previous questions and to ask fresh ones. So the living interaction precedes.[10]

In this process Latin American evangelicals also found valuable parallels and coincidences with the questions being explored by evangelicals in other parts of the world,[11] with the insights of the Anabaptist tradition creatively uncovered by John Howard Yoder,[12] with the probing and questioning of Jacques Ellul into Scripture, tradition, and sociology,[13] and with the post-imperial missiology of men such as John Stott, Michael Green, Andrew Walls, and Lesslie Newbigin.[14]

Evangelical Theology in Latin America

In the last two decades, evangelical theologians in Latin America[15] have entered in an active and fruitful dialogue at a global level. The main foci of that dialogue have been the Lausanne Movement, the Theological Commission of the World Evangelical Fellowship, and the International Fellowship of Evangelical Mission Theologians. In the case of Latin America most of the contributors to this dialogue have come from the Latin American Theological Fraternity founded in 1970.[16] Within these circles, and in spite of the hostility of some conservative missiolo-

---

10. Stott and Coote, 334.

11. See for instance the confluence of fifteen authors from around the world in their commentary of the Lausanne Covenant, C. René Padilla, 1976.

12. Especially his books *The Original Revolution* (Scottsdale: Herald Press, 1972) and *The Politics of Jesus* (Grand Rapids: Eerdmans, 1972). For an explanation of the relevance of the Anabaptist position for Latin America see Samuel Escobar, "The Kingdom of God, Eschatology and Social and Political Ethics in Latin America," *Theological Fraternity Bulletin (TFB)* Buenos Aires 1 (1975): 1–42.

13. The relevance of Ellul's insights for Latin America comes from his effort to read Scripture and the Christian tradition from his French context, which has been subject to the same ideological influences prevalent in Latin America. Ellul is a lay theologian who has not lost his Protestant identity.

14. For a description of post-imperial missiology and its ideological and theological sources see Samuel Escobar, "A Movement Divided: Three Approaches to World Evangelization Stand in Tension with One Another," *Transformation* 8(4): 7–13.

15. In the Spanish language the word "Evangélico," which would be the literal translation of "Evangelical," is used as a synonym of "Protestant." However, since the sixties church life and theology have developed in two streams within the Protestant minority: "ecumenical Protestantism" for some of the oldest churches related to the conciliar ecumenical movement, and "evangelical Protestantism" that in its ethos and theology would be closer to the position to which we usually refer with the term "evangelical" in English. This position is also shared by some of the largest Pentecostal communities.

gists in the United States,[17] the concerns and the reflection rising from the life of evangelical churches in Latin America have entered the global dialogue. This has proved the validity of the conviction that

> We should seek with equal care to avoid theological imperialism or theological provincialism. A church's theology should be developed by the community of faith out of the Scripture in interaction with other theologies of the past and present, and with the local culture and its needs.[18]

Evangelical thinkers in Latin America have worked in a two-pronged theological approach. On the one hand they have carried out a *critical task*, which has included an ongoing debate with the Liberation theologies that dominated the theological scenario in the last two decades. Such a critical task in some ways was a continuation of the debate with the Protestant predecessors of these theologies.[19] The most extensive and organic works embodying this critical approach come from Andrew Kirk,[20] Emilio A. Núñez,[21] and Samuel Escobar.[22] More

---

16. For a history of the Latin American Theological Fraternity see Anthony Christopher Smith's *The Essentials of Missiology from the Evangelical Perspective of the "Fraternidad Teológica Latinoamericana"* (Southern Baptist Theological Seminary, Louisville, Kentucky, Ph.D. dissertation, 1983), which focuses on the Fraternity's missiology. For dissertations about other aspects see Dieumemme E. Noelliste, *The Church and Human Emancipation: A Critical Comparison of Liberation Theology and the Latin American Theological Fraternity* (Evanston: Garrett Evangelical Theological Seminary, Ph.D. dissertation, 1987); Valdir Raul Steuernagel, *The Theology of Mission in Relation to Social Responsibility within the Lausanne Movement* (Chicago: Lutheran School of Theology, Ph.D. dissertation, 1988) and Daniel C. Elliott, *Theology and Mission from Latin America: The Latin American Theological Fraternity* (Wheaton College, M.A. Thesis, 1992).

17. Brazilian missiologist Valdir Steuernagel (*The Theology of Mission in Relation to Social Responsibility within the Lausanne Movement*) has documented the debates and the hostility of North American missiologists from the "Church Growth" school against Latin American Evangelical theologians (see especially 164 ff., and 224 ff.).

18. Stott and Coote, 334.

19. Protestant antecedents of Liberation theologies are studied by Alan Neely, *Protestant Antecedents of the Latin American Theology of Liberation* (Washington, D.C.: American University, Ph.D. dissertation, 1976). Several Latin American evangelicals offer a critical approach in C. René Padilla, 1974.

20. *Liberation Theology* (Atlanta: John Knox Press, 1975).

21. *Liberation Theology* (Chicago: Moody Press, 1985).

22. *La fe evangélica y las teologías de la liberación* (El Paso: Casa Bautista de Pulicaciones, 1987), and *Liberation Themes in Reformational Perspective* (Sioux Center: Dordt College, 1989).

recently several other contributions were gathered in a volume outlining an Anabaptist commentary about Liberation theologies.[23] What is distinctive of the evangelical stance is an emphasis on the primacy of biblical authority in their theological method and the insistence on keeping evangelistic activity at the center of the mission of the church. However, their critical task has also developed into a clarification of the theological assumptions—not always explicit—of the so-called Church Growth mission theory with its overwhelming institutional and propagandistic weight.[24]

On the other hand, evangelical theologians have given themselves to the *constructive task* of developing a theology of mission that would express the dynamic reality and the missionary thrust of their churches in Latin America. They have been working to provide a solid biblical basis for new patterns of evangelism and discipleship, in continuity with their heritage of a Bible-centered form of presence and mission committed to spiritual and social transformation. They have worked on the assumption that if commitment to biblical authority is going to do more than simply pay lip service to biblical truth, a fresh exploration is required into the depths of the biblical text, with the questions raised by the Latin American context. Moreover, commitment to biblical authority should not be limited to certain beliefs in the area of soteriology, but also to fresh explorations into a biblically-based social ethics.

An eloquent example of this twofold approach may be found in the dense pages of *Mission between the Times*.[25] In this important book and other writings[26] René Padilla offers a missiological reflection based on detailed exegesis of the biblical text. Orlando Costas' approach was evangelical in its inspiration and emphasis but less polemical against Liberation theologies, and at the same time more pragmatic about Church Growth missiology. His book *Christ outside the Gate*[27] and his posthumous work *Liberating News*[28] show him at his best in the way of formulating a theology of contextual evangelization and mission. In

23. Daniel Schipani, ed., *Freedom and Discipleship* (Maryknoll, NY: Orbis, 1989).

24. Wilbert Shenk, ed., *Exploring Church Growth* (Grand Rapids: Eerdmans, 1983).

25. C. René Padilla, *Mission between the Times* (Grand Rapids: Eerdmans, 1985).

26. Padilla has edited several collective volumes by evangelical theologians, such as *Fe cristiana y Latinoamérica hoy* (Buenos Aires: Ediciones Certeza, 1974); *The New Face of Evangelicalism* (Downers Grove: InterVarsity Press, 1976); *Nuevas alternativas de educación teológica* (Buenos Aires/Grand Rapids: Nueva Creación/Eerdmans, 1986).

27. Orlando E. Costas, *Christ outside the Gate* (Maryknoll: Orbis, 1982).

28. Costas, *Liberating News* (Grand Rapids: Eerdmans, 1989).

both books Costas takes Liberation themes but works with them so as to incorporate the missionary thrust and the evangelistic passion of the evangelical perspective. Another important distinctive of Costas' work is his effort to take seriously the dialogue with missiology and ecclesiology from mainline and ecumenical theologians.[29]

Without any pretension of being exhaustive in relation to themes or authors we see evangelical reflection focusing around a cluster of themes of immediate concern to evangelical churches. There are five main areas of research and exploration. First, what could be described as the search for a pneumatic and contextual hermeneutics, in which René Padilla[30] and Emilio A. Núñez[31] have been more explicit. Second, the development of a missiological Christology, with several Latin American contributions that we will consider in detail in this chapter. Third, a holistic missiology with contributions in the area of soteriology from Mortimer Arias,[32] in anthropology from Sidney Rooy[33] and Tito Paredes,[34] in historical theology from Valdir Steuernagel[35] and Samuel Escobar.[36] The fourth area is what we could call a grassroots and post-western ecclesiology with contribution from Guillermo Cook,[37] John Driver,[38] and René Padilla.[39] The fifth emerges from the Pentecostal movement and centers on a missiological pneumatology[40] and a self-

29. Costas' doctoral dissertation (*Theology of the Crossroads in Contemporary Latin America* [Amsterdam: Rodopi, 1976]) dealt with the missiology of the Ecumenical theologians of Latin American Protestantism.

30. "Biblical Foundations: A Latin American Study," *Evangelical Review of Theology* 7(1): 79–88.

31. *Liberation Theology* (Chicago: Moody Press, 1985).

32. *Announcing the Reign of God* (Philadelphia: Fortress Press, 1984); *The Great Commission* (Nashville: Abingdon Press, 1992).

33. "A Theology of Humankind," *Exploring Church Growth*, Wilbert Shenk, ed. (Grand Rapids: Eerdmans, 1983), 191–206.

34. *El evangelio en vasos de barro* (Lima: Presencia, 1990).

35. *The Theology of Mission in Relation to Social Responsibility within the Lausanne Movement* (Chicago: Lutheran School of Theology, Ph.D. dissertation, 1988).

36. *Christian Mission and Social Justice* (Scottsdale: Herald Press, 1978).

37. *The Expectation of the Poor* (Maryknoll, NY: Orbis, 1985).

38. *Contra Corriente, Ensayos sobre la eclesiología radical* (Guatemala: Semilla, 1988).

39. "A New Ecclesiology in Latin America," *International Bulletin of Missionary Research* 11(4): 156–164.

40. Norberto Saracco, "Espíritu y Palabra en la Comunidad Evangelizadora," in CLADE II, *La Evangelización en los Años 80* (Mexico: Fraternidad Teológica Latinoamericana, 1979); "El Evangelio de Poder" (Quito: CLADE III paper, 1992).

critical Pentecostal ecclesiology.[41] These theologians are all engaged in active evangelistic teaching and pastoral tasks in Latin America or the Hispanic world of the U.S. Their themes and style are closely related to the way in which they practice their faith in daily ministry, more than to the demands of academic debate in the European or North American setting.

The Rediscovery of Key Biblical Themes

The crucial—but not uncontroversial—set of biblical themes for the global dialogue today is that referring to social and economic realities. Economic systems are experienced by people in different ways, according to the level of society in which they move, or to the region of the world in which they live. Only a Christian conscience, shaped by biblical truth and responsive to the Spirit's drive, will enable Protestants in the First World to detect and grasp the anguish of those who experience the reality of the global economic order built by the West, not as its beneficiaries but as its victims. The theological task of the future will involve the sensitivity to read Scripture anew with that kind of awareness, and in this evangelicals in Latin America have a long and cherished tradition.

The missionary pioneers of evangelical theology in Latin America were very explicit about the social significance of the Gospel and Christian conversion. It might be said without exaggeration that it was the Protestant presence that brought back to Latin America the conviction that there is an intimate relationship between personal faith in Jesus Christ and ethics. Already in 1942 Stanley Rycroft, formerly a Presbyterian missionary in Peru, wrote that

> The impact of Evangelical Christianity on the great social problems of the Latin American republics is producing a growing consciousness among thoughtful people that Christianity demands something more than outward conformity or even intellectual assent. It has in it the seeds of social righteousness and justice, for when men become truly Christian they cannot avoid adjusting their human relationships if they "hunger and thirst after justice" at all.[42]

The theological conviction behind this fact was also expressed clearly by John A. Mackay, who was an influential educator and evangelist

---

41. Ricardo Gondim Rodrigues, "El Evangelio de Poder" (Quito: CLADE III paper, 1992).

42. Stanley Rycroft, 1942, 159.

among students in Latin America before coming to work in theological education at Princeton. Thus he wrote: "In the wake of meeting God in the full Christian dimension of that encounter, man is seized by a force and inspired by a vision which moves him to struggle on for the achievement of God's purpose both within him and through him."[43]

A fresh reading of the Bible within the social crisis of the sixties in Latin America caused theologians of every tradition to rediscover some aspects of the biblical message that had remained obscure, unknown or even purposefully forgotten. It became necessary to acknowledge that themes such as *justice*, *poverty*, *oppression*, and *liberation* are not accidental departures here and there from the great lines of biblical teaching. They are teachings which cannot be separated from the core of God's self-revelation through Jesus Christ. They are intrinsic to other themes such as revelation, relationship with God, repentance, and the nature of Christian life. The understanding of every point of biblical teaching requires adequate regard to the wholeness of the message. The Exodus story, for instance, has to be understood in its unique particularity and then placed within the totality of God's revelation.

When such understanding is carried to its logical consequence it acquires a missiological dimension. Without a story that includes Creation, Covenant, Desert, Promised Land, Exile, the Messiah, the Cross, and the Resurrection, there is no key to understand the Exodus in a way that it becomes a word for the present. Emilio A. Núñez has said: "Before the Exodus Israel was already a people with a long history in which their monotheistic faith, the knowledge of Yaweh the Lord stands out."[44] It was for that particular people and not for any other nation that God performed his liberating event:

> The foundation and frame of reference for the theological significance of that great liberating event are found in the covenant by which God committed Himself to His people—beginning with Abraham—to bless them and make of them a means of blessing for all the families of the earth. It was in faithfulness to that commitment that Yahweh intervened on behalf of His people, liberating them from slavery in Egypt.[45]

---

43. John Alexander Mackay, *Christian Reality and Appearance* (Richmond: John Knox Press, 1969), 17.

44. Emilio A. Núñez, *Liberation Theology* (Chicago: Moody Press, 1985).

45. Núñez, 191.

That particularity gives to the liberation act proclaimed and described in the Bible a unique form, content, means, and atmosphere, which have to be taken seriously when the reader today intends to use it as a paradigm for missionary action—"God does not merely 'act in history,' God acts in history in *particular ways*."[46] God's historical project begins with his people though it is intended for all humankind. From this understanding of the particularity of God's action in the world through his people comes the evangelical criticism of the way in which Latin American Liberation theologies read the Exodus.

In order to understand Liberation theologies it is important to remember that the Christianization of Latin America came as part of the Iberian conquest in the sixteenth century. As a missiologist wrote recently, "The Iberian expansion presented a new feature in terms of the history of missions: for the first time on a major scale, missions were allied with secular power in a way that gave them the ability to coerce their audience and not to persuade them."[47] Already in those days there were missionaries and theologians like Bartolomé de las Casas who contrasted that warlike missionary methodology with the Biblical view.[48] But the military method was the predominant one and so a feudal social order, justified by theological discourse, was established in Latin America. When these countries became independent from Spain, mostly between 1810 and 1824, the Catholic church remained ideologically allied to the colonial epoch, and became a symbol of conservatism.

As we entered the second part of our century, some Catholic missionaries and theologians came to the conclusion that their Christian duty was to cooperate with political projects aimed at the destruction of that old order built during centuries of dependence and oppression, which was now in its capitalistic phase. The way ahead was a form of liberation that would come by the use of Marxist social analysis and the organization of people for revolution.[49] The presupposition was the

46. John Howard Yoder, "Withdrawal and Diaspora: The Two Faces of Liberation," *Freedom and Discipleship*, Daniel Schipani, ed. (Maryknoll, NY: Orbis, 1989), 76–84.

47. Charles Taber, *The World Is Too Much with Us* (Macon: Mercer, 1991), 21.

48. A selection of the writings of Las Casas which present this view is George Sanderlin, ed., *Witness* (Maryknoll, NY: Orbis, 1992).

49. Míguez Bonino (1983), 77–78, describes this "historical project" in a way similar to Gustavo Gutiérrez (1973), 237. For Gutiérrez' revision of his use of Marxist analysis see the new edition of his classic work, *A Theology of Liberation* (Maryknoll, NY: Orbis, 1988), 156–61.

Marxist tenet that history moves towards socialism. Revolution was the way to liberation, and Christians were called to take part in that revolution. Thus Liberation theologies came to be, and theology was defined as the reflection of Christians on this new historical praxis, in light of God's Word.

The Exodus became a favored motif of this new theological approach. The perspective of social analysis was used to understand the present condition of Latin America, and also to understand the biblical story of the Exodus as an historical event.[50] The contention of evangelical theologians is that to adopt a Marxist reading of the Exodus is to push the biblical view into the mold of the Marxist version of the Enlightenment. Padilla says that, "A far better alternative is theology that reads the Bible on its own terms and refuses to force it into an ideological straight jacket, consequently imposing its own limitations on the Word of God."[51] The edifice of Liberation theologies will need serious repair as it has become affected by the collapse of regimes that applied the Marxist ideology in Eastern Europe.

We believe with Yoder that, "the seriousness with which we should take the centrality of Exodus in the Hebrew Canon forbids our distilling from it a timeless idea of liberation that we would then use to ratify all kinds of liberation projects in all places and forms."[52] Rather than ratifying Marxist political projects with biblical language, evangelicals propose to explore and develop the transformational potential of their distinctive missionary presence in Latin American societies. This gives special relevance to the search for a missiological Christology, because the church proclaims that the existence of the universe and human history can only be understood within the purpose of God, manifested in Jesus Christ by the power of the Holy Spirit. "With the coming of Jesus Christ all barriers that divide humankind have been broken down and a new humanity is now taking shape *in* and *through* the church."[53]

---

50. For a careful discussion of this point in Daniel Schipani, ed., *Freedom and Discipleship* (Maryknoll, NY: Orbis, 1989). A detailed evangelical analysis is found in Emilio A. Núñez, *Liberation Theology* (Chicago: Moody Press, 1985).

51. Daniel Schipani, ed., *Freedom and Discipleship* (Maryknoll, NY: Orbis, 1989), 47.

52. John Howard Yoder, "Withdrawal and Diaspora: The Two Faces of Liberation," *Freedom and Discipleship*, Daniel Schipani, ed. (Maryknoll, NY: Orbis, 1989), 84.

53. Padilla, *Mission between the Times* (Grand Rapids: Eerdmans, 1985), 142.

Origins of Evangelical Christology in Latin America

A brief historical reference is necessary in order to grasp the continuing relevance of some older questions. Because Latin America was already a Christianized continent when the early Protestant missionaries came to it, Christology became the first privileged theme demanded by their missionary theology. The most lasting contribution, because of its contextual frame and evangelistic thrust, came from Scottish Presbyterian John Alexander Mackay (1889–1983). After sixteen years as a missionary (1916–1932) Mackay became a mission executive and then President of Princeton Theological Seminary.[54] A missiological exploration around the theme of Christ in Latin American culture was the central concern that he developed in his classic work *The Other Spanish Christ*.[55]

What Mackay found striking in the Creole Christ of Latin America was what he described as his lack of humanity, the fact that he appeared almost exclusively in two dramatic roles, "The role of the infant in his mother's arms, and the role of a suffering and bleeding victim. It is a picture of a Christ who was born and died, but who never lived."[56] This Creole Christ was for Mackay a "southamericanized" version of the Christ of Spanish religion, in which he had become the center of a cult of death. Following the analysis of Unamuno and other Spanish philosophers, Mackay observed that the dead Christ was seen as only an expiatory victim. Moreover,

> He is regarded as a purely supernatural being, whose humanity being only apparent, has little ethical bearing upon ours. This docetic Christ died as a victim of human hate, and in order to bestow immortality, that is to say a continuation of the present earthly, fleshly existence.[57]

Mackay's missiological agenda as an evangelist and a teacher to Latin American youth in the twenties and thirties was designed as an evangelical response to the kind of Christendom without Christ that he found in those lands. At the top of this agenda was Christology, and the way in which he outlined the task has become decisive and influential even in our time. Mackay's books in Spanish are masterful works in their contextual presentation of the Jesus of the Gospels. They develop

---

54. See biographical note, Samuel Escobar, "The Legacy of John Alexander Mackay," *International Bulletin of Missionary Research* 16(3): 116–22.

55. (New York: Macmillan, 1933).

56. Ibid., 110.

57. Ibid., 98.

the agenda that is summarized in the following extended quotation. Responding to an interlocutor pointing out that Christ as a child and a victim corresponded to the two central truths of Christianity, the Incarnation and the Atonement, he said:

> Yes, but incarnation is only the prologue of a life, while atonement is into epilogue. The reality of the former is unfolded in life and guaranteed by living; the efficacy of the latter is derived from the quality of the life lived. The Divine child in His Mother's arm received His full significance only when we see the man at work in the carpenter's shop, receive the Spirit in the Baptismal waters of Jordan, battle hungry and lonely with the tempter, preach the glad tidings of the Kingdom of the poor, heal the sick and raise the dead, call the heavy laden and children to His side, warn the rich and denounce hypocrites, prepare His disciples for life and Himself for death, and then lay down His life not as a mere victim of hate or destiny but voluntarily and in dying ask His Father to forgive His slayers. In the same way the Crucified, in mortal anguish on the cross is transfigured when we think that in life he had experienced the temptations of a strong man and overcame them. It was the man who died, the true, the second Man, the Lord from heaven as man, such a man as never has been nor shall be.[58]

Mackay added to these proposals his concern about the need to proclaim Jesus as the resurrected Lord, because in Latin America the vision of the risen Christ "has been no less dim than that of the historical Jesus."[59] Because the true Lordship of Christ had not been acknowledged in South American religion, "He remains to be known as Jesus, the Saviour from sin and the Lord of all life."[60] At this point Mackay also underlined a theme that was distinctive of his theology: the difference between an attitude of distant admiration of Jesus that he described as "the balcony" and one of committed discipleship, for which he used the metaphor of "the road." Because Jesus is Lord he is to be followed on the road which is the place where life is lived in the midst of tensions, where conflicts and concerns become the soil from which ideas are born. Thus discipleship is the ground of true theology, "Truth as it relates to God is always existential in character, involving a consent of the will as well as an act of understanding. Assent may be given on the

---

58. Ibid., 110–11.
59. Ibid., 112.
60. Ibid., 117.

Balcony, but consent is inseparable from the Road."[61] The praxis of obedience to Jesus Christ is then the way of access to the truth of God.

The theology of Mackay had a definite missionary and evangelistic thrust.[62] He developed an apologetic missionary approach which explored deep seated points of contact between the Gospel and the Latin American soul shaped by the Iberian culture. Well into the fifties Mackay's agenda was being pursued by the first generation of Latin Americans that tried to articulate their evangelical faith in a contextual manner. Some of the first theological works originally written by Protestants in Spanish were journalistic and homiletical in style but they embodied a rich biblical Christology, in an effort to communicate the Gospel to large audiences that were ignorant of the main aspects of the life and teachings of Jesus.[63]

The revival of Christology within Roman Catholicism came much later and the course of events was different.[64] Vatican II with its emphasis on the use of Scripture and a contextual liturgy in the vernacular prompted a renewal in which the rediscovery of the Jesus of the Gospels was an important component. The words of the mass in Spanish to the tune of folkloric rhythms from Mexico, Chile, or Argentina was for many Catholics in Latin America the first intelligible contact with the Christological core of the liturgy. A paraphrase of the Gospels versified with the metric of the gaucho popular poetry of Argentina, became a best-seller through which many young people understood for the first time the life of the incarnate Jesus, as "one of us."[65] On the other hand, the presence of a new wave of North American and European Catholic missionaries, with a missionary style that emphasized "presence" rather than "conquest," pointed out the validity of the practice of Jesus as a missiological model. These facts brought into Catholicism a renewed

---

61. John Alexander Mackay, A *Preface to Christian Theology* (New York: Macmillan, 1941).

62. Mackay summarized his missionary theology in a book which is still relevant, *Ecumenics: The Science of the Church Universal* (Englewood Cliffs: Prentice Hall, 1964).

63. Such is the case of classic books by Gonzalo Báez-Camargo, e.g., *Las Manos de Cristo*, 2d ed. (Mexico: CUPSA, 1985).

64. The Spanish version of *Jesus Christ Liberator: Critical Christology for Our Time* by Leonardo Boff (1978), first appeared in 1974. In the preface of the book Héctor Borrat presents it as "the first systematic Christology published in Latin America," but he acknowledges that Protestants were far ahead of Catholics in the study of that theme, *Jesucristo el liberador* (Buenos Aires: Latinoamérica Libros, 1974), 11.

65. Amado Anzi S. J., *El Evangelio Criollo* (Buenos Aires: Editora Patria Grande, 1964).

Christological search which followed along the lines of Mackay's agenda, though it was not directly related to it.

As is well known, student militancy and revolutionary pressures, the triumph of the Cuban Revolution, and the failure of U.S.-oriented development policies, brought the social question to the forefront in the late sixties and the seventies. It can be shown by historical observation[66] that some forms of Catholic missionary experience within these conditions were the "praxis" that preceded the theological formulations of Liberation theologies, especially their Christology. In 1982 René Padilla offered a descriptive and critical summary of this Christological search as it was exemplified by the Jesuit theologian Jon Sobrino, from El Salvador, comparing it with parallel developments in Africa and Asia.[67] It is not our task in this chapter to consider this new form of Catholic Christology, but, returning to the agitated days of the sixties and seventies, we will consider how the Christological search was also intensified in an ethical direction among evangelicals in Latin Ameria. [68]

From Christology to Social Ethics

Justo L. González, now a well-known theologian and historian in the English-speaking world, who originally came to North America from Cuba, wrote in 1965 his short but very influential book, *Revolución y Encarnación*.[69] It was a study of the Johannine material in the New Testament as a way of calling evangelicals to become aware of the kind of docetic Christology into which they had fallen, and that was proving sterile especially in relation to social ethics. Coming out at the time in which social activism and revolutionary militancy had increased to critical levels in Latin America, González' book was an effort to develop a social ethic that would use a Christological paradigm as a foundation. This book was followed in 1971 by *Jesucristo es el Señor*,[70] in which González outlined with great clarity the development

---

66. Samuel Escobar, "Missions and Renewal in Latin American Catholicism," *Missiology* 15(2): 33–46.

67. Vinay Samuel and Chris Sugden, eds., *Sharing Jesus in the Two Thirds World* (Grand Rapids: Eerdmans, 1983).

68. The historical and theological processes of these years have been covered extensively by Emilio A. Núñez, *Liberation Theology* (Chicago: Moody Press, 1985) and Samuel Escobar, *La fe evangélica y las teologías de la liberación* (El Paso: Casa Bautista de Publicaciones, 1987).

69. (Rio Piedras, Puerto Rico: La Reforma, 1965.)

70. (San José/Miami: Editorial Caribe, 1967.)

and the meaning of the doctrine of the Lordship of Jesus Christ. Both books in a way summarized a contextual interpretation of Christology as a way to figure out the nature and mission of the church. Though both had a definite pastoral intention which accounted for their clear, brief, and straightforward style, they were based on the careful historical research of González' well-known works on the History of Christian Thought.

González refined some points of the argument during a colloquium on Social Ethics in which he concluded that there was almost general agreement "to reject the docetism of those who see no other task than that of saving souls for a future life . . . (and) to reject the ebionism of those who imagine that their action in society and in history is going to establish the Kingdom of God."[71] In one of his most recent books, González has deepened the analysis of Christological themes within the larger Trinitarian thrust of his exposition. Working from the concerns of the Hispanic context in the United States, he has explored both the social context and the social connotations of the development of Christological dogma and has insisted in his attack on gnosticism and docetism:

> Docetism, while seeming to glorify Jesus, in truth deprived him of what in the New Testament is his greatest glory: his incarnation and suffering on the cross. In the last analysis, what docetism denied was not only the reality of the incarnation and the suffering of Jesus but the very nature of a God whose greatest victory is achieved through suffering and whose clearest revelation is in the cross.[72]

During the same period, several members of the Latin American Theological Fraternity were engaged in evangelistic work, especially among students and professional people. In the late fifties and during the sixties it became natural and necessary for them to follow Mackay's Christological agenda, and to focus their public announcement of the Gospel on campuses on the basic facts of Jesus' actions and teachings as presented in the Gospels. These were unknown to the average student at that time. In some cases an apologetic note about the historicity of Jesus became necessary due to the debate with Marxist interlocutors in the academic and intellectual world.[73] The material developed in workshops and courses all over Latin America was summarized in Escobar's

---

71. Padilla (1974), 166.
72. Justo L. González, *Mañana Christian Theology from a Hispanic Perspective* (Nashville: Abingdon, 1990), 143.

presentation at the First Latin American Congress of Evangelism held in Bogotá, Colombia, November 1969.[74]

One outcome of the Bogotá Congress was the formation of the Latin American Theological Fraternity in 1970. A central concern of the founders was the development of a contextual theology of evangelization. Their explorations converged with the work being developed by evangelical theologians in other parts of the world. Padilla and Escobar found great affinity with what John Stott had started to develop in his series of Bible studies at the World Congress of Evangelism in Berlin, October 1966, especially in his emphasis on the "Great Commission" as it is presented in the gospel of John.[75] Evangelical work around this subject in Latin America became an important contribution to the Lausanne Congress in 1974 and to the Lausanne Covenant.[76] The "Response to Lausanne," drafted by the Radical Discipleship group incorporated aspects of the ongoing Christological reflection that could not be incorporated into the Covenant.[77] The most recent work of evangelicals from Latin America in the area of Christology has to be understood within the frame of this historical development.

An important self-critical discovery of those years was that the same docetism that Mackay had criticized among Roman Catholics had soon started to develop also among evangelicals. This development could be traced back to the negative effect of post World War II independent missionary efforts from North America that were heavily influenced by Dispensationalism, the mentality of the Cold War with its suspicion about social change, and the delayed effects of the Liberal-Fundamentalist debates.[78] The fact is that on the basis of missionary experience, theological dialogue, and research in texts, René Padilla

---

73. Samuel Escobar and René Padilla, *¿Quién es Cristo Hoy?* (Buenos Aires: Certeza, 1970).

74. The text of this presentation was published in English as part of a symposium edited by Brian Griffiths, *Is Revolution Change?* (London: InterVarsity Press, 1972).

75. A recent book by Mortimer Arias, *The Great Commission* (Nashville: Abingdon Press, 1992), develops these themes in a more contemporary key.

76. John R. W. Stott, *The Lausanne Covenant: An Exposition and Commentary*, Lausanne Occasional Papers No. 3 (Wheaton: LCWE, 1975).

77. For a careful chronicle and analysis of the Lausanne process, and the Latin American participation in it, see Valdir Raul Steuernagel, *The Theology of Mission in Relation to Social Responsibility within the Lausanne Movement* (Chicago: Lutheran School of Theology, Ph.D. dissertation, 1988), 124–69.

78. Brian Griffiths, ed., *Is Revolution Change?* (London: InterVarsity Press, 1972), 85–86.

came to the conclusion that the problem was not limited to Latin America. Actually, evangelicalism around the world had been affected by docetism:

> Despite its theoretical acknowledgment of Christ's full humanity, evangelical Christianity in Latin America, as in the rest of the world, is deeply affected by docetism. It affirms Christ's transforming power in relation to the individual, but is totally unable to relate the Gospel to social ethics and social life. In our case Mackay's challenge remains unmet.[79]

A Missiological Christology

As we have seen, by the logic of the Christendom of Latin America, Catholics and Protestants alike will necessarily enter the Christological debate as soon as they try to think their faith or figure out their identity and mission. In fact, as Míguez Bonino has expressed it, their task will be to identify the Christologies that already exist in this nominally Christian continent, and to subject them to a psycho-sociological and theological interpretation.[80] However, in the evangelical exploration there is a unique distinctive that has to be clarified and stressed. It is found in the evangelistic thrust of evangelical theology which has been so aptly expressed by Orlando Costas:

> Theology and evangelization are two interrelated aspects of the life and mission of the Christian faith. Theology studies the faith; evangelization is the process by which it is communicated. Theology plumbs the depth of the Christian faith; evangelization enables the church to extend it to the ends of the earth and the depth of human life. Theology reflects critically on the church's practice of the faith; evangelization keeps the faith from becoming the practice of an exclusive social group. Theology enables evangelization to transmit the faith with integrity by clarifying and organizing its content, analyzing its context and critically evaluating its communication. Evangelization enables theology to be an effective servant of the faith by relating its message to the deepest spiritual needs of humankind.[81]

This emphasis makes evangelical theologizing different from the forms of Protestant theology stemming from churches that have aban-

---

79. René Padilla and Mark Lau Branson, *Conflict and Context: Hermeneutics in the Americas* (Grand Rapids: Eerdmans, 1986), 83.

80. José Míguez Bonino, ed., *Faces of Jesus* (Maryknoll, NY: Orbis, 1984), 2.

81. Orlando Costas, *Liberating News* (Grand Rapids: Eerdmans, 1989), 1.

doned a vital concern for evangelization. These tend to focus more on the correction of abuses inside the existing churches or the search for relevance in the socio-political struggles of our day.[82] It is also different from the Catholic approach in which the sacramental dimension of the presence of the Roman Catholic Church in Latin America is taken as the basis for assuming that the population is already Christian. With this presupposition evangelization is understood more as a call to commitment and discipleship, without a call to conversion. What we find in authors like Padilla, Costas, and Núñez is a missiological thrust in which the evangelizing capacity of the churches is a definite and influential presupposition and a prerequisite of theological discourse.

In this moment of transition in Latin America, the search for a Christological missiology has come from the crisis of the traditional models of mission. René Padilla has been the theologian who has worked more consistently in the development of that agenda. He believes that there is a common Christological concern in the work of theologians from Asia, Africa, Latin America, and the ethnic minorities of North America and Europe:

> The images of Jesus Christ imported from the West have on the whole been found wanting—too conditioned by Constantinian Christianity with all its ideological distortions and cultural accretions, and terribly inadequate as a basis for the life and mission of the church in situations of dire poverty and injustice. This has led to the search for a Christology which will have as its focus the historical Jesus and provide a basis for Christian action in contemporary society.[83]

The term "historical Jesus" for Padilla does not refer to the technical expression usually associated with the Liberal theology of the last century in which "historical" would mean "the product of the historical-critical method."[84] Evangelicals in Latin America would share what Padilla considers a fundamental premise of his Christology, "that the Gospels are essentially reliable historical records and that the portrait of

---

82. This is, for instance, the general thrust of the writings of many of the Protestant authors from Latin America in a recent anthology, Dow Kirkpatrick, ed., *Faith Born in the Struggle for Life* (Grand Rapids: Eerdmans, 1989).

83. Vinay Samuel and Chris Snugden, eds., *Sharing Jesus in the Two Thirds World* (Grand Rapids: Eerdmans, 1983).

84. Walter A. Elwell, ed., *Evangelical Dictionary of Theology* (Grand Rapids: Baker, 1984), 584.

Jesus that emerges from them provides an adequate basis for the life and
mission of the church today."[85]

The Latin American context forces the question of the need to
rediscover and expound the concrete actions of Jesus as they were
reported by the evangelists so that they may be grasped, contemplated,
and understood as the shaping patterns for contemporary discipleship.
This theological task extends to the wealth of biblical data that lies
behind the creedal systematizations in which "the Christian message
was cast into philosophical categories, and the historical dimension of
revelation was completely overshadowed by dogma."[86]

To the degree in which the missionary movement and teaching in
churches limit themselves to transmitting Christology mainly as propositional truth defined in the Nicean or Chalcedonian formulas, they
transmit images of Christ that may be "useful for personal piety or civil
religion, but . . . neither faithful to the witness of Scripture concerning
Jesus Christ nor historically relevant."[87] The creedal formulations defining the deity and the humanity of Jesus Christ became obstacles to
grasping the dimensions of humanity which are very important for shaping life and mission today. Emilio Núñez in his study of Liberation theologies acknowledges that "this new emphasis on the humanity of
Christ is a reaction to the lack of balance in a Christology that magnifies
the deity of the Word incarnate at the expense of his humanity."[88] He
goes on to describe the way in which Latin American evangelicals
received an Anglo-Saxon Christology that was the result of the liberal-
fundamentalist debate:

> Thus what was emphasized in Evangelical conservative Christology
> was necessarily the deity of the Logos, without denying his humanity.
> We were presented with a divine-human Christ in the theological for-
> mula; but in practice he was far removed from the stage of this world,
> aloof to our social problems.[89]

This biblical clarification does not dismiss the validity and usefulness of
the traditional creedal statements, but it takes them for what they are, a
form of Christian tradition that should always be open to confrontation

---

85. René Padilla and Mark Lau Branson, *Conflict and Context: Hermeneutics in the Americas* (Grand Rapids: Eerdmans, 1986), 83.

86. Ibid.

87. Ibid.

88. *Liberation Theology* (Chicago: Moody Press, 1985), 236.

89. Ibid.

with Scripture.[90] The confrontation of creeds with Scripture, both understood within their historical context, helps us to appreciate the validity of the creeds, and at the same time to recover depths of meaning in Scripture that might have remained in the shadows due to the historical relativity of the definitions. [91]

When Scriptures are viewed afresh, one of the first questions becomes "Who was Jesus of Nazareth?" Padilla has gathered material from the Gospels around some features of Jesus' work which "could not but puzzle people in general, provoke suspicion in many and infuriate those who held positions of privilege in the religious-political establishment."[92] The picture obtained is eloquent and challenging: Jesus spoke with authority despite his lack of theological study, he claimed to be related to God in a unique way, he was a friend of publicans and sinners, he affirmed that God's kingdom was present in history and manifest in the healing of the sick, he concentrated his ministry on the uneducated, the ignorant, and the disreputable, he attacked religious oppression and rejected empty religious ceremonies, he condemned wealth and regarded greed as idolatry, he defined power in terms of sacrificial service and affirmed nonviolent resistance, he summoned his followers to social nonconformity patterned after his own. For Padilla the consequence is clear:

> If the Christ of faith is the Jesus of history, then it is possible to speak of social ethics for Christian disciples who seek to fashion their lives in God's purpose of love and justice concretely revealed. If the risen and exalted Lord is Jesus of Nazareth, then it is possible to speak of a community that seeks to manifest the kingdom of God in history.[93]

A second important set of questions has to do with the way in which Jesus accomplished his mission. Bible exposition within the frame of missiological reflection was the agenda followed by Padilla as he explored the marks of Jesus' ministry. His basic assumption was that, "To be a disciple of Jesus Christ is to be called by him both to know him

---

90. For this point see the fascinating debate about Padilla's Christological proposal in the consultation on "Hermeneutics in the Americas, Conflict and Context: Hermeneutics in the Americas," René Padilla and Mark Lau Branson, eds. (Grand Rapids: Eerdmans, 1986), 92–113.

91. For a recent exploration along these lines see the excellent work of Justo L. González, *Mañana Christian Theology from a Hispanic Perspective* (Nashville: Abingdon, 1990).

92. Padilla and Branson, 87.

93. Ibid., 89.

and to participate in his mission. He himself is God's missionary par excellence, and he involves his followers in his mission."[94] Jesus' mission includes "fishing for the Kingdom," in other words the call to conversion to Jesus Christ as the way the truth and the life. It is this conversion to him that stands as the basis on which the Christian community is formed.

Mission includes also "compassion" as a result of immersion among the multitudes. Neither a sentimental burst of emotion nor an academic option for the poor, but definite and intentional actions of service in order to "feed the multitude" with bread *for* life, as well as Bread *of* life. Mission includes "confrontation" of the powers of death with the power of the Suffering Servant, and thus "suffering" becomes a mark of Jesus' messianic mission and a result of power struggle and human injustice.

Through creative contextual obedience Jesus' mission becomes not only a fertile source of inspiration, but also has the seeds of new patterns that are being explored today through practice and reflection, such as simple lifestyle, holistic mission, the unity of the church for mission, the pattern of God's Kingdom as a missiological paradigm and the spiritual conflict involved in mission.

A third area of inquiry centers around the question, "What is the Gospel?" The most enthusiastic calls for missionary activism stem from sectors of evangelicalism in which this question appears irrelevant. As Yoder observed concerning one of the expressions of this sector, the Church Growth missiology: "It is assumed that we have an adequate theology that we received from the past . . . we do not really need any more theological clarification. What we need now is efficiency."[95] Padilla believes that as a result of this assumption on the part of many evangelicals, "the effectiveness of evangelism is measured in terms of results, with little or no regard for faithfulness to the Gospel."[96] This concern is not limited to Latin America. Missiologists who are exploring what it means to evangelize and be missionary in North America today also believe that the question is important. Thus George R. Hunsberger says:

---

94. René Padilla "Bible Studies," *Missiology* 10 (3): 319–38.

95. John Howard Yoder, "Church Growth Issues in Theological Perspective," *The Challenge of Church Growth*, Wilbert Shenk, ed., (Elkhart, IN: Institute of Mennonite Studies, 1973).

96. René Padilla, *Mission between the Times* (Grand Rapids: Eerdmans, 1985), 62.

The central question of theology—What is the gospel?—must be asked in more culturally particular ways. And the more particular the question the more will be our sense that the answer will emerge in unexpected ways. It will come more out of Christian communities which increasingly learn the habit of "indwelling" the Gospel story so deeply that it shapes their life of common discipleship.[97]

These important questions that should be asked with regard to the life and mission of the church today are related to the content of the Gospel because "the *what* of the Gospel determines the *how* of its effects on practical life."[98] Grasping the wealth of meaning of the Gospel in the biblical revelation, and the demands of the obedience of faith, is the only way out of the prison of the predominant "culture Christianity" in North America which is also being exported, especially through the mass media. Padilla stresses the eschatological and soteriological dimensions of the Christian message centered in the person of Jesus Christ. In Him, through the pattern of promise and fulfillment, the Old and the New Testaments are related. From a careful exposition of the Gospel centered around a solid Christological core, Padilla derives the conclusion that if "the apostolic mission is derived from Jesus Christ . . . He is the content as well as the model and the goal for the proclamation of the gospel."[99] Consequently, Christian preaching has to be molded by the Word of God and not by a mere search for relevance:

> Preachers for whom relevance is the most basic consideration in preaching are frequently mistaken—they fail to see the link between relevance in preaching and faithfulness to the Gospel . . . there is nothing more irrelevant than a message that simply mirrors man's myths and ideologies![100]

The consequence of this fact is critical in two directions. It rejects the unilateral stress on the humanity of Jesus that reduces Christian action to mere human effort. Thus it becomes necessary to criticize the Christology of some Liberation theologians like Jon Sobrino for not taking seriously the wholeness of the gospel; "it is no mere coincidence that Sobrino should see the Kingdom of God as a utopia to be fashioned

---

97. George R. Hunsberger, "The Newbigin Gauntlet: Developing a Domestic Missiology for North America," *Missiology* 19 (4): 406.

98. Padilla, op. cit., 62.

99. Ibid., 62.

100. René Padilla, "God's Word and Man's Myths," *Themelios* 3 (1): 3.

by men rather than as a gift to be received in faith."[101] Unacceptable also are Liberation Christologies that overemphasize the political dimension of the death of Jesus at the expense of its soteriological significance. Padilla, for instance, accepts the truth based on examination of the texts of the Gospels that the death of Jesus was the historical outcome of the kind of life he lived, and that he suffered for the cause of justice and challenges us to do the same. However, he thinks that warnings are necessary because

> Unless the death of Christ is also seen as God's gracious provision of an atonement for sin, the basis for forgiveness is removed and sinners are left without the hope of justification . . . salvation is by grace through faith and . . . nothing should detract from the generosity of God's mercy and love as the basis of joyful obedience to the Lord Jesus Christ.[102]

On the other hand, Padilla criticizes the managerial forms of missiology in evangelicalism which in their concern with methodology disregard questions about the content of the gospel.[103] Serious work is needed in order to provide a contextual reading of Scripture in response to the question "What is the gospel?" However, this is disregarded or overlooked by the Church Growth theory which espouses what Charles Taber calls "a narrowed-down version of the evangelical hermeneutic and theology."[104] From the Christological basis of his way of understanding the gospel, Padilla questions the rigidity of the structural-functional model of cultural anthropology used by Church Growth because it produces a missiological approach "tailor made for churches and institutions whose main function in society is to reinforce the status quo."[105] He also questions the extreme individualism of those missiologies which have lost the biblical wholeness:

> The salvation that the Gospel proclaims is not limited to man's reconciliation to God. It involves the remaking of man in all the dimensions

---

101. Vinay Samuel and Chris Sugden, eds., *Sharing Jesus in the Two Thirds World* (Grand Rapids: Eerdmans, 1983), 28.

102. Ibid.

103. I have described managerial forms of missiology in "A Movement Divided: Three Approaches to World Evangelization Stand in Tension with One Another," *Transformation* 8(4): 7–13.

104. Wilbert Shenk, ed., *Exploring Church Growth* (Grand Rapids: Eerdmans, 1983), 119.

105. Ibid., 301.

of his existence. It has to do with the recovery of the whole man according to God's original purpose for his creation.[106]

This holistic dimension of the gospel allows us to understand the New Testament teaching about the nature of human beings, which is offered within a missiological context. Christology is the key for anthropology because to begin with, as Rooy says, "Everyone's relation to God in Christian anthropology is defined by each individual's relation to Jesus Christ."[107] This is the basis for important safeguards against the pitfalls of hermeneutical procedures such as those of the reductionist anthropology of the Church Growth school that limits itself to read into the biblical text the values of contemporary American social sciences. Rooy elaborates this point:

> The historical significance of the incarnation reaches backward and forward. Christ's life, death and resurrection mark the crucial point of human history—we might call them the mountain pass of creation's course. The same road stretches meaningfully back from the summit's peak to creation beginning and continues its meandering progress to the destiny of humankind. The basic affirmations of humankind's identity as the one created in the image of God and responsible for the tending and development of natural reality remain valid. These affirmations are reconstituted in the reconciling work of Jesus Christ, the authentic image of God, the new person.[108]

In their debate with Church Growth missiology and its proposed method of "homogeneous units" based on race or class, Rooy and Padilla have insisted on the community dimension of the New Testament teaching about the new man, especially as Paul teaches it in the Ephesian epistle. They develop from this text an ecclesiology that derives from the work of Jesus Christ, because the new humanity is humankind in Jesus Christ: "The 'one new man' here is clearly a new humanity, the church composed of what was formerly two, that is Jews and Gentiles."[109] Through careful exegesis Padilla proves that apostolic missionary practice aims "at forming churches that would live out the unity of the new humanity in Jesus Christ."[110] The "newness" that Paul is proclaiming is closely connected with his own missionary work as a

---

106. René Padilla, *Mission between the Times* (Grand Rapids: Eerdmans, 1985), 79.

107. Sidney H. Rooy, "A Theology of Humankind," *Exploring Church Growth*, Wilbert Shenk, ed. (Grand Rapids: Eerdmans, 1983), 198.

108. Ibid.

109. Ibid., 199.

110. René Padilla, *Mission between the Times* (Grand Rapids: Eerdmans, 1985), 160.

Jewish man who happens to be a missionary to Gentiles. And precisely what he is doing is founding churches, communities of new people which are to express the novelty brought by the Gospel, even if that novelty brings all the pastoral questions that fill his Epistles. As Padilla concludes, "The impact that the early church made on non-Christians because of the Christian brotherhood across natural barriers can hardly be overestimated."[111]

The growing involvement of Latin American evangelicals in the political arena of their countries brought a new agenda to theological reflection.[112] It came first as part of the work on the Kingdom of God[113] and it followed the specific work of a consultation about evangelicals and political power.[114] The approach to the issues of Justice and Power was basically Christological in the work of Padilla, developing from the eschatological dimension of his Christology. This was operative in his critical evaluation of culture, and the understanding of the forces hostile to the Kingdom of God that presently enslave human beings and tend to undermine the Church's identity and distort her mission. There is an Antichrist at work in the world, that has to be named and unmasked at the same time at which Jesus Christ is proclaimed as Lord.

> The challenge of the moment is not to criticize the governments in religious language but rather to confront the values and attitudes that make it possible for our people to be domesticated by advertising; it is not to oppose the official myths with other secular myths but rather to point to the judgment of God on every attempt to build the Kingdom of God without God. Since the coming of Christ, the key to history is to be found in his death and resurrection, and the proclamation of the Gospel places humanity face to face with only one alternative—Christ of Antichrist. [115]

From such a stance come the theological elements that will enable churches to avoid the corrupting comfort of the Constantinian pitfall in one extreme and the contradictions of otherworldliness in the other.

---

111. Ibid., 165.

112. An account and evaluation of this process and recent events in René Padilla, "Latin American Evangelicals Enter the Public Square," *Transformation* 9(3): 2–7. Cf. a brief account of the ongoing theological work on these issues in the Fraternidad Teológica Latinoamericana (FTL), *Boletín Teológico* 9(3): 2–7.

113. René Padilla, 1975.

114. Pablo Deiros, ed., *Los evangélicos y el poder político en América Latina* (Buenos Aires/Grand Rapids: Nueva Creación/Eerdmans, 1986).

115. René Padilla, *Mission between the Times* (Grand Rapids: Eerdmans, 1985), 127.

Mission from the Periphery

Two significant trends at the end of this century will have a bearing on the development of new missionary patterns, and we think that part of the agenda for theology in the future will be to explore ways they might become part of a coherent missiology with a global thrust. On the one hand as Yoder has pointed out, "It is one of the widely remarked developments of our century that now one dimension, now another, of the ecclesiastical experience and the ecclesiological vision once called 'sectarian' are now beginning to be espoused by some within majority communions."[116] It may be that as Christians and churches search for more faithful patterns of obedience to Jesus Christ, they increasingly find themselves going through the experience of disestablishment in societies that hold some form of "official" Christian identity. They have discovered, like "sectarians" of the past, that they must learn to live as "resident aliens."

On the other hand we observe today what missiologist Andrew Walls describes as "a massive southward shift of the center of gravity of the Christian world, so that the representative Christian lands now appear to be in Latin America, Sub-Saharan Africa, and other parts of the southern continents."[117] This being the case, the existence of thriving churches in what used to be called the Third World, confronts the old European or North American churches with a new set of questions, and new ways of looking at God's Word. It is important to keep in mind what Walls deduces from this fact even if some may consider what he says as an exaggeration:

> This means that Third World theology is now likely to be the representative Christian theology. On present trends (and I recognize that this may not be permanent) the theology of European Christians, while important for them and their continued existence, may become a matter of specialist interest to historians . . . The future general reader of Church history is more likely to be concerned with Latin American and African, and perhaps some Asian, theology.[118]

With all their purported Latin Americanism most Liberation theologies were still part of a western discourse, played to the tune of Marx

---

116. John Howard Yoder, *The Priestly Kingdom: Social Ethics as Gospel* (Notre Dame: University of Notre Dame Press, 1984), 5.

117. Andrew Walls, "The Gospel as the Prisoner and Liberator of Culture," *Evangelical Review of Theology* 7(2): 226.

118. Walls, 226–27.

and Engels, Moltmann, or the European theologians of Vatican II. Even though they were located in the frontier situations between affluence and misery they still moved within the categories of Enlightenment theology. We must be prepared for something different if we are going to take seriously the emergence of new churches as part of the "southward shift of the center of gravity of Christianity" to which Walls referred. The new pastoral situations and theological questions are coming from churches which move in the frontier between Christendom and Islam, churches surrounded by cultures shaped by animism or great ethnic religions, ethnic churches in the impoverished heart of secularized western cities, thriving Pentecostal churches in Latin America, or old churches in post-Marxist eastern Europe. These are the missionary churches of today and tomorrow and the ears of the missiologist should be tuned to their message, their songs and their groans, at the same time that they are attentive to the Word of God.

The ideas of a missiology that comes from the periphery of the modern world may have some merit as we explore the future. During a theological consultation about Christology, Argentinean Pentecostal Norberto Saracco explored the significance of the Galilean origin of Jesus' ministry.[119] His approach was not an effort to find in the context in which Jesus lived, situations comparable to our contemporary ones that would lend themselves to an "almost magical relationship that does not take seriously the text nor our situation."[120] Saracco preferred to explore the meaning of the options chosen by Jesus for his own ministry, "which were both relevant to the context and in accordance with his redemptive project."[121]

Orlando Costas pursued this point in a more extensive reflection, and developed a creative summary of a new dimension for a Christological missiology.[122] Concentrating on the gospel of Mark, he explored a model of evangelization rooted in the ministry of Jesus. It could be characterized as an evangelistic legacy, "a model of contextual evangelization from the periphery."[123] He placed special significance on Jesus' choice of Galilee, a racial and cultural crossroads, as the base for his mission. He explored also the significance of Jesus' identity as a

---

119. Saracco, Samuel and Sugden (1983), 33–41.
120. Saracco, ibid., 33.
121. Ibid., 33.
122. For a bibliography about the sources of this approach to the significance of Galilee for Jesus' mission, see Costas, *Liberation News* (Grand Rapids: Eerdmans, 1989).
123. Ibid., 49.

Galilean, and of Galilee as an evangelistic landmark and the starting point of the mission to the nations, with its universal implications. Costas' understanding of his own contemporary context emphasized the "peripheral" nature of some of the points and places where Christianity is more dynamic today. His missiological proposal is that "the global scope of contextual evangelization should be geared first and foremost to the nations' peripheries, where the multitudes are found and where the Christian faith has always had the best opportunity to build a strong base.[124]

At some point the "sectarian" vision to which Yoder referred, coming from the periphery of official Catholic and Protestant versions of history, may have a fertile encounter with the theological questions coming from missionary churches on the peripheries of the contemporary world. As Jews and Gentiles came together through community events in the early church, new community events will be necessary in which the reconciliation of Christians from the North and Christians from the South takes place as they experience what it means to become a "new humanity," and they theologize about it. Because, as Padilla has stated,

> The missiology that the church needs today is not one that conceives the people of God as a quotation taken from the surrounding society but one that conceives it as 'an embodied question mark' that challenges the values of the world . . . Only a missiology in line with the apostolic teaching and practice with regard to the extension of the Gospel will have a lasting contribution to make toward the building of this kind of church—the firstfruits of a new humanity made up of persons 'from every tribe and tongue and people and nation' who will unitedly sing a new song to the Lamb of God.[125]

---

124. Ibid., 67.
125. Wilbert Shenk, ed., *Exploring Church Growth* (Grand Rapids: Eerdmans, 1983), 301–2.

The Identity of Protestantism in Latin America

Antônio Carlos Barro

Introduction

Only recently have Latin American historians and theologians begun to look at Protestantism to understand its identity. This search has led to a critical perspective and an awareness that not everything done by the missionaries was appropriate. On the basis of that critique we have begun to construct an autochthon (or indigenous) theology that reflects the situation of Latin America.

Because of the character and values that motivated the Protestant missionaries coming to Latin America, the Protestant church has had difficulty discovering its own cultural and theological identity. Rubem Alves, one of the strongest critics of Protestantism from within, points out:

> What we have in our hands is disappointing. Having gathered the results of the thoughts produced and sown by Protestantism over more than a hundred years in Brazil, we sense a strong odor of degeneracy, decadence and precocious senility.[1]

Enrique Dussel, the Roman Catholic historian and theologian agrees, "Theologically, until the works of Rubem Alves and Míguez Bonino . . . there is no [Protestant] movement [in Latin America] that deserves to be considered."[2]

Alves and Dussel may not reflect the majority theological view in Latin America, yet their lament was echoed by Orlando E. Costas[3] when

---

1. Rubem Alves, "As Idéias Teológicas e os seus Caminhos Pelos Sulcos Institucionais do Protestantismo Brasileiro," *História da Teologia na América Latina* (São Paulo: Edições Paulinas, 1981), 127.

2. Enrique Dussel "Hipóteses Para una História da Teologia na América Latina," *História da Teologia na América Latina* (São Paulo: Edições Paulinas, 1981), 175.

3. Orlando E. Costas, *El Protestantismo en America Latina Hoy: Ensayos del Camino (1972–1974)* (Costa Rica: Publicaciones INDEF, 1975), 2.

he pointed out the necessity of having a historical treatment of the development of Latin America Protestantism to understand its present behavior. Such a treatment would help us identify the factors that molded and determined the lifestyle of the church and its effects on the history of Latin America.

This is the purpose of this paper: to provide a brief historical review of mainline Protestantism in Latin America and the contribution it made to the formation of our cultural and theological identity. I will take into consideration the kind of Protestantism brought by the North American missionaries, their perspective on Latin America, and their motivation to evangelize it. Then I will show some of the results of this missionary work in today's church, and the challenge ahead for the Protestantism in Latin America.

North American Perspective of Latin America

A proximity to its neighbor from the North and the increase of commerce and travel helped to make the conditions of the Latin American people known in North America. Because of that, the missionaries who went to work in Latin America had already formed an idea of the social, cultural, and religious life of the people there. The following extracts will give some idea of the missionaries' perspective on Latin America.

Perspective on Social and Cultural Life

According to Hubert W. Brown[4] the condition of the Latin American people at the end of the last century was not favorable. He quoted a missionary in Mexico, as saying that "thousands of men are such habitual drinkers that they never do a day's work; others are unable to perform full labor because of the injurious effects of drink."[5] Regarding family life, he observed that a great proportion of men were unfaithful; children were polite but not very obedient and prevarication was not sufficiently punished; young men did not respect women. "The marriage rite is often more honored in the breach than in the observance."[6]

Among the early writings about Latin America, Bishop Thomas B. Neely gave us a complete overview of the Latin Americans. The people, he said, were courteous with polished manners[7] and were lovers of plea-

---

4. Hubert W. Brown, *Latin America: The Pagans, the Papists, the Patriots, the Protestants and the Present Problem* (New York, Chigago, Toronto: Fleming H. Revell Company, 1901), 262ff.

5. Ibid., 263.

6. Ibid., 263–68.

sure and fond of display.[8] Neely then compared life in Latin America with life in the United States, Canada, or Great Britain. Individual morality, he affirmed, was much lower on the average in Latin America than in these countries. People lacked conscience and failed to reflect morally on what they thought or did. Intemperance pervaded all classes of society, and a great variety of intoxicating beverages were used. Sexual purity was not generally maintained and indecent language and action were observed even in the homes. There was a tendency, he believed, to disparage home life and the moral tone of the home was immeasurably inferior to the average home in the U.S. or Canada. His conclusion was, "The home lacks a wholesome happiness such as is generally found in these countries."[9]

Neely continued his observations by saying, "It is quite common for unmarried couples to live together as though they were married," which led to illegitimacy and abandoned babies. He conceded that the moral standard in U.S. and Canada was not perfect, but it was infinitely higher than that in South America. The contrasts between a Protestant nation and a Catholic nation were evident to Neely. So he asked, "Is South America in need of our best social ideals?" His answer, "Protestant mission will take her only these."[10]

According to Neely, the difference in the moral and social life between the North and South was caused by several factors: base character of the first settlers; low racial influences; Roman Ecclesiasticism; the effect of the inquisition; lack of education and priestly immorality. Not only was the moral and social life lower in the South, but the political aspect received a similar judgment from Neely. The first settlers who went to the U.S. did so for freedom, a protected home, and an unshackled conscience. On the other hand, for those who went to South America, the motives were greed and gold. The basis of every good thing in the United States was the Bible, while in South America there was no open Bible. The problem in South America was that the people did not have the fundamental principles that made for a sound political and a wholesome social life.[11] Neely's conclusion was predictable:

---

7. Thomas B. Neely, *South America: Its Missionary Problem* (New York: Educational Department, The Board of Foreign Missions of the Presbyterian Church, USA, 1909), 123–24.

8. Ibid., 125.

9. Ibid., 125–30.

10. Ibid., 130–32.

11. Ibid., 132–49.

The best ideals and achievements of Protestantism are needed by South America for her social and political development. Give the Spanish, the Portuguese, the aborigines, and the mixed races the same Biblical and Protestant principles, and, as they accept and conform thereto, there will result the same conception and actualization that is found among other peoples who have been favored with and blessed by these vital, purifying, and ennobling principles.[12]

Robert E. Speer, the great promoter of missions from the Student Volunteer Movement for Foreign Missions, wrote *South American Problems* in 1912, in which he surveyed many aspects of the South American life and religion. To him, "The fundamental problem in South America is ethical."[13] He described the people there in this way:

They . . . have their noble qualities . . . they are warm-hearted, courteous, friendly, kindly to children, respectful to religious things, patriotic to the very soul; but the tone, the vigor, the moral bottom, the hard veracity, the indomitable purpose, the energy, the directness, the integrity of the Teutonic people are lacking in them.[14]

"The continent wants character."[15] As one can see, the qualities in the South Americans were those pertaining to an "easy going character" with which the Latin American people have been characterized until today. These were not qualities that build a nation, nor do they contribute to the improvement of society as a whole.

By inference, one can conclude: the qualities that the Latin Americans lacked, in opposition to the Anglo-Saxons people who have them all, were those of real importance for progress and self-determination. That is why Latin America was seen as backward and the Northern people as well advanced. To say the least, at the end of last century and the beginning of this century, Latin America did not enjoy a good reputation among North American Protestants.

Since Protestant missionaries and writers viewed everything through their religious and national lenses, what they found in Latin America did not match life back home. Consequently, they helped to disseminate concepts, real and fictitious, about Latin America that persist even today. Particular problems or situations were generalized and

---

12. Ibid., 149–50.

13. Robert E. Speer, *South American Problems* (New York: Student Volunteer Movement for Foreign Missions, 1912), 73.

14. Ibid., 73–74.

15. Ibid., 81.

applied to every people and country as if Latin America was only one nation. Latin America was also compared to the U.S., but they forgot that the former was composed of many nations with different peoples and cultures, while the latter had a more homogenous population, coming basically from one part of the world. Missionaries were "unable to understand some deep differences between their culture and the local culture," says W. Wedemann.[16]

Perspective on Religious Life

Perhaps there is nothing that played a more important role in the evangelization of Latin America than the anti-Roman Catholic sentiment found among the Protestant missionaries. This sentiment was also found among the liberal politicians and the educated members of Latin America society more or less around the time of the independence of the Latin America countries. These all had grown tired of the Roman Catholic church controlling almost everything in society and government. H. M. Goodpasture puts it this way:

> Liberal parties and Freemasonry sprang up in almost every country to carry forward the ideas of the eighteenth-century Enlightenment. One of their principal targets was the power exerted over society by the clergy. The liberal parties of the various republics differed in many ways, but in one respect they were unified: they wished to reduce clerical influence in all sectors of society.[17]

The growing independence movement in Latin America and the separation between the State and the Roman Catholic church opened up the way for Protestant missionary work. A new avenue was laid before the missionaries that generated excitement. "Thank God that the wall of Romish exclusivism, higher than the Chinese wall, has been broken down, and that all America is now open to the ingress of a new and holier influence."[18]

The kind of Christianity brought by the Roman Catholic church was regarded as feeble and false. Speer quoted A. G. Simonton, the pioneer of Presbyterianism in Brazil: "It is said that no people can be without a religion; if so, few nations can be much more destitute than

---

16. Walter Wedemann, *A History of Protestant Missions to Brazil, 1850–1914* (Ann Arbor: University Microfilms. Ph.D. Southern Baptist Theol. Seminary, 1977), 151.

17. H. McKennie Goodpasture, *Cross and Sword: An Eyewitness History of Christianity in Latin America* (Maryknoll: Orbis Books, 1989), 120 .

18. Brown, 173–74.

Brazil."[19] Later, H. W. Brown pointed out, "Whatever the Roman Catholic church did do, during the three long centuries of her undisputed sway, she did not give the people the Word of God."[20] This sentiment was prevalent among the majority of the missionaries and missions to Latin America. Bishop Neely characterized Romanism in Latin America in this way: (1) It was medieval; (2) It was opposed to Protestantism and the new intellectual and individual freedom which it represented; (3) It was imported from Spain and Portugal and represented a bigoted and unrelenting type of religion; (4) It was a militant Romanism; (5) It was the church of the cruel Inquisition; (6) It proceeded from an isolated Roman Catholic church (isolated from Europe and from progress); and, (7) It was a church affected and modified by its contact with Indian paganism.[21]

Because of this, he concluded, the "Roman Church in South America has been a sad failure."[22] And, it "has been weighed in the balances and found wanting."[23] According to the missionaries, the Roman church failed to provide education and to elevate the culture of the people. That church was also blamed for the slow progress found in Latin America, when compared to the progress found in Europe and the States. However, most important, the church was condemned for not bringing true Christianity to Latin America. Speer pointed out, "The great mass of the South American people have not been given Christianity."[24] Four years later, H. C. Stuntz put it this way, "South America does not have the gospel. Her millions have almost no means of finding their way to Christ. They do not have the Word of God."[25] The cause for this situation is that "the Roman Church is not a preaching Church."[26]

This anti-Catholic sentiment was found not only among the missionaries, but also among the new believers in Latin America. E. Carlos Pereira, a Brazilian minister, after his participation at the Panama Congress (1916), wrote *O Problema Religioso da America Latina* (The Religious Problem of Latin America). For him, "Romanism was nothing

19. A. G. Simonton quoted in Speer, 221.

20. Brown, 199.

21. Neely, 158ff.

22. Ibid., 162.

23. Ibid., 181.

24. Speer, 168.

25. Homer C. Stuntz, *South American Neighbors* (New York, Cincinatti: The Methodist Book Concern, 1916), 105.

26. Ibid., 106.

more than a corrupted Christianity."[27] The conclusion of his book is intense and revelatory of the spirit of the day; "Outside Rome, inside Christianity."[28]

The consequence of this anti-Catholic sentiment was clear: Latin America, they concluded, needed to be re-evangelized and as such, it was in fact a mission field. Neely was very emphatic in his plea for the evangelization of that continent. "A new religious force is absolutely needed, and this must be supplied by Protestantism."[29] South America needed to be rescued and the work in need was threefold: (1) To provide strong religious influences for the Protestants; (2) to give the pure gospel to the people who have been brought under the teaching of Romanism; and, (3) to evangelize the incoming immigrants before they are controlled by the conditions and Roman environment of South America.[30]

The conditions in South America impelled Speer to "acknowledge that our Protestant Missions in South America are to people whom the Roman Catholic church calls Roman Catholics. And these Missions must be justified on this basis."[31] According to H. W. Brown, the missionary enterprise to Latin America was criticized in some quarters with the argument that the Roman Catholic Church is a Christian church and better adapted than Protestantism to the character and conditions of the Indo-Latin races of America. His answer was, "it is only necessary to point out the superstitious practices sanctioned by Romanism, together with the religious destitution of the people, and, in contrast, the spiritual work that Protestant missions are doing." He concluded, "In the struggle against ignorance and superstition, let our watchword be: All America for Christ!"[32]

Motivation to Evangelize Latin America

Behind every enterprise there is a driving force which we call motivation. The dictionary defines motive as "the object influencing a choice or prompting an action." According to Gerald H. Anderson:

---

27. Eduardo Carlos Pereira, *O Problema Religioso da America Latina* (São Paulo: Empresa Editora Brasileira,1920/1916), 207.

28. Ibid., 442.

29. Neely, 184.

30. Ibid., 233–42.

31. Speer, 142.

32. Brown, 13–14.

The overarching motive for missions . . . was love for Christ and obedience to the Great Commission for the salvation of souls. Underneath, however, was the compelling idea, developing, since the 1840's, of America's Manifest Destiny—of a national mission assigned by Providence for extending the blessings of America to other peoples.[33]

Latin American countries began to be evangelized in the 1850s, when the Manifest Destiny theory was taking shape. Therefore, it is of supreme importance to see how it came to influence the missionary work in those places. But beyond that, an honest approach to the subject of missionary motivation has to look also at the "love for Christ and obedience to the Great Commission" as motives for mission. This is our intention in this section.

Love for Christ and Obedience to the Great Commission

In 1810, the American Board of Commissioners for Foreign Missions (ABCFM) was formed to promote missions within the Congregational and the Presbyterian churches. The Board's concept of missions is representative of the North American missionary thought of those days. Hence, it is important to study the Board's reports to understand what was behind the missionary enterprise. Some examples follow.

In the paper *The Present Duty of the Church to the Heathen World*, presented in the Annual Report of 1844, we read,

The object which our Savior had in view, when he said to his disciples, 'Go ye, therefore, and teach all nations, baptizing them in the name of the Father, and of the Son, and of the Holy Ghost,' was to secure the spread of his gospel throughout the earth; and not till it shall have been carried to every nation and tribe and family, will the command cease to be obligatory. At the present moment, however, more than six hundred millions of our fellow men are living in ignorance of the only way of salvation; hence it is the obvious and imperative duty of the church to send the gospel to these perishing multitudes, with the least possible delay.[34]

At the end of that report the following conclusion was reached, "The command of Christ, unrepealed and yet not obeyed, has come

---

33. Gerald H. Anderson, "American Protestants in Pursuit of Mission: 1886–1986," *IBMR* 12(3): 98.

34. American Board of Commissioners for Foreign Missions, "The Present Duty of the Church to the Heathen"(1844), 48.

down to us, 'Go ye into all the earth, and preach the gospel to every creature.'"[35]

Years later, at the Annual Meeting of 1852, another important report was delivered. It was called, *The Grand Motive to Missionary Effort*. This paper is important because it not only delineates the right motive for missionary effort, but points to those motives which are not of primary significance for this enterprise. The five secondary motives, according to this report, are: (1) the physical, social, and temporal wretchedness of the heathen; (2) the power of pledges and resolutions; (3) the success of the missionary work; (4) the denominational *esprit du corps*, the pride of the church and, (5) the awful doom which awaits those who live and die within the precincts of pagan idolatry.[36]

The paper proceeds to point out a higher motive for missions. First, the question, "What then is the high, commanding motive which includes every other, and without which all secondary and subordinate considerations soon lose their power and value?[37] And the answer:

> What can it be but *love to Christ who first loved us*. The love of Christ, shining out from the cross, has enkindled a responsive love in the heart of the Christian. And of the earliest emotions of the regenerate soul, commingling itself often with the first swelling tide of the gratitude for its own deliverance, is the desire to speak of Christ to others.[38]

And as such, "This motive has no limits to its sway, but is boundless and inexhaustible, as the love of Christ itself."[39] Therefore, one has to understand that love for Christ was the cause of mission, the desired consequence being the conversion of the nations to God.

The concept of love for Christ and obedience to the Great Commission is clearly present in missions to Latin America. A. G. Simonton wrote in his diary on Oct. 10, 1857 (two years before his arrival in Brazil), "Whatever the results to me, I am ready to move [into a missionary career], and I feel, more than ever, that this is the duty ahead for me."[40] There was for him a sense of obligation, a command to obey. He was

---

35. Ibid., 53.

36. Ibid., 22–23.

37. Ibid., 24.

38. Ibid.

39. Ibid., 24.

40. A. G. Simonton quoted in Maria Amelia Rizzo, *Simonton: Inspirações de uma Existência* (São Paulo: Grafica São José, 1961/2), 23.

aware of the difficulties ahead, but he was confident that God would guide his steps and provide for every need.[41]

However, there was something more than just a sense of obligation to fulfil. Simonton had a sensitive heart and his desire to please God can be seen throughout his diary. On Dec 2, 1859, he wrote, "I intensively feel the necessity of a clear knowledge of Christ and the perception of his presence and love. Being a missionary without a ardent love for Christ and zeal for souls is a bad business. I will renew my commitment."[42] Simonton's ministry was short, though greatly blessed. Due to contraction of Yellow Fever, he died on Dec. 9, 1867. A year before his death he wrote, "I long for a fire baptism that will consume my dross, and for a heart totally dominated by Christ."[43] In Simonton we find a love for Christ and the desire to save souls as part of his motivation.

Another example is provided by James H. McLean, missionary to Chile in 1906. He wrote *The Living Christ for Latin America*, and at the end of his book he states, "Latin America calls for our best. Latin America calls for men and women filled with that unquenchable love which is the breath of the living Christ."[44] There is no question that love for Christ and the desire to see the nations converted to God played an important role in the development of the missionary enterprise to Latin America.

The Doctrine of Manifest Destiny

According to Anderson,

> The doctrine of Manifest Destiny had its roots in the concepts of Anglo-Saxon racial superiority, of America as the center of civilization in the westward course of empires, the primacy of American political institutions, the purity of American Protestant Christianity, and the desirability for English to be the language of humanity.[45]

My purpose here is to look for this doctrine in the missionary work in Latin America. Again, it is useful for a broader understanding to see this thought in the *American Board* and then I will try to determine if this concept was present in mission to Latin America.

---

41. Ibid., 24.

42. A. G. Simonton quoted in Rizzo, 60.

43. Ibid., 121.

44. James H. McLean, *The Living Christ for Latin America* (n.p.: The Board of Foreign Missions and the Woman's Boards of Foreign Missions of the Presbyterian Church, USA, 1916), 182.

45. Anderson, 98.

The paper *Obligations of America Christians to Foreign Missions* was presented at the ABCFM's Annual Meeting of 1865 and it reflects many of the points outlined by Anderson. The paper points to three aspects why American Christians were obligated to missions: national history, national prosperity and, national honor.

National history: There was a firm belief that the land of America was preserved by God to be given to the Pilgrims. That is why the land was undiscovered and unoccupied for many years. The Pilgrims did not come earlier because they were not ready. They had to be purified from problems prevalent in Europe.

> And when the set time had come; when our fathers had gained the discipline and the manhood which they needed, this goodly land, another Canaan, was given to them. The Angel of the Covenant led them forth, as the shepherd his flock; and his hand was against their enemies. To us he may say, as he said to Israel of old, "No man has been able to stand before you unto this day."[46]

According to the report, it was God's desire that a Protestant people might possess the land and hold the key of the Pacific.[47] Biblical language, as we have seen, is used for America. Even the North's victory over the South is seen in the divine context. God saved the North and surrounded the South with strong delusions. To what end? That America might be a missionary country. The first settlers, says the report, "came to found a state, but it was a *missionary state*."[48] The preservation of the state and the missionary enterprise were closely connected. We read,

> Modern missions, in their broader import, date from the close of the last century. And it was just then that our country began to recover from its desperate struggles with England, and reap the benefits of a stable government, and gather the rich harvest of the carrying trade, which the wars of Europe threw into our hands. And since that time, just so fast as God has opened the world to the gospel of his Son, just so fast has he given us the ability to proclaim that Gospel.[49]

And the natural conclusion, "Who can resist the inference? It is as if a voice from 'the excellent glory' had said to us, 'I have filled your garners, that you may feed the perishing.'"[50]

---

46. Ibid., 30.
47. Ibid., 31.
48. Ibid.
49. Ibid., 32.
50. Ibid.

National prosperity: Under this topic the report observed: "The nearest glance at our country shows that everything has been framed upon a scale of unequal magnificence."[51] The report goes on to describe how God in his grace gave the North American people an unmatched richness from one coast to another.

National honor: There is an intimate connection of missions with national honor. It is worthwhile to quote the report here:

> To the full measure of our due, and beyond that measure, perhaps, we covet the respect, spontaneous, undissembled, of our fellow-men. But how shall we best secure it? . . . We must render our country radiant with the blessings of righteousness and truth; and then, with a generous self-forgetting philanthropy, strive to make the destitute and wretched, wherever found, sharers of our joy . . . Let [the] deed become the germ of a loftier purpose. With a far richer boon, let us go forth to the ends of the earth.[52]

As one can see, there was a genuine desire to help those in distress. However, the ulterior motive was to show a national honor. "And when one people after another shall rise up and call us blessed, the world will know it, and delight to do us honor. Such triumphs are sure and final."[53]

The Manifest Destiny concept can also be found in the missionary work to Latin America. Antonio Mendonça[54] believes that in general the missionary growth at the 19th century's last quarter was a product of the national expansionist sentiment combined with theological motives. Hubert B. Brown, in his *Latin America*, includes the idea of Manifest Destiny. According to him, Latin America was a continent in crisis because of the kind of Christianity there. The Roman Catholic church was felt to be responsible for the terrible situation of Latin America, as we already pointed out. Moreover, the North American churches were obligated to do missions in Latin America. Brown says, "Look then for a moment at the size of our Western Hemisphere, in which the United States plays the most prominent role. Our position entails religious as well as political obligations to the rest of our fellow Americans."[55] Latin America was seen as a small child that needed to be under the mother-

---

51. Ibid.
52. Ibid., 34.
53. Ibid.
54. Antônio Gouvêa Mendonça, *O Celeste Porvir: A Inserção do Protestantismo no Brasil* (São Paulo: Edições Paulinas, 1984), 57 .
55. Brown, 15.

hood of the United States because its "future will be so closely united with our own."[56]

Years later, Thomas B. Neely[57] stated, "The Protestant nations of the world must sustain missions in South America, and the greatest responsibility naturally and providentially rests upon the Protestants of the United States and of Canada." Later he clarifies his points:

> South America is an America. It is our nearest continent and because of proximity the greatest obligation rests on the people of North America. Furthermore, the United States is in South America. What is more, the United States has become a South American power. It is on the Isthmian Canal Zone. It is true it is only a strip ten miles wide and about forty-seven miles long, but it is territory in South America. There the flag of the United States flies, there are American officers, American soldiers, and American courts.[58]

Therefore, geographically, the United States was naturally responsible for Latin America, and religiously, United States was providentially responsible. The interest of one nation and the interest of God were united for the cause of missions in Latin America. The negative aspects of the doctrine of Manifest Destiny are evident, but one has to recognize that underneath this doctrine there was the desire to see the nation serving others to honor God. This is very clear when the issue of *national prosperity*[59] was presented. The question regarding prosperity was, "Are we ourselves both object and end?" The answer was negative. Love for property cannot surpass love for the Savior.

The Results of the Missionary Work

When the modern missionary movement gained momentum in the western world, and in our case the United States, many young people were challenged to give their lives to the missionary cause. There was a sense of urgency. "They [Christians] can evangelize the whole world in less than half a century."[60] This was not only a catchword, but was also one of the driving motives for missions. Further we read in the same document:

56. Ibid., 16–17.
57. Neely, 249.
58. Ibid., 287.
59. ABCFM, 33.
60. Ibid., 48.

We have the ability to carry this gospel, in less than half a century, to sixty millions of our benighted fellow men. God is saying to us, from each opening page of his providence, by every fresh display of his grace, 'To this generation of Christians is tendered the privilege of doing, under my guidance, the noblest work which man has ever undertaken or conceived.'[61]

The gospel, they believed, had to be preached to the nations which were perishing without the knowledge of Jesus Christ, and Matthew 28:18 became a paradigm for mission.

The difficulty facing these missionaries-to-be, though it was not recognized at the time, was a complete lack of preparation for missions. This challenge was overcome by the zeal and enthusiasm for the missionary task. Passion for the heathen souls, eagerness to communicate the gospel and the urgency of the task did not allow them to expend precious time in preparation. Contributing to this was the fact that seminaries were set up to train local pastors for the North American context rather than missionaries. Thus, the missionaries, by and large, whatever they lacked in cultural sensitivity, had a good theological training. With that and a great amount of goodwill they set out for the mission field to conquer the world for Christ. Once on the mission field, it was only natural that the majority of them would work and preach the gospel as if they were in North America.

Another problem that arose was that the new converts did not have any idea what kind of church they were looking for. We should bear in mind that mission in Latin America was primarily anti-Catholic and, as such, the model provided by that church had to be disregarded both by the missionaries and the new believers. The missionaries came to build a new church and to bring the pure gospel of Jesus Christ. The new believers, in accepting this offer, were also breaking with the old structures of the Roman Catholic church, and indeed the culture of the land. As Rubem Alves points out, "frequently, to be converted to Christ signified an alienation from the mother culture."[62] The problem soon became acute: what kind of church should come into existence?

The new converts had no clue about that. Hence the answer had to be found with the missionaries and the answer that they had was also the only one they knew: to establish the kind of church they were most

---

61. Ibid., 53.
62. Rubem Alves, *Dogmatismo e Tolerância* (São Paulo: Edições Paulinas, 1982), 64.

familiar with, i.e., the church in the U.S. Ironically, Protestantism eventually took the shape in Latin America which it intended to destroy, i.e., another foreign religion with all the elements that were strange to the Latin American people. The difference this time was that Protestantism was not forcibly imposed upon the people as Catholicism was. It was freely and wilfully accepted by those who wished to change religious loyalty. However foreign the product, this fact must not be forgotten. I will describe now some of the characteristics of the Protestant church which came into being as a result of the missionary work.

A Conservative Church

The people in Latin America at the time of the coming of the missionaries were a blend of European, African, and native pre-Columbian peoples. Furthermore, we should remember that Portugal and Spain were influenced by the Moors who occupied those lands for many centuries. From that heritage Latin America possessed an Arabic element in its culture. Portugal and Spain were counted among the least progressive nations in Europe and did not participate very much in the development achieved by the other European nations. Culturally then, the Latin Americans inherited a conservative worldview.

Moreover, Latin America was religiously conservative because of the Roman Catholic influence on society. People were, most of the time, passive in their relationship to the church. The Pope's words and the bishop's power could never be questioned. People were not educated to think for themselves. Catholic influence in education was very strong and widespread. We should remember that the Roman Catholic church was the official church in many Latin America countries, and as such, it had the power to dictate what should and what should not be taught in schools. What people learned was what the church told them, and what the church told them was hardly conducive to progress.

If Latin America was conservative, so were the missionaries who came to minister there. They were women and men of a pietistic faith and indomitable desire to bring the pure gospel to the people. In the case of Brazil, Paul E. Pierson states that the majority of the early missionaries were graduated from Princeton and other seminaries in the United States.[63] These missionaries belonged to the Old School Presbyterianism. Thus they brought with them theological influences from people

---

63. Paul E. Pierson, *A Younger Church in Search of Maturity: Presbyterianism in Brazil from 1910 to 1959* (San Antonio: Trinity University Press, 1974), 95 .

such as: Charles Hodge, J. H. Thornwell, and R. L. Dabney, all champions of the Old School orthodoxy.

Leonard J. Trinterud points out that,

> Despite what Hodge and the other Princeton professors thought of themselves, throughout the nineteenth century they found themselves unable to understand the popular religious movements of the day. The popular movements in turn rejected Princeton as 'high-toned,' 'book learned,' and interested only in the upper classes.[64]

If this was so, we have grounds for believing that this same sentiment was prevalent among most of its students. Most of the missionaries who came from that tradition carried with them this inability to understand the religion of their host land or popular religion of any kind. Contributing to this inability was the inflexible leadership found at Princeton. When Hodge returned to Princeton from a trip he made to Germany, he found there a leadership style whose motto was: allow no changes. "This position Hodge loyally accepted and supported."[65] We should note that it was from listening to a sermon from Charles Hodge that Simonton had his thoughts directed to missions.[66] One can only ponder how much of the environment found at Princeton influenced the new missionaries and the development of their work in the mission field.

Báez Camargo and K. G. Grubb point out another interesting factor that determined the conservatism of the missionaries: the proximity of Latin America to the United States. They assert that, "The quality of the missionary force has suffered from proximity to the United States; geographical conditions have not demanded that degree of independent thinking which more distant fields encourage."[67] National leadership were formed with the same conservative characteristics because they modeled themselves after the missionaries. The new leaders had to show their loyalty to the missionaries and prove that they were able to take over leadership and assume the job, otherwise the missionaries would not feel confident to relinquish their position.

---

64. Leonard J. Trinterud, "Charles Hodge (1797–1878): Theology-Didactic and Polemical," *Sons of the Prophets*, ed. Hugh T. Kerr (Princeton: Princeton University Press, 1963), 29.

65. Ibid., 30.

66. M. Richard Shaull, "Ashbell Green Simonton (1833–1867): A Calvinist in Brazil," *Sons of the Prophets*, ed. Hugh T. Kerr (Princeton: Princeton University Press, 1963), 119; Pierson, 19 ff.

67. Gonzalo Báez Camargo and Kenneth G. Grubb, *Religion in the Republic of Mexico* (London, New York: World Dominion Press, 1935), 120–21.

During the 1930s, with the arrival of the so called "faith missions" in Latin America, another element was added to the conservatism found there, i.e., fundamentalism. "These groups," according to R. K. Dehainaut, "for the most part, place their primary emphasis on individual conversion, are pietistic, anti-Catholic, anti-World Council of Churches, and are politically conservative."[68]

The Latin American soil continues to be a fertile land for fundamentalistic ideas. According to Julio de Santa Ana, fundamentalism weakened the understanding of the Bible because it did not take into consideration the context where people live.[69]

A "World Negating" Mentality

"Individual salvation was the main thrust of the 'true' Christianity brought by Protestants."[70] This fact was a reflection of the missionaries' background. They lived in an age where revival played an important role in their lives and in the missionary movement. Revival called attention to the sinfulness of society and, consequently, underneath the acceptance of Jesus Christ as personal Savior there was an appeal to reject the world and its corrupted nature. This helped to develop the "World Negating" mentality that accompanied a more pietistic lifestyle.

In Latin America there is a tendency to blame Pietism for the church's lack of responsibility in the various aspects of society. Carmelo E. Alvarez points out that, "In 1900 . . . the missionaries were . . . very much pietistic in their religious practice; they did not dance or smoke and they were conservative in biblical and theological issues." And he concludes, "Those who know the composition of the majority of the Protestant Churches in Puerto Rico will note the great influence of that practice in the life of the churches."[71]

At this point there is no doubt that the Protestant churches in Latin America are churches divorced from its reality. Regarding Presbyterianism in Brazil, Pierson pointed out, "the piety . . . expressed could also

---

68. Raymond K. Dehainaut, *Faith and Ideology in Latin America Perspective* (Guernevaca: Centro Cultural de Documentacion, 1972), 5–12.

69. Julio de Santa Ana, *Protestantismo, Cultura y Sociedad: Problemas y Perspectivas de la Fè Evangelica en America Latina* (Buenos Aires: Editorial La Aurora, 1970), 143–50.

70. Walter Wedemann, 127.

71. Carmelo E. Alvarez "Las Misiones Protestantes en Puerto Rico," *Lectura Teologica del Tiempo Latinoamericano: Ensayos en Honor del Doctor Wilton M. Nelson* (Costa Rica: Seminario Biblico Latinoamericano, 1979), 233.

degenerate into a selfish concern for one's own salvation in the life to come and a religion indifferent to the needs of others in this world."[72] Any attempt to see the world differently was undermined, because the church had no relationship with the things of the world. Unfortunately, the situation is very much the same today. We live in a continent where death overcomes life; oppression and misery are normally accepted as part of one's destiny in life; corruption is pervasive and found in every sector of society. What, then, is the role of the church in this situation? Omar Arboccó writes on the Evangelical church in Peru:

> The church, due to its formation and limited vision, does not say anything, it is voiceless to this sick society and is corrupted by the collective and personal sin. The effect of this indifference, has provoked a divorce between the church and society. The church is forgetting the biblical mandate of being 'light to the world' and 'salt of the earth.'[73]

This divorce, Arboccó points out, is a product of a church with no adequate theology and theologians. It might be possible that the main cause for this lack is due to missionary paternalism demonstrated at the beginning of their labor. This paternalism blocked much of the initiative of the new believers in search of an authentic Latin American form of Christianity. The result of this attitude is a generalized disorientation found among the evangelical churches. We did not have a pattern to follow and as such everything must be created anew. It also explain why Liberation theology has found a niche among the young evangelical theologians in Latin America and has become the new paradigm for doing theology in Latin America.

We pointed out above that the missionaries went to Latin America to preach the pure gospel and there was a sense of urgency in their mission. As a consequence, they did not see themselves as initiators of political changes. Webster E. Browning wrote, "It will be well . . . to keep mission within its proper limits, with an absolute disassociation from political parties or pretensions."[74] Eventually, the new believers came to develop the same aversion to politics and society's social problem.

The fact remains that if the missionaries felt that this particular

---

72. Pierson, 96.

73. Omar Arboccó, "Modelo de Mision: Iglesia Evangelica Peruana," *Consulta Nacional Sobre la Mision de la Iglesia* (Lima: Concilio Nacional Evangelico del Peru, 1987), 70–71.

74. Webster E. Browning, *The River Plate Republics* (London, New York: World Dominion Press, 1928), 77.

form of mission was not part of their task, they could at least try to open the eyes of the national churches to the problems found in society and encourage them to be more involved in society. However, they continually saw the Protestant churches as "too small to take part in the social field, and their wisest strategy for the present lies in building up their own membership."[75]

The missionary's goal was to reach the individual, with the hope that in due time society would be renewed as well.[76] Hence, the vocation of the missionaries could not be diverted from this preeminent goal. The activities of education, medical and social work "are only indirectly related to the inner life and spiritual well-being of the Church."[77] This mentality that the gospel is first concerned with the spirit and only secondarily with the body was developed from the beginning of Protestantism in Latin America. As a result, as soon as some people began to challenge the church to be concerned with life in this world, these people were labeled as "liberal" and some were accused of leaning toward the "social gospel." In some cases they were silenced and expelled from the church.

In Latin America today, evangelicals still tend to look on involvement in politics or serious promotion of social causes as none of their business. Churches are now divided on this issue because of a lack of understanding of what the gospel is. For most of our churches, the gospel is only related to heaven above and the preaching of the gospel continues to address only those areas pertaining to spiritual issues. Right now in Brazil the talk of the moment is about "spiritual battle," which is another issue imported to us through literature and guest lecturers from the U.S.

Another reason for this "world negating" mentality was the moralistic attitude and influence of the missionaries upon the new believers. Since the missionaries found a continent lacking moral qualities, they had a tendency to exclude themselves from any activity where Roman Catholic people were involved. Everything in society was wrong and depraved and thus any involvement was rejected. An illustration of this fact is in the area of music. Latin American sounds and instruments were not permitted in the worship service because they were associated

---

75. Kenneth G. Grubb, *An Advancing Church in Latin America* (London, New York: World Dominion Press, 1936), 64.

76. Ibid., 23.

77. Ibid., 31.

with a non-Christian culture. It is only a decade or so ago that our people began to use the instruments of the land and to create new songs that
are truly Latin American. I should note, however, that the resistance to
this trend is still very strong in our churches.

This exclusivistic attitude was transmitted to the new church and it
persists to the day. We evangelicals in Latin America consider ourselves
far superior to any other people, and as such we have a tendency to manifest a sentiment of indifference for what non-evangelicals are or do.
They are not worthy to be associated with. However, this sentiment will
change as soon as those people "accept Jesus Christ as Lord and Savior"
and join our church.

An Anti-Ecumenical Christianity

The militant anti-Catholicism which was present in most of the
missionary work contributed to an attitude of disdain towards the
Roman Catholic people in Latin America. This disdain is now part of the
"Protestant culture" in our lands. It is something that we learn, develop,
and transmit to our children and to the new believers as they join our
churches.

Because of this antagonistic attitude we have developed a sense of
identity where we are better then everybody who is not Protestant. Morally we are superior people just as religiously we are saved and they are
not. As a consequence, we are always crusading against the Roman
Church in order to save some of its people and rescue them from their
errors. Because of this, it is very hard for the evangelical churches to
have any association with the Catholics. This association goes against
everything we are. It damages our evangelical tradition of noninvolve-
ment with them. The tragic aspect of this attitude is that the evangelicals
transfer their religious rejection to everything that the Roman Catholic
Church promotes or is involved with. For instance, if there is a housing
project in a city which is going to benefit the poor population, but the
Catholics are involved, then our tradition tells us not to participate.

This anti-Ecumenical attitude is also reflected between the Protestant churches as well. Besides some evangelistic campaign, very little
has been done by the evangelical churches to show their unity and solidarity with one another. Unfortunately, we inherited from the missionaries a kind of lone ranger identity. Every group thinks that they are better
than the others, and, as a consequence, dialogue between them is almost
nonexistent. There is no trust between churches and leaders so as to
form a strong body of believers.

A God-Loving People

In the predominant theological reflection on the missionary work in Latin America there has been a lack of balance. Too often Latin American theologians fail to recognize the positive aspects of this missionary work. Báez Camargo and Grubb acknowledged that, "Fine examples . . . of sacrifice and devotion have been given by some missionaries, whose example of faith the Mexican churches might well follow."[78]

Occasionally, theologians remember the positive aspects of the missionary work in Latin America. Míguez Bonino, for instance, points to four areas Protestantism addressed: doctrinal; liturgical; ethical; and social, cultural, and political. In this regard, Protestantism served the Latin American people well, because it broke the Roman Catholic religious and cultural monopoly that was obstructing access to modernity, that despite its faults, was the coming wave of history.[79]

Jean-Pierre Bastian mentions at least three essential aspects of the Protestant ecclesiology in Latin America: (1) calling to conversion; (2) the priesthood of all believers; and (3) the central role of the Bible.[80] Gonzalo Castillo-Cárdenas points to the following as positive aspects of Protestantism. It brought opposition to (1) a superficial Roman Catholic religion; (2) syncretistic practices; (3) a divorce between religion and morals; (4) ignorance of the Scriptures; and (5) the religious passivity of the people. "These are and continue to be the great motives that give validity and power to the Latin American Protestant movement."[81]

It is important to highlight the doctrine of the priesthood of all believers. Though its full application is still wanting, there is no doubt this idea has made a big impact on the people in Latin America who were used to the model presented by the Roman Catholic church with its heavy dependency on professional and foreign clergy. The practical side of this doctrine was, "every believer as evangelist."[82] Robert Wood, a Catholic priest, argues that one of the factors of Protestant church growth in Latin America is the creation and establishment of a native

---

78. Báez Camargo and Grubb, 122.

79. Míguez Bonino (1970), 35.

80. Jean-Pierre Bastian, "Hacia una Nueva Eclesiología Evangélica Desde los Pobres," *Cristianismo y Sociedad* 18(64): 28.

81. Gonzalo Castillo Cárdenas, "El Cristianismo Evangelico en America Latina," *Cristianismo y Sociedad* 2(5): 63.

82. A. E. Fernandez Arlt,"The Laity in the Latin American Evangelical Churches: 1806-1961," *The Layman in Christian History*, eds. Stephen C. Neill and Hans-Ruedi Weber (Philadelphia: The Westminster Press, 1963).

clergy and hierarchy. In contrast, he points out that "the Catholic Church in Latin America still depends heavily on foreign clergy after four hundred years."[83]

Brazil, for instance, was privileged to have a strong national leadership from the beginning of the missionary work. José Manoel da Conceição, a former Roman Catholic priest, was the first Latin American to be ordained as a minister in a Protestant church and he left a significant mark in the life of the Presbyterian Church of Brazil. In 1867, only eight years after Simonton's arrival, three Brazilians were to reside with him for theological training.[84] According to Wedemann,[85] "by 1914 there was already a Brazilian Protestantism in Brazil." Though the Roman Catholic church had some national priests, it never approached the Protestant church in this respect.

A positive aspect that we inherited from the missionaries' strong morality is the certainty that we are a different kind of people and as such we cannot compromise our faith in Christ by following some of the customs of our lands. Evangelicals are known all over Latin America for their commitment to family, work, and a strong Christian ethic. Our lifestyle is so well known by society in general that when an evangelical commits a mistake of some proportion, he or she will be condemned because expectations are much higher.

Finally, we need to mention that from the missionaries' love for Christ we Latin American Christians acquired a genuine desire to follow the Lord and suffer the consequences of this choice. We are still discriminated against, for example, by the secular media and by the government which always favors the Roman Catholic church. Our people are known as "Bible People" for their profound love for the Word of God. Thousands of illiterate people learn how to read using their Bibles as a textbook. We have maintained our evangelistic zeal and are committed to see the Kingdom of God expand in our lands.

What is Ahead for the Church in Latin America

Since the 1950s Latin American theologians have pointed out that Protestantism is now calling for a theology that reflects the Latin American situation. We recognize this and sense it is necessary to press for-

---

83. Robert Wood, *Missionary Crisis and Challenge in Latin America* (St. Louis and London: B. Herder Book Co., 1964), 55.

84. Pierson, 24.

85. Wedemann, 241.

ward. The problem is that up to this point theology is divorced from practice, and as such, what the theologians say is not what the church does. If the theology is at a crossroad in Latin America, this is not the same with the church. The church continues its journey and most of the time it ignores the theologians, leaving them behind as they dialogue at the crossroads.

This happens for the simple reason that the majority of the Latin American theologians are progressive, having been influenced by Liberal and Liberation theology. On the other hand, the majority of the churches in Latin America are very conservative. Therefore, the theologians talk about the ideal church that they dream one day will come into being, and the real church already thinks and operates as if it had reached that stage. We have here two roads that seldom cross despite all the efforts and impatience of the theologians.

Let me illustrate this point quoting from Castillo Cárdenas. He wrote,

> we feel entangled in a net of traditions, practices, ecclesiastical ideal, 'programs,' etc., that obstruct the movement of our churches into the dynamic situation where we live. All these were brought as an ecclesiastical outfit by the missionaries' agencies. For the mission of the younger church of today, the problem is not only that this outfit was imported, but that it does not meet the need of the contemporary mission situation. This, partially explains the evangelical difficulties of the moment.[86]

Here is one of the main challenges in Latin America: There is a need to break with the missionary's legacy. We agree that it is essential to look for new methods to meet the need of the Latin American people; that we need a theology born and reflected from the people's context; that we need to be closer to them. However, one should note that Cárdenas wrote the above almost thirty years ago, and up to the present Latin American theologians are still echoing the same strains. It appears that nothing has changed and the church has yet to hear their cry.

If the traditional churches in Latin America keep moving in the same direction they are now following, one can reach only one conclusion: the future does not belong to them in Latin America. Part of the Roman Catholic church is being renewed by the *Comunidades Eclesiais de Base* and is growing and moving toward people's need. For the first

---

86. Castillo Cárdenas, 63.

time in Latin America part of the Catholic church is doing something in favor of the people. This church as a whole is influenced and guided by Liberation theology. The problem ahead is that in its journey, it is losing the pastoral side of theology. Since social problems are getting bigger every day, there is not much time to deal with the spiritual problems of the people. Here is where Pentecostalism meets the need of the Latin American people. It is true that Pentecostalism continues to think as it has since its beginning, but it provides mechanisms to bring renewal into its life. It basically continues to be a church alienated from society, emphasizing the division between the sacred and secular. But it is a growing church and it fills the vacuum left by the CEBs and traditional churches.

In summary, we have one church (CEB) addressing the social needs of the people, and the other (Pentecostal) addressing the spiritual needs. The struggle for the traditional churches lies between these two churches. However, they tend to put aside any talk about social concerns as well as about Pentecostalism. The mainline churches are fixed with the idea that they are of a higher quality than the CEBs and the Pentecostals.

Having the CEBs addressing social issue, and the Pentecostals addressing spiritual needs of the people, the question then is: what is left for the churches established by the missionary movement? The conclusion is that the future for them is not bright and it appears that their splendor is peacefully resting in the past.

However, we do not want to finish this work on a negative note. There is always hope. Waldo A. Cesar pointed the way out: "we need to accept the awakening of God's Spirit, because it is not history, or politics, or power structures, or even the organized church (they are mere instruments) that can give motives for the fight in this world, and capacity to encounter the so-called secular. Only God can do it."[87]

In conclusion, our identity will be found and shaped as we experience God in our journey toward the consummation of the Kingdom. This journey, we need to bear in mind, happens in the midst of our Latin American people and in the pathways of our land. We need to empty ourselves of some past presuppositions which go against our people and our culture and start to love them as Christ does. "For Christ and Latin America" must again, and in a new way, be our motto.

---

87. Waldo A. Cesar, "Problemas e Tendências do Protestantismo Contemporâneo," *Cristianismo y Sociedad* 3(7): 25.

Contributors

Antônio Carlos Barro was born in Marilia, State of Sao Paulo in Brazil. A graduate of Fuller Theological Seminary with a Ph.D. in Intercultural Studies, he is now the Senior Pastor of Igreja Presbiteriana de Londrina (Presbyterian Church of Londrina) in Brazil.

Anthony Balcomb was born in Pietermaritzburg, South Africa in 1947, and raised in Northern Rhodesia (now Zambia). He received his Ph.D. from Natal University. During the last 15 years he has been in church ministry in South Africa. He is currently the Director of Studies of the Evangelical Theological House of Studies in Pietermaritzburg, South Africa. He is the author of *Third Way Theology: Reconciliation, Revolution, and Reform in the South African Church During the 1980s*. His book *No Easy Way of Dying: True Confessions Of A White Believer in Africa* will be published soon.

Kwame Bediako received his Ph.D. from Aberdeen. He is a minister of the Presbyterian Church in Ghana and the Director of the Akrofi-Christaller Memorial Centre for Mission Research and Applied Theology in Ghana. He is the author of the book *The Gospel and Contemporary Ideologies*.

Samuel Escobar was born in Arequipa, Peru. He received his Ph.D. from Universidad Complutense in Madrid, Spain in 1989 on "Paulo Freire: A Political Pedagogy." He is the Thornley B. Wood Professor of Missiology at Eastern Baptist Theological Seminary, and has served as Associate General Secretary for the International Fellowship of Evangelical Students and as the Director of Inter-Varsity Christian Fellowship of Canada.

Evelyn Miranda-Feliciano is the Executive Director of the Institute for Studies in Asian Church and Culture. She is an author of nine books for young people on family, culture, and socio-political themes. As a contributor to Christian magazines and theological journals in the U.S. and in Europe, she is currently working on a writing project sponsored by the David C. Cook Foundation and the Jim Johnson Writer's Fund.

Ken Gnanakan was born in India. He studied theology at the Melbourne Bible Institute in Australia and received his Ph.D. from King's College, University of London. Actively involved in theological education in Asia, he is the General Secretary of the Asia Theological Association and the Executive Director of the Asian Center for Theological Studies in India.

David Lim has an M.Div. from Asian Theological Seminary (ATS) and a Ph.D. from Fuller Theological Seminary. He served as Academic Dean of ATS, and is presently the Pew Lecturer on Two Thirds World Theology and the Associate Dean of the Oxford Centre for Mission Studies while on a leave of absence from the Center for Community Transformation (Philippines), where he serves as Training Director. His mission foci have been professionals, urban poor, Muslims, and Chinese Buddhists in the Philippines.

Cyril Okorocha was born in Owerri, Nigeria in 1948. He is an ordained Priest in the Anglican Church and holds a Ph.D. in Missiology from the University of Aberdeen. He was elected the West Africa Coordinator of the International Fellowship of Evangelical Mission Theologians, Pioneer General Secretary and National Coordinator of Africa Theological Fellowship in Nigeria, and is also the Associate Secretary for Mission and Evangelism and Officer for the Decade of Evangelism of the Anglican Communion.

Miroslav Volf was born in Yugoslavia. He has a Ph.D. from Tübingen University, and is Associate Professor of Systematic Theology at Fuller Theological Seminary. Volf has written numerous articles on theology and the current state of the former Yugoslavia. His books include *Work In the Spirit: Toward a Pneumatalogical Theology of Work*, *"Raspeti Bog" Teoloske meditacije o Santicevu vjerskom pjesnistvu* (*"Crucified God" Theological Meditations on the Poetry of Aleksa Santic*), and *Zukunft der Arbeit—Arbeit der Zukunft* (*The Future of Work—The Work of the Future*).

William Dyrness is Professor of Theology and Culture, and is the Dean of the School of Theology at Fuller Theological Seminary. Dyrness has taught at Nairobi Evangelical Graduate School of Theology in Kenya and at Asian Theological Seminary in the Philippines. He is the author of *Learning about Theeology from the Third World* (1990) and *Introduction to Cross-Cultural Theology* (1992).